Pretty People

STAR
★★★★★★★★★★ AMERICAN CULTURE / AMERICAN CINEMA
DECADES

Each volume in the series Star Decades: American Culture/American Cinema presents original essays analyzing the movie star against the background of contemporary American cultural history. As icon, as mediated personality, and as object of audience fascination and desire, the Hollywood star remains the model for celebrity in modern culture and represents a paradoxical combination of achievement, talent, ability, luck, authenticity, superficiality, and ordinariness. In all of the volumes, stardom is studied as an effect of, and influence on, the particular historical and industrial contexts that enabled a star to be "discovered," to be featured in films, to be promoted and publicized, and ultimately to become a recognizable and admired— even sometimes notorious—feature of the cultural landscape. Understanding when, how, and why a star "makes it," dazzling for a brief moment or enduring across decades, is especially relevant given the ongoing importance of mediated celebrity in an increasingly visualized world. We hope that our approach produces at least some of the surprises and delight for our readers that stars themselves do.

ADRIENNE L. McLEAN AND MURRAY POMERANCE
SERIES EDITORS

Jennifer M. Bean, ed., *Flickers of Desire: Movie Stars of the 1910s*

Patrice Petro, ed., *Idols of Modernity: Movie Stars of the 1920s*

Adrienne L. McLean, ed., *Glamour in a Golden Age: Movie Stars of the 1930s*

Sean Griffin, ed., *What Dreams Were Made Of: Movie Stars of the 1940s*

R. Barton Palmer, ed., *Larger Than Life: Movie Stars of the 1950s*

Pamela R. Wojcik, ed., *New Constellations: Movie Stars of the 1960s*

James Morrison, ed., *Hollywood Reborn: Movie Stars of the 1970s*

Robert Eberwein, ed., *Acting for America: Movie Stars of the 1980s*

Anna Everett, ed., *Pretty People: Movie Stars of the 1990s*

Murray Pomerance, ed., *Shining in Shadows: Movie Stars of the 2000s*

Pretty People

Movie Stars of the 1990s

EDITED BY

ANNA EVERETT

RUTGERS UNIVERSITY PRESS

NEW BRUNSWICK, NEW JERSEY, AND LONDON

LIBRARY OF CONGRESS CATALOGING-IN-PUBLICATION DATA

Pretty people : Movie stars of the 1990s / edited by Anna Everett.
    p. cm. — (Star decades : American culture / American cinema)
    Includes bibliographical references and index.
    ISBN 978–0–8135–5244–6 (hardcover : alk. paper)
    ISBN 978–0–8135–5245–3 (pbk. : alk. paper)
    ISBN 978–0–8135–5325–2 (e-book)
    1. Motion picture actors and actresses—United States—Biography. I. Everett, Anna,
1954–   .
  PN1998.2.P75   2012
  791.4302'80922—dc23

                                          2011023339

A British Cataloging-in-Publication record for this book is available from the British
Library.

Visit our Web site: http://rutgerspress.rutgers.edu

Manufactured in the United States of America

For my darling mother, Lena. RIP

CONTENTS

ACKNOWLEDGMENTS

Collaborative productions are often marked by remarkable and inspiring creativity as well as trying experiences. This volume is no exception. I am very lucky to have had the opportunity to work with my talented and dedicated co-authors, whose remarkable creativity through trying times inspired me during each phase of this volume's completion. I am honored to acknowledge the amazing work of my collaborators: Melvin Donalson, Mary Beth Haralovich, Karen Hollinger, Tracey Hoover, Mia Mask, Toby Miller, R. Barton Palmer, Donna Peberdy, Murray Pomerance, Laura Isabel Serna, and Linda Ruth Williams. Thank you all so much; I remain in your debt. I also want to express my deepest gratitude to Adrienne L. McLean, Murray Pomerance, and Leslie Mitchner, whose incredible patience and faithful support were indispensable throughout this book's circuitous journey from start to finish. Working with the three of you has been an unforgettably rewarding intellectual and professional experience. I will always be grateful for the invitation to participate in this important series. In addition, I thank the editorial team at Rutgers University Press for the care taken with making this volume a beautifully artistic production. I must add that my work on this volume would have been diminished greatly without a major contribution from my research assistant, Andrew Flanagan—thank you. I am also grateful for the support of my colleagues at the University of California, Santa Barbara, especially the faculty, staff, and students in the Department of Film and Media Studies. I want to extend a special word of thanks to the smart and engaged students in my new Stars in the Media class for their enthusiasm and feedback that helped so much during the final stages of this book. Last, but certainly not least, I am delighted to acknowledge the unwavering support and assistance of Aldon L. Nielsen for his personal, intellectual, and professional generosity and constancy.

While this was a team effort by many smart and devoted people, I must take responsibility for any shortcomings that may be associated with this volume, which I certainly hope are few and far between.

Pretty People

INTRODUCTION

★☆☆☆☆☆☆★★★★

Stardom in the 1990s

ANNA EVERETT

> Everybody *wants* to be famous. Nobody *needs* it.
> —Jayne Cortez

Hollywood stardom was transformed in fundamental ways in the 1990s, as was the nation itself during this final and revolutionary decade of the twentieth century. The period saw much of American society upended and reordered, with many social, cultural, political, and economic institutions radically altered. Among those affected was the phenomenon of film stardom as an index of changing national values and societal norms. Significant changes to familiar social scripts about identity norms, in terms of gender, race, ethnicity, age, class, sexuality, and nationality, tracked more consistently with the *fin de siècle* demands of American multiculturalism and transnational capitalism's globalization imperatives. Equally important were such epochal technological advances as Englishman Tim Berners-Lee's invention of the World Wide Web and web server software systems in 1991 that changed society forever. And in 1993, twelve years of Republican dominance of the White House came to an end with the inauguration of Arkansas governor Bill Clinton as president; he would subsequently become the first Democrat to be twice elected president since Franklin Roosevelt.

Other major U.S. events of the decade included the opening of the Mall of America, the largest mall in the country, in Minnesota; the Persian Gulf War and the 24/7 news cycle responsible for what became known as the "CNN effect"; David Dinkins taking office as mayor of New York and Douglas Wilder as governor of Virginia, the first African Americans to hold these positions (Wilder becoming the nation's first African American governor since Reconstruction); the debut of Netscape's web browser and Microsoft's Windows 95 operating system, presaging the dotcom boom; the Anita Hill/Clarence Thomas hearings, in which Hill accused of Thomas of sexual harassment and the Senate considered and later approved his nomination to the Supreme Court; the beating of motorist Rodney King by four Los Angeles policemen, followed by the release of the videotape that captured the incident, the trial and acquittal of the officers, and rioting in the city; the ratification of the North American Free Trade Agreement (NAFTA); the approval of women for combat roles in the U.S. military; O. J. Simpson's acquittal on the charge of murdering ex-wife Nicole Brown Simpson and Ron Goldman; deadly high school shootings in Kentucky, Arkansas, Oregon, and Colorado; the senseless murder of Matthew Shepard in Wyoming because of his homosexuality; Bill Clinton's denial, then confession, of his sexual encounter with intern Monica Lewinsky in the White House, leading to his impeachment; Michael Jackson's marriage to Lisa Marie Presley; Tejano singing sensation Selena Perez's murder by her fan club president; and the dominance of pop music charts by boy bands such as the Backstreet Boys, 'N Sync, and Boys II Men. All these could be said to have exerted an influence on the emergence of new types of Hollywood stars and the shifting contours of stardom and celebrity.

The point of this select historical mapping is to situate the shifts and mutabilities in stardom production and consumption at this time within an incredible array of drastic changes across the spectrum of U.S. life and culture. This distillation of nineties-era occurrences is not meant simply to echo Orrin E. Klapp's notion of stardom's ideological function as societal reinforcement and perpetuation, hegemonic seduction, and transcendence as a safety valve for discontent (qtd. in Dyer, *Stars* 24). Rather, our consideration of contemporaneous stardom at the intersection of these and many other historic events highlights Shmuel N. Eisenstadt's cogent observation about the power of charismatic personalities at times of sociocultural change: "Charismatic appeal is effective especially when the social order is uncertain, unstable and ambiguous and when the charismatic figure or group offers a value, order or stability to counterpoise this" upheaval (qtd. in Dyer, *Stars* 31). And while the charismatic appeal of film stars in the nineties was no less pivotal or effective in American cultural negotiations of major change, progress, and setbacks than in past decades, Marcia Landy's assertion that "the phenomenon of stardom raises questions about the nature of cinematic representation as a literal reproduction of reality" (x) has particular resonance at century's end.

The fact that *fin de siècle* American society was in a state of flux is quite apparent. Consequently, the very nature of cinematic representation and its sister phenomenon of stardom evolved accordingly. As film exhibition saw the advent of the NC-17 rating (replacing the X rating along with its stigma), in film production doors also opened. The politics of multiculturalism propelled widespread acceptance of major stars from all racial and ethnic groups, civil rights advancements produced tolerance for novel filmic narratives about gender and sexual normativity, and sweeping technological changes affected film art and commerce while engendering new practices of audience participation and new formations of fan cultures. Tried and true formulas for maintaining traditional and classic film stardom persisted and became even more entrenched—the James Bond franchise returned with *GoldenEye* (1995), which became the most profitable of all Bond films to date with earnings of $353 million worldwide—but newer modes of stardom production, manipulation, institutionalization, and intensification were on the horizon, especially with the rise of the World Wide Web and other digital media technologies.

Specifically, what digital media proffered for nineties-era film stars (established and emerging) were new avenues to stardom and fan communities, self-regulating promotion, and evolved types of interactive fandom that included new outlets for global circulation of star discourse, both inside and outside mainstream media's hegemonic control structures. In terms of counterhegemonic societal narratives and scholarly interest in popular and participatory cultures, audiences, and fandom, Henry Jenkins convincingly makes the case for the game-changing arrival of digital media technologies during the nineties:

> The concept of the active audience, so controversial two decades ago, is now taken for granted by everyone involved in and around the media industry. New technologies are enabling average consumers to archive, annotate, appropriate, and recirculate media content. Powerful institutions and practices (law, religion, education, advertising, and politics, among them) are being redefined by a growing recognition of what is to be gained through fostering—or at least tolerating—participatory cultures. . . . Something was in the air in the early 1990s that would have resulted, one way or another, in the academic "discovery" of fandom. (1–3)

With the turn to audience and reception studies in the nineties as a result of the highly influential Birmingham School of cultural studies, the star phenomenon and star studies, among other popular culture institutions and practices, were upended. Leading the charge was the eighties- and nineties-era televisual institutionalization of stardom and celebrity as everyday discourses in the home. TV shows such as "Entertainment Tonight" (1981–) and its copycats "Inside Edition" (1989–) and "Extra" (1994–), among others, set the stage for advertising and promotion in the post-studio era that was determined by the film industry itself. Most striking in this regard was the explosive growth of the Internet, advanced computer games, and other digital media technologies. More than anything else, the Internet successfully built upon the everyday star discourse of celebrity journalism on TV. This emergent web-based celebrity helped transform stardom and its discursive practices very significantly, laying the foundation for a sort of hyper-stardom and hyper-fandom feedback loop of participatory media culture that continues to develop exponentially in the new millennium. The advent of new media culture and an expanded star discourse in the 1990s certainly laid the foundation for the emergence of twenty-first-century blogs, vlogs, and social media. However, in the nineties, networked media culture was more commonly expressed through such identifications as user groups, usenets, webrings, drums, and listservs, among others. Key among the uses of this expanded media environment was the not surprising development of fan and official movie star websites as the decade came to a close.

☆☆☆☆☆ Beyond Whiteness in the Cult of Celebrity

Although the development of computer-generated digital and convergence cultures signified a major paradigm shift in the production and consumption of stars and stardom, more significant, arguably, was the integration of black, Asian, Latina/o, feminist, queer, working-class, and other marginalized groups into the firmament of Hollywood stardom. For example, it was the system of star tokenism that produced the star turns of Anna May Wong and Sessue Hayakawa in the 1910s, 1920s, and 1930s; Carmen Miranda and Caesar Romero in the 1940s; Nancy Kwan, Sidney Poitier, Dorothy Dandridge, and Rita Moreno in the 1950s and 1960s; Pam Grier, Richard Roundtree, Bruce Lee, and Richard Pryor in the 1970s; and Eddie Murphy, Jennifer Beals, and Michael Nouri in the 1980s, to name but a few. And while the majority of these later actors produced stellar individual performances, often in supporting film roles, a number of racially and ethnically defined performers in the 1990s became bona fide movie stars who carried major films and led those films to amazing box-office success.

Among stars of this caliber were Denzel Washington, Andy Garcia, Halle Berry, Will Smith, Wesley Snipes, Jennifer Lopez, and Antonio Banderas. And while these stars have competed successfully within a framework that Gwendolyn Audrey Foster calls "an emphatically white heterocentric world" and its expressive Hollywood media industry, most important is that on their individual paths to stardom they successfully negotiated the challenges of white privilege. Still, Foster explains it thus: "We may still live in a world of white dominance and heterocentrism, but I think we can agree that we are in the midst of postmodern destabilizing forces when it comes to sexuality and race. Though the dominant cinema and the media continue to norm whiteness and heterosexuality, it seems to take [a] Herculean effort to maintain the binaries necessary to stabilize white heterotopia and supremacy" (7).

In addition to some Herculean challenges to Hollywood's normative whiteness posed by the growing influence and boxoffice power of the stars mentioned above and others as well, a revitalized ethnic and racially informed independent cinema movement also contributed significantly to the decade's multicultural and pluralist star constellation. This movement consisted of independent and specialty films replete with Chicana/o-Latina/o, Native American, African American, and Asian American stars and star texts, though not necessarily in equal measure. Not since the race films of the 1910s and 1940s and the blaxploitation film movement of the 1970s have distinctive independent American cinema movements recoded the nation's film culture beyond hegemonic whiteness. This means that celluloid racial passing in blackface, brownface, redface, and yellowface was no longer *de rigueur* as American film audiences increasingly embraced racial diversity in the cinema. Discussing the crossover experience in what he calls "the Hispanic Specialty Films," David Rosen asserts, "The 1980s will long be remembered as the 'golden age' of American independent film-making, particularly for 'specialty' or art films" (241). In Rosen's view, "More independent films [were] produced during the decade than ever." Moreover, he credits the successful 1980s' independent film with launching the important careers of actors and directors like Edward James Olmos, John Sayles, Spike Lee, and Susan Seidelman, among others (241).

By the 1990s, then, this nexus of racial diversity and stardom helped to advance a new representational economy more reflexive of America's actual demographic composition and striking cultural complexities. For example, rather than reifying or naturalizing America's anxious color consciousness, film culture and discourses of stardom promoted new casting strategies and politics of colorblindness exemplified by Denzel Washington's powerful starring role in *The Pelican Brief* (1993). In her *New York Times* film review, Janet Maslin informed the nation rather off-handedly that "Mr. Washington plays Gray Grantham, the brilliant black newspaper reporter who was white in Mr. Grisham's novel" (17 December 1993). Despite critical accolades for the film in terms of Washington's and Julia Roberts's star performances, the film failed to transcend the historic miscegenation taboo whereby sex/romance between black males and white females is historically forbidden. Making this point in different terms, Maslin writes, "Mr. Grisham . . . did close his book with a clinch and a promise of romance between Darby and Gray. The film, which thrives on the comfortable chemistry between its two stars, isn't quite gutsy or color-blind enough to do the same."

Whereas mainstream film studios were not ready to go there, independent filmmakers Spike Lee and Mira Nair readily delved into the thickets of interracial romance with their respective hits *Jungle Fever* (1991) and *Mississippi Masala* (1991). In the former, Wesley Snipes portrays architect Flipper Purify, a philandering black husband involved in a torrid extramarital love affair with his white secretary, Angie Tucci (Annabella Sciorra). In the latter, Sarita Choudhury stars as Meena from India by way of Uganda, who falls in love with African American Demetrius, the romantic lead (Denzel Washington). Dana A. Luke, a fan of *Mississippi Masala*, posted an insightful user comment about the film on IMDb.com. Recognizing the film's message about racism's destructiveness even outside the familiar black/white racial binary, he comments: "In short, this movie doesn't come at you as 'I'm a preachy race relations movie' but rather as a sweet love story that gets waylaid by issues of race and color in a believable way. I saw this movie for the first time when it came out in 1991, and thought it was good. I saw it again last night (1998) and like a fine wine or cheese it's getting even better with age" (Luke, "Gets even better with age," IMDb.com, 28 February 1999). Later into the decade, as the above films successfully broached the miscegenation taboo, Columbia Pictures entered the fray with *Fools Rush In* (1997), a romantic comedy featuring an interracial cast including Matthew Perry and Salma Hayek. Perry, whose stardom accrued largely to his television celebrity in a number of successful shows—most famously as Chandler Bing in the long-running and hugely successful sitcom "Friends" (1994–2004)—was pursuing a Hollywood film career with this starring role. For her part, Hayek, also a successful television actor, was already on track for establishing her film stardom, having been cast in such indie and mainstream films as *Mi vida loca* (1993), *Desperado* (1995), *Fair Game* (1995), and *Fled* (1996).

Fools Rush In and *Pelican Brief* helped lay the foundation for big film studios to move beyond their own taboos on representing interracial love. As Mary Beltrán and Camilla Fojas remind us, the Supreme Court's overturning of laws against interracial romance with the 1967 *Loving v. Virginia* decision emboldened many to support "the multiracial or mixed race movement." Moreover, Beltrán and Fojas observe that "the number of mixed race youth has continued to increase, as mixed marriages and families are increasingly commonplace. By the 1990s, organizations advocating for mixed race individuals and families were able to successfully . . . change the

Salma Hayek as Cora, a love interest in the action film *Fled* (Kevin Hooks, MGM, 1996). Hayek's obvious star quality makes an impression even in this bit part early in her career. Courtesy Photofest New York.

categories on the census to reflect racial multiplicity" (6). And although Hollywood was not leading the charge for changing the discourse, many of its most popular, charismatic stars have certainly made this subject more interesting and visually pleasing to contemplate.

☆☆☆☆☆ Chick Flicks amid the Masculinist Action Film Juggernaut

Specific film stars and changing processes of star making and unmaking in the nineties are clear indices of stardom's enduring cultural clout. But the politics of gender in Hollywood's star system were not truly progressive. This claim is easily supported by the glaring disparity between the number of big-budget and high-concept Hollywood films opened by female stars and those starring their male counterparts.

As a case in point, among the ten highest-grossing films of the decade, the only films with women in the lead were star vehicles for Julia Roberts, Jodie Foster, and Whoopi Goldberg. If we extend the count to include the twenty highest-grossing films, women stars fare marginally better. The highest grossing films with women in lead roles, according to Box Office Mojo's "Yearly Box Office" tabulations, were *The Silence of the Lambs* (1991), with Jodie Foster; *Sleeping with the Enemy* (1991), *My Best Friend's Wedding* (1997), and *Runaway Bride* (1999), all with Julia Roberts; *Sister Act* (1992), with Whoopi Goldberg; *Fried Green Tomatoes* (1991), with Kathy Bates; *The Prince of Tides* (1991), with Barbra Streisand; *The Hand That Rocked the Cradle* (1992), with Annabella Sciorra; *Sister Act 2: Back in the Habit* (1993), with Whoopi Goldberg; *The Client* (1994), with Susan Sarandon; *Dangerous Minds* (1995), with Michelle Pfeiffer; *While You Were Sleeping* (1995), with Sandra Bullock; *Congo* (1995), with Laura Linney; *The First Wives Club* (1996), with Goldie Hawn; *Scream* (1996) and *Scream 2* (1997), with Neve Campbell; *Contact* (1997), with Jodie Foster; *I Know What You Did Last Summer* (1997), with Jennifer Love Hewitt; *Shakespeare in Love* (1998), with Gwyneth Paltrow; and *Stepmom* (1998) and *Notting Hill* (1999), with Julia Roberts.

Most striking here is the incredibly small number of women stars who had more than one film among the ten or twenty highest grossing. Only Roberts stands out, the five films she carried as lead actor making her the decade's undisputed box office queen. Although Foster, Goldberg, and Campbell each led two very successful films in the nineties, only Foster's did not include a sequel. As for the others, their individual star turns were not insignificant. All told, these women's experiences with 1990s-era stardom are symptomatic of a particular set of challenges to an altered film-going culture confronted with audience fragmentation along gender lines and ever proliferating hybrid film genres, new entertainment rivals such as computer gaming, and mega-theme parks. Nonetheless, as a percentage of the film industry, female stars, their audiences, and their fervent fan bases maintain a strong hold despite the dominance of masculinist action films, safe family films, animated children's films, and digitally enhanced science fiction and technoir films endemic to the times.

The derisive label "chick flick" also functions to marginalize the star power and contain the star image of otherwise very talented and charismatic women performers. In his elaboration on Klapp's one-dimensional female type called "the pinup," Dyer reminds us that its function reifies "woman as sexual spectacle and sex object" (*Stars* 50). The "chick flick" label that came into wide usage in the nineties seems to recall and revivify this discursive limitation, as it confines women stars and their audiences. A subtext of the "chick flick" idea might well be a contemporary redux of Christine Gledhill's insights about the diminution of melodrama's worth inhering to its status as a woman's form (207).

At the same time, the fact that contemporary women tend to embrace the term is inescapable. Perhaps it is a move of recuperation or reinscription. Be that as it may, many young actors, particularly Meg Ryan, Julia

Meg Ryan as bookstore owner Kathleen Kelly in *You've Got Mail* (Nora Ephron, Warner Bros., 1998). Ryan's appealing girl-next-door persona helped to popularize email and online dating. Courtesy Photofest New York.

Roberts, Demi Moore, Whitney Houston, and Sandra Bullock, have accrued a very popular and diverse body of work that often gets enfolded within this quite elastic conceptual rubric. If Joan Crawford was the face of melodrama in classical Hollywood (Gledhill 207), then Meg Ryan can be considered the face of the 1990s chick flick. Exploring at length the predicament of women stars during the decade makes it apparent that the majority of the essays in this volume will concern male performers as a matter of course.

☆☆☆☆☆ New Star Trends and Structures: Stars as Brands

The foregoing discussion has articulated several significant contours of contemporary stardom that help distinguish its unique practices, manifestations, challenges, and opportunities at the close of the millennium. In addition to situating stardom within a context of dramatic and fundamental changes throughout America, what remains is the work of delineating how individual film stars contributed to and expressed their own brands of star discourse as part of a larger media ecology at work. A key conceit in star studies now is exploring the persistence of stardom in the age of digital reproduction, and what this persistence means for stars themselves. In *Understanding Celebrity*, Graeme Turner comments on the power of film stardom in the nation's obsession with celebrity. He observes that "the development of the film star is perhaps the most elaborate and socially grounded instance of the broad phenomenon of modern celebrity" (14). Turner also points us in the direction of Andrew Wernick, who advances the point in this way: "A star is anyone whose name and fame has been built up to the point where reference to them, via mention, mediatized representation or live appearance, can serve as a promotional booster in itself" (qtd. in Turner 9).

These observations are crucial as we contemplate the modern star as protector of his or her own media brand. During the 1990s, many stars seemed cognizant of how the Hollywood star system, like many successful blue-chip American business enterprises, was an industrial and cultural self-perpetuating institution devoted to both the pursuit of historic global profits and expanded audience appeal. It is hardly surprising that celebrity and stardom as discourses of exceptionalism and simultaneous averageness (the "all that" rhetoric of star making and unmaking) would engender reality TV and individual homepages, fan websites, and even official star web pages online.

This brings us to the discussion of stars as specific celebrity brands consistent with the times. The eleven essays compiled here provide a breadth and depth of new research that make understanding the specificities of stardom in the 1990s quite clear and worthwhile. And while this collection addresses some of the most successful and influential film stars of the era, it also engages with those stars whose impact on the culture of stardom is not necessarily defined by consistently high box-office numbers but who instead are more appreciated for their roles in resetting the coordinates of stardom for a new age. These thoughtful and insightful works owe much to the impressive corpus of critical, historical, theoretical, ideological, and popular writing on stars, stardom, and star-gazing over the past century. As a result, these essays are very much in dialogue with the important contributions and established paradigm-setting works of Richard Dyer, Christine Gledhill, Jackie Stacey, Adrienne L. McLean, James Naremore, Janet Staiger, Murray Pomerance, Barry King, and Richard deCordova, to name only a few among many brilliant researchers who help us make sense of our star-struck culture throughout the decades.

In "Arnold Schwarzenegger: Corporeal Charisma," Linda Ruth Williams opens the dialogue with an astute analysis of one of Hollywood's mega-male stars and his remarkable and unique star text that must be read through the actor's excessive and imposing physical body. And although trading in bodies—particularly the body beautiful—has been the stock in trade of cinema from its inception, Williams pushes forward to explicate how Schwarzenegger adroitly managed and manipulated all aspects of his spectacularly hard body for commercial gain, and to form a transmedia branding system over which he maintained ultimate proprietorship. Through her study, we see how audience reception of Schwarzenegger's body and star text is not so easily managed or contained in terms of stabilizing his masculine image. As Williams puts it, "Schwarzenegger provoked extensive critical response during the 1990s, and writers usually start with his body as a way of thinking about his body of work." For Williams his body is a "crystallization of the decade's most successful genre: action. Perhaps in no other genre (with the possible exception of pornography) is the body of the film and the body of the star so synonymous." Most insightfully, she continues, "The story of Schwarzenegger's stardom is also a story of extreme self-control that reverberates" throughout his career in bodybuilding, in business, and in blockbuster movies.

Karen Hollinger's probing essay "Jodie Foster: Feminist Hero?" shifts our focus to an important consideration of Hollywood's gender discourse at decade's end with an unflinching gaze upon A-list women stars and their situatedness vis-à-vis late-twentieth-century second wave, third wave, and even postfeminist imperatives. Hollinger deconstructs Foster's star image, personal life, and iconic character performances as they intersect with feminist ideals. What her research and analysis uncover are, as Hollinger puts it, the "difficulty involved in making female Hollywood stars into iconic feminist figures" when the bifurcated actual person and the star-image that is Jodie Foster is "a study in contradictions." One special strength of Hollinger's research is its tracking of Foster's career from child star to Hollywood ingénue to Yale graduate to heroic Academy Award–winning woman star to film director to more traditional female co-star and then to a closeted and ultimately out lesbian. Using a combination of academic and popular criticism, Hollinger interrogates claims about Foster as a new type of female star whose film choices and private life positioned her as a feminist hero at one point. As Foster's career matured, especially when she became a director and producer, Hollinger notes that Foster's feminist fans/audiences became disappointed when she failed to "develop a Hollywood cinema that is 'women-centered'" or an embodiment of feminist ideals.

In "Denzel Washington: A Revisionist Black Masculinity," Melvin Donalson provides an invaluable primer on the changing racial dynamics in Hollywood and in society at large through his examination of the meaning of Denzel Washington's transcendent star image and personal achievements in Hollywood during the 1990s. Among Donalson's insightful revelations are that Washington's stardom revised and liberated the black male image from the shackles of ghetto-centricity and neo-minstrelsy historically associated with black masculinity, and that Washington's stardom hinged on first becoming a crossover success with mainstream white audiences. Through an analysis of six iconic Washington films, he addresses the question of why Washington became more of a crossover star than his predecessors. Donalson's study leaves no doubt that Washington's credentials were impeccable and that he possessed the requisite sex appeal and glamour. And, as Donald Bogle wrote, "Lo and behold, the guy could act." Donalson reminds us that Washington successfully translated his televisual celebrity into cinematic superstardom. Additionally, he makes the case that although "one black actor can't carry the burden," Washington has done more than any other actor to redefine black masculinity onscreen, and outside the norms of society's usual racial scripts. Perhaps most cogent in Donalson's study is that he conveys the import of Washington's professional and good-Joe type of film characters as counterbalances to the "pervasive black ghetto male images in the 'hood films of the early 1990s."

Addressing the quintessential female superstar and boxoffice queen of the decade is R. Barton Palmer's essay "Julia Roberts: Cultural Phenomenon." Palmer deciphers a crucial element in Roberts's undeniable onscreen magnetism and overall cultural capital, which he locates in the uncanny private-life parallels to her popular film characters' fictional lives. Palmer sees *Notting Hill*, especially, as a "displaced star biography." For Palmer, then, "*Notting Hill* is not only a romantic comedy, but also a woman's picture—and on both its fictional and metafictional levels. The film traces a pattern of maturing self-awareness that is connected not only to romantic fulfillment, but also and, arguably more importantly, to the full acceptance of the responsibilities and discontents of cinematic stardom." Interestingly, Palmer intimates that Roberts's fans willfully and pleasurably conflate the romantic travails and victories found in Roberts's film heroines with her own highly publicized romantic entanglements. As he puts it, "Like Julia Roberts, [*Notting Hill*'s] Anna is not forced to choose between a husband and happy domesticity, on the one hand, and a satisfying career, on the other. Quite the contrary. *Notting Hill* makes it quite clear that the relationship with a man who comes without the baggage of his own career completes rather than replaces Anna's professional life, promoting the notion of a woman liberated and empowered rather than entrapped by romance, with her drive for success at least as important as what personal happiness her glamour and charm might win for her." What makes Roberts's postfeminist star image so compelling and a cultural phenomenon, as Palmer suggests, is that like so many men in society, Julia Roberts manages to have it all—career, romance, and ultimately a happy ending, both onscreen and off.

From boxoffice queen to boxoffice king, Murray Pomerance's essay "Leonardo DiCaprio: King of the 'World'" enables us to appreciate the unpredictable nature of mega-celebrity as he takes us through the process of DiCaprio's incremental and accelerated moves up the ladder to A-list Hollywood stardom. During his early journeyman years in such films as *What's Eating Gilbert Grape* (1993), *This Boy's Life* (1993), *The Quick and The Dead* (1995), and *The Basketball Diaries* (1995), and television shows "Santa Barbara" (1983–1993) and "Growing Pains" (1985–1992), the young actor developed the "Good Bad Boy" persona that typified a large portion of DiCaprio's career throughout the nineties. As Pomerance describes the persona, "He could show popular and appealing qualities as a promising, heterosexual, sport-loving, competitive, appropriately aggressive, and yet sweet and adorable male figure." Most important to DiCaprio, Pomerance argues, "was the idea of producing an 'acting tour de force,'" which he accomplished to astonishing effect in the most financially successful film of the decade, *Titanic* (1997). Most important for star studies in the nineties was DiCaprio's precipitation of an obsessive fandom associated with the film, the "Titaniacs," largely comprising young girls. As Pomerance notes, these fangirls were "bug-eyed observers who had seen the film more than ten times before a year was out," catapulting the film to a shocking $200 million box office record and "Leo" to mega-watt stardom.

Helping us to grasp further the new racially and ethnically diverse star universe of the era is Laura Isobel Serna's essay "Andy Garcia, Antonio Banderas, and Edward James Olmos: Stardom, Masculinity and 'Latinidades.'" In her analysis of these three very distinctive and individuated film stars, Serna unpacks and calls into question what Frances Aparicio calls "the ways in which the entertainment industry, mainstream journalism, and Hollywood have homogenized all Latinos into one undifferentiated group." For her, the media embrace of Garcia, Banderas, and Olmos (in films, on television, and in print) signifies a representational shift, of sorts, from the familiar pattern of discursive foreignness and racial otherness positioned completely outside the U.S. social and cultural mainstream. Simultaneously, however, she cautions against blindly accepting media "construction[s] of the mainstreaming of Hispanic culture." Moreover, she argues that "Latino film stars [get] mobilized as highly visible representatives of a perceived sea change in American culture at large." Representing the so-called "Latino Boom" in Hollywood during the nineties, Serna penetrates the particular star function of these charismatic stars. For her, then, these stars "share the experience of being read as Latino," while each star "presented a differently inflected version of socially acceptable Latino masculinity." Banderas is codified as the Latin lover, Garcia is representative of Latin passion, assimilation, and family values, and Olmos is "an ethnic star unflinchingly committed to his community." All three, Serna demonstrates, convey a sense of individual exceptionalism. She is very attentive to the specificities of each performer's star image and personal lives, as well as how Olmos, Garcia, and Banderas cultivate a growing Latina/o audience while advancing claims to cultural citizenship and cultural belonging in the United States.

With "Tom Hanks and Tom Cruise: The Box Office and 'True Masculinity,'" Mary Beth Haralovich presents a fascinating look at two of the decade's most successful male stars. As articulated by Haralovich, Hanks and Cruise are the contemporary embodiments of classical Hollywood-era male movie-star types and the quintessence of contemporary or nineties-era new masculine star images. That is, both performers are variations on popular masculine types, types capable of portraying all-American maleness from across the masculine continuum, from heterosexual normativity to homosexual alterity, from macho tough guy to sensitive male in touch with his feminine side. However, Haralovich carefully distinguishes between these men as specific image types and real individuals, revealing remarkable points of convergence and divergence between them. For example, she reminds us that the comedy genre catapulted both Toms' careers upward. Second, she outlines two kinds of economic power and two kinds of popular masculinity engulfing these stars in the 1990s. In Haralovich's formulation of their differences, Tom Hanks typified the "Ordinary Guy" and Tom Cruise became the "Intense Guy." Her scrupulous research makes manifest behavioral aspects of this particular difference. When questions about Hanks's and Cruise's sexuality titilated the media early in the decade, questions associated primarily with their gay performances in *Philadelphia* (1993) and *Interview with a Vampire* (1994), respectively, Cruise defended his heterosexuality vehemently while Hanks, by contrast, was untroubled: his "ordinary guy" masculinity was stable. In terms of their up-close-and-personal online participation in new media culture, Haralovich notes that Cruise's official website is "robust and strong," whereas Hanks's MySpace page reveals a "regular guy."

A crucial significance of Haralovich's star study turns on her ability to demystify the ideological power and function of stardom. In terms of what stardom *does*, Hanks's huge popularity helped make "a success of the mainstream message film," as when Hanks and director Steven Spielberg received the highest civilian honor from the U.S. Navy for *Saving Private Ryan* (1998); and it confronted America's homophobia and asserted the moral high ground, tackling the stigma of homosexuality and AIDS in *Philadelphia*. As individual stars, Haralovich makes the point that Cruise's star image combines "charming vulnerability" and "cocky young guy" bravado; also, his visible maturation has led him to be favorably compared to mature matinee idols of previous generations. Hanks's star image consists of thoughtful acting and a physical malleability that fully embodies a personality, bringing likeability and humanity to flawed and extraordinary male roles through his ordinary body, poignant eyes, and beefy face. In terms of his retro Hollywood appeal, Hanks is favorably compared to Spencer Tracy and Jimmy Stewart.

Mia Mask's essay "Angela Bassett and Halle Berry: African American Leading Ladies," is an uncompromising treatise on the predicament of black women stars in Hollywood at this time. In her balanced analysis of these contrasting and powerful icons of black female beauty, complexity, resilience, and agency, Mask situates Bassett's and Berry's career choices, personal lives, and star images within the contexts of Hollywood's persistent institutional racism and a resurgent black independent film movement often plagued with its own problematic gender discourse. She discloses how Bassett and Berry offer interesting case studies of "the choices black actresses must make to succeed in an otherwise exclusionary, white, heterosexist, and predominantly male industry." Mask tracks their respective career trajectories and also takes note of each woman's "distinct brand of charisma: Bassett embodies black bourgeois respectability, unconditional maternal love, and sociopolitical responsibility. Berry aligned herself with hip-hop culture, urban sassiness, and coquettish sexuality in a multicultural era." Another key insight that Mask brings to her study is sensitivity to these women stars' dialogic encounter with the changing sociocultural realities of American civil society, particularly in terms of race and identity politics. Mask comments, for instance, that "interracial relationships figured prominently in Berry's early screen persona and throughout her career. Bassett veered away from risqué and taboo roles."

From a discussion of ascendant black women's stardom, we move to Donna Peberdy's compelling critique of cinematic discourses on the politics and crises of white masculinity in the era of multiculturalism. In "Michael Douglas: An Ordinary Man," Peberdy takes account of a specific subset of Douglas's *oeuvre* during the nineties that illustrates a discernable departure from the familiar narratives and characters of his earlier films. Her concern is with challenging academic and popular media reductions of Douglas's star image to the endangered "Average White Male" type. The Douglas films that constitute Peberdy's primary objects of analysis are the neo-noir "erotic thrillers" *Basic Instinct* (1992), *Disclosure* (1994), and *A Perfect Murder* (1998); and the "pathetic masculinity" films *Falling Down* (1993), *The Game* (1997), and *Wonder Boys* (2000). Her research revises the essentialized view of Douglas's screen persona as the epitome of contemporary masculinity in crisis, a reified case of the idiolect of the star. More simply put, this means that recurring elements of a star performance carryover from role to role. "In Douglas's case," Peberdy argues, "a recurring theme in his 'Average White Male' roles is the presentation of ordinariness." Significantly, her star study looks at Douglas's nineties films as the first to figure him as middle-aged, and even graying: "It is the new emphasis on age that marks Douglas as different. His graying hair suggests an aging Douglas, not the timeless and unchanging Douglas from *Fatal Attraction*, *Basic Instinct*, and *Disclosure*."

In "Pierce Brosnan: Licensed to Sell," Tracey Hoover and Toby Miller investigate one of the more interesting practices of the stardom phenomenon in the nineties, the star's management and manipulation of his star image as a proprietary brand. Hoover and Miller make a convincing case for Pierce Brosnan as one of the era's most astute operators in this mode of celebrity publicity and promotion. Recognizing Brosnan's role in the revivification of the Bond film franchise, they map and scrutinize his amazing business acumen as well as his fierce protection of his personal and professional autonomy. "Brosnan," they assert, "is very careful about his star signage as a commodity fetish, having brought a celebrated case before the World Intellectual Property Organization (WIPO) over the domain name <piercebrosnan.com> to get a Canadian website shut down for using it without permission. WIPO established in its decision that the sign 'Pierce Brosnan' has 'secondary meaning'; that is, everything done under it is associated in the public mind with the person, Pierce Brosnan. As a consequence, the actor has trademark-protection rights over his name." Clearly, during this era, Brosnan's name was licensed to sell masculine cool.

Finally, in "Keanu Reeves and Johnny Depp: Hollywood and the Iconoclasts," I take on what I term the "masculinity reset" as codified in the star images and personal lives of Depp and Reeves, young Hollywood's most iconoclastic players. Each in his turn, I contend, contributed significantly to reformulations of "cinematic codes of masculinity, and, by extension, gender significations at large." And this as normative heterosexual behaviors and values "were shifting and becoming much more fluid than in past eras." Like other nontraditional masculine types in the cinema, Reeves and Depp

Jennifer Lopez featured in an early supporting role in *Blood and Wine* (Bob Rafelson, Twentieth Century–Fox, 1996). Lopez's Gabriela "Gabby" is a Cuban nanny/housekeeper, a beauty who steals the hearts of rival petty criminals Alex (Jack Nicholson) and Victor (Michael Caine). Courtesy Photofest New York.

often struck a gentle and sometimes effete masculine figure that threatened to destabilized masculine orthodoxy and gender performativity especially in opposition to women's prescribed roles. But, as I note, by the century's end different registers of gender and other identity politics were in the offing, whereby social movements advancing gender equity made rigid social, cultural, and political positions less tenable. Moreover, the study engages with the changing nature of American attitudes toward people of mixed-race lineage, which was a very important element in both young actors' unique features and alluring visual appeal beyond the discourses of white privilege, the miscegenation taboo, and the tragic mulatto/a figure.

For me, Reeves's and Depp's stardoms were also imbricated within the technological revolution of the World Wide Web and the evolution of cyberculture and convergent media processes. Also, I argue that fierce and active fans of the charmingly roguish or so-called "Hollywood bad boys" were innovative in their devoted fandom, as Depp's and Reeves's fans were among the first to establish fansites for their favorite American idols. Culling a range of popular and journalist reportage and academic treatises on stardom, celebrity, cultural, and historical work, I take seriously claims that both Depp and Reeves were major catalysts for much of what distinguishes star culture in the nineties from other historical periods.

Considering the breadth and scope of the essays collected in this volume, it will become evident that the work presented here is steeped in the excellent research and scholarship on star studies that precede it, while advancing innovative and insightful research perspectives, methods, and tenets of its own and in terms responsive to new realities and developments in today's film and media industries and cultures. And while an encyclopedic examination of the many shifts and changes transpiring in stardom and the important stars at its core is outside the parameters of this project, the authors here have endeavored to produce as thoughtful, provocative, and forward-looking a volume as possible from their individual research interests and vantage points. It is important to acknowledge at this point a necessarily selective process in the choice of stars featured in this work. And since some of the stars discussed here are not as highly positioned inside the Hollywood A-list hierarchy as others, for this volume it was essential to represent a diversity of stars from across the racial and ethnic spectrum. One glaring lack in this area is the growing number of Latina stars that emerged during the decade. However, the significance of Jennifer Lopez and Salma Hayek, for example, is considered in the chapter "In the Wings" at the end of the book. Ultimately, the essays in this volume provide an exciting and effective primer on film stars in the 1990s.

Arnold Schwarzenegger
Corporeal Charisma

LINDA RUTH WILLIAMS

In 2003 the American Film Institute published lists of the fifty greatest heroes and fifty greatest villains in U.S. movie history, accompanied by a three-hour broadcast on CBS hosted by Arnold Schwarzenegger. Schwarzenegger's Terminator character was the only role to appear on both lists, by virtue of the *volte-face* taken between *The Terminator* in 1984 and its first sequel, *Terminator 2: Judgment Day*, in 1991. For French theorist Edgar Morin, stars are godlike because they weld hero to villain in a way that is beyond human, which in itself might seal Schwarzenegger's profile as exemplary 1990s star. The move from destroyer to protector has been read as highly symptomatic of a shift enacted by many a Hollywood male at the start of the 1990s—action stars morphing into softer thespians, killers becoming dads, insensitive hulks discovering their sensitive side. Everything

Arnold Schwarzenegger has done in his forty-year career has been forged on a monumental scale, and the pirouette from villain to hero was replete with era-defining significance. Indeed, his shape-shifting has always seemed emblematic of its moment.

The story of Schwarzenegger's stardom is also a story of extreme self-control that reverberates through the institutions and individuals around him (a self-control that becomes controlling)—control over his body, a body shaped and remolded in the bodybuilding career that preceded his movies; in fierce self-promotion as he entered film in the 1970s and 1980s; and in the pathway he negotiated through key Hollywood genres in the 1990s, all accompanied by the hard-working publicity machine assisting his every move. "Modesty is not a word that applies to me in any way—I hope it never will," Schwarzenegger has asserted (qtd. in Morin 66).

Schwarzenegger's rise to stardom can be framed through a number of familiar star trajectories and myths. He is the immigrant from old Europe making good in the new world, though unlike his studio-era ancestors he didn't have to perfect an American accent or Anglicize his name to secure fame.[1] He is the exploitation performer who, by 1990, had risen to the top of the Hollywood A-list. John Ellis has discussed how stardom is a negotiation of apparent "ordinariness" and glamorous remoteness (91). But this resoundingly New Hollywood star has striven to forge an identity that is anything but ordinary. More like the godlike figures of studio-era Hollywood Babylon, Schwarzenegger wants visibly to be as extraordinary as possible. Extratextual glimpses of the Schwarzenegger-Shrivers jet-skiing in Florida do little to suggest a sense of an average family man mucking in with the kids. Stardom, as mentioned above, is often theorized as a contradictory state—stars speak to a variety of audiences and shape-shift if the market requires it, but profound contradictions might open up between public/private elements of a star profile and between what a star projects at different moments of his or her career.

The balance between (pseudo) private and public, hammered out by publicists, agents, and the industries that circulate star images, is often precarious. Elements of private life and screen persona don't necessarily fit together, and poorly matched suture lines enable contradictory messages to leak out. But Schwarzenegger does not look as contradictory as many of his forebears or contemporaries—his public image is of total identification between self and role, with little else seeping through the cracks. Indeed, there aren't many cracks—in public and private he appears a man of steel, welded into his iconic form through the furnace of self-will and exercise. Which is not to say that there is no contradiction about Schwarzenegger or the roles he plays, but rather that contradiction is manifestly present on the glossy surface of his star body. He is both old and new—old world, old-style hero, working in New Hollywood, from and for the Baby Boom generation. He is branded as hyper-masculine despite starting in a sport that is associated with semi-naked posing, male spectacle, and gay visual consumption. He mocks "girlie men" yet, in his willingness to exhibit himself, has been read as a muscled-up version of one.[2]

He is an American star par excellence, but an American star with a residual German accent who, with a special dispensation, retained his Austrian citizenship when he was naturalized as American in 1993. Certainly his Europeanness has not always worked in his favor: Schwarzenegger is not just a white star, he's a whiter than white star, anxious enough about his Austrian heritage to investigate his father's involvement with the Nazi Party during World War II. He has even argued that the residual accent is not a performance failure but a deliberate affectation, which endearingly reminds his fans that "I am indeed a mortal human being" (qtd. in Van Scheers 208). His Europeanness, branded as hard-working brawn rather than effete culture, has contributed to his universal marketability and, as I discuss toward the end of this chapter, he took the global marketplace far more seriously than many of his peers.

By the 1990s Schwarzenegger's brand had been forged in a number of arenas, each informing the other, with cinema just one element in the firmament of his marketable products, identities, and merchandise. The oft-repeated story of the poor boy from an obscure Austrian village who took to sport partly on the encouragement of his brutal father, partly to escape that brutal father, is told in parallel with the story that at the tender age of ten little Arnie determined that one day he would make his way to the USA and get very, very rich. He started off as a bodybuilding brand, with an empire of merchandise radiating out from his multiple physical successes: before he ever hit cinema screens he was making money with businesses supplying sports equipment (first, a mail order business marketing products under the name "Arnold Strong," also his first screen name [see Schwarzenegger and Hall 108]; and second, through property investment). The Schwarzenegger brand is not, then, just a figurative way of framing his approach to movie stardom; he sells products with various permutations of his name wrapped around them, and not just around theatrically released movies.

By the 1990s the power of his brand was also highly evident in the home viewing market. Schwarzenegger's crest of stardom was pushed along as VCRs and DVDs entered the living room with his name prominently affixed to the packaging: he was the Video Software Dealers Association star

of the year in 1990 (Prince 116). Star studies have focused on the inter-
play between ancillary marketing texts and cinematic images (Catherine
Deneuve and Chanel No. 5; Sharon Stone wearing Gap outfits; see Thompson and Epstein, respectively). In this period Schwarzenegger made this a
plainly visible part of the well-oiled machine of the multitasking brand
that spoke his star machismo in various consumer tongues. All his products (film/video texts you can watch, gyms you can exercise in, books and
political messages you can be inspired by) send out a mutually reinforcing
and market-compatible message: strength is good, power is good, money
is good.

The 1990s were particularly significant for Schwarzenegger. This was
the moment when he consolidated his family-friendly, cross-genre appeal,
crucial to his world domination bid. And though as the decade progressed
his box office returns diminished somewhat—*Last Action Hero* (1993) was
his first flop; *Batman & Robin* (1997) was also a critical and commercial
failure—he had learned the message of flexibility and diversification. In
1986 he made a good marriage to political royalty (Maria Shriver, John F.
Kennedy's niece), and by the 1990s they were building a family. Action
cinema also took a familial turn at this point, and Schwarzenegger became
the perfect product to capitalize upon this shift. As the decade progressed
he forged an extracurricular persona that straddled politics and entertainment. His support for the Republican Party was rewarded with his being
named the chair of the President's Council on Fitness and Sports from 1990
to 1993 under George H. W. Bush, who called him "Conan the Republican."
Schwarzenegger's sports star persona became the rock upon which his film
star persona was built, and onto that superstructure political stardom was
welded, secured with his election as California governor in 2003. These
three formations of stardom were systematically bolted onto each other as
the decade dawned and progressed.

Onscreen he adopted a kind of bolted-together stardom, too, which
took a number of different shapes and turns as he identified what was
lacking in his personal firmament and attempted to plug a new personal
"talent" into the gap, comedy being the most cynical add-on. Charisma
emerges in the conjunction of these moving parts. It is not a deific effusion
as borne out by Hollywood stars of old, but something far more fleshily
grounded and commercially manufacturable in response to need. Charisma,
for Schwarzenegger, is something that emerges first from the built-up
body, second from the versatility and multiple roles it plays. It effuses from
fleshly manifestation and the manufacture of persona, like the reek of
body fluids.

★★★★★ Charisma, Charm, and the Corpus

> When we speak of charisma, we are transported to the domain of the heroic, the extraordinary, the magical. And, unlike in life, the film charisma is not dissipated and routinized. Congealed in the emulsion, it is released by the projector to radiate again and again.
>
> —Lorraine Mortimer, in Morin viii

> I knew I had an advantage over most bodybuilders: when you have the size, the whole rough cut, you can sculpt it into a masterpiece. . . . I chiseled and polished, rendering that animal mass I'd brought from Europe down to the work of art I wanted. I'd had jewel-like abdominals for the first time.
>
> —Arnold Schwarzenegger to Douglas Kent Hall, 1977

Schwarzenegger provoked extensive critical response during the 1990s, and writers usually start with his body as a way of thinking about his body of work. The body as sexual-cultural symptom becomes the embodied crystallization of the decade's most successful genre: action. Perhaps in no other genre (with the possible exception of pornography) are the body of the film and the body of the star so synonymous. This is not simply because Schwarzenegger's body is so massive and manifest, but because the male body in particular was a key focus for theorists of the politics of spectacle and stardom when Schwarzenegger's global star was ascendant. Critical writing on action cinema as it emerged as a discrete focus for film studies in the early 1990s started not with the narrative or formal hallmarks of the genre, but with the bodies of its stars. Susan Jeffords and Yvonne Tasker in particular drew parallels between the hard bodies onscreen and the hard right-wing politics of the Reagan and Bush eras, though there is also a strong focus on these bodies as suffering and damaged.

Thus the spectacle of action was framed not simply through its central technology so expertly wielded by Schwarzenegger—Uzis, Harley-Davidsons, Glock 9mms (another famous Austrian export)—but the movement of, damage to, and generally spectacular excesses of the human body in extreme form. In *Eraser* (1996) he suffers a nail through the hand, a spike through the thigh, and a bullet in the shoulder, while in *End of Days* (1999) he is dangled from a window sill with his hand embedded in broken glass, run over by a train, strangled, stitched, thrashed by a baseball bat–wielding gang of Satanists, and, perhaps most undignified of all, beaten up by a demonically impelled Miriam Margolyes. In *Terminator 2* (1991) he is repeatedly shot, run over by a truck, and finally dissolved in molten steel. Examples like this can be found in most of Schwarzenegger's films; the spectacle of male suffering is as ubiquitous in action cinema as that of tooling up. Such images are salaciously presented, appealing to a sadomasochistic aesthetic, and demonstrating, above all, that Schwarzenegger can take it.

Stardom is extra- as well as intratextual, and it may well be that the measure of his success is that we know Schwarzenegger without ever having seen a Schwarzenegger film. His signature elaborate action set-pieces are almost stand-alone cinematic vignettes, perhaps arbitrarily exchangeable across and between movies. In *Eraser* he shoots his way out of a plane, sets fire to one of its engines, loses his parachute, and then catches up with it midair. The plane then chases him through the sky and, still dangling from the parachute, he shoots straight into the cockpit before landing in a breaker's yard. Compare, or exchange, this with the crane sequence in *Last Action Hero*, the Harrier sequence in *True Lies* (1994), and the subway sequence in *End of Days*, and a star profile begins to emerge wrought in the interchangeable bolted-together parts of high octane, kinetically edited, rock-music spectacle, all orchestrated around the exploits of a body by turns imperiled and heroic.

Star quality has often been defined through charisma, though this is usually quite diffusely articulated and tied to the body through glamour or beauty. Introducing Edgar Morin's seminal 1972 text *The Stars*, Lorraine Mortimer writes that stardom lies "at the crossroads of what we call the 'aesthetic,' the 'magical,' and the 'religious'" (in Morin vii). Star charisma is also highly corporeal; as Mortimer also suggests in my epigraph above, it is brought by the star's body into the body of the film. Schwarzenegger is more superman than deity, sporting the body of a hero driven by an iron will, and larger than life. Yet so brazen is he about the manufactured nature of the body that he has written a book about how to achieve it: *Arnold: The Education of a Bodybuilder*, first published in 1977, but a bestseller in the 1990s. Part 1 is a muscle-obsessed autobiography; part 2 is Arnold's bespoke training program and diet, which rode the crest of his success on the big screen with reprints and new editions. The program is perhaps parodied in the training schedule to which he subjects his small charges in *Kindergarten Cop*—"Time to turn this mush into muscles!" he declares. This ex-Mr. Olympia, Mr. World, and Mr. Universe spent the 1990s connecting übermensch to mortal, the extraordinary to everyday, though he is never quite a regular Joe. Given Schwarzenegger's later "Governator" role and his developing political profile during the decade, it is also interesting that for other writers—including most significantly Richard Dyer mediating Max Weber—star power and political power have the same mesmeric origins. For Weber charisma is "a certain quality of an individual personality by virtue of which he [*sic*] is set apart from ordinary men and treated as endowed with supernatural, superhuman or at least superficially exceptional qualities" (qtd. in Dyer, *Stars* 30).

Dictionary definitions present charisma as mingling the political with the religious—a charismatic person has a magnetic charm and has been favored by the gods. Charisma, then, is a bearing that suggests the star's right to dominate the space he or she inhabits. Schwarzenegger's charisma is rooted in straight corporeal prowess, augmented by the damageable/unconquerable quality the body exudes while engaging in performed acts of derring-do. The self-reflexive postmodern sense of irony lent by some of his films, his infamous one-liners, and the self-promoting/self-mocking biographical stories both reinforce and contradict the iron man persona, but all these elements work together to suggest a man in command of screen space and personal fate. "We must not regard Arnold as the new Laurence Olivier," Paul Verhoeven said of him; "He is more of a Charlton Heston. His strength is his charisma" (qtd. in Van Scheers 209).

But Dyer goes further when he suggests that the well-timed, well-placed charismatic star emerges in response to contradictory social impulses and forces, glamorously and symbolically making sense of his or her moment. Quoting S. N. Eisenstadt, charisma is most effective "when the social order is uncertain, unstable and ambiguous and when the charismatic figure or group offers a value, order or stability to counterpoise this" (31). Schwarzenegger was one such figure. To paraphrase Dyer on Monroe, in the late 1980s and throughout the 1990s Schwarzenegger seems to "be" the very tensions that ran through U.S. culture. Such tensions are well documented in studies of gender, action, and cinema at this time. Mark Gallagher argues that "cinematic and literary representations of male action compensate for threats to stable, traditional masculinity, threats posed by economic and cultural changes affecting men's roles in the workplace and in the domestic space." For Gallagher, figures such as Schwarzenegger offer viewers "utopian solutions to social problems, privileging the transformative effects of physical agency" (3). With male identity widely viewed as crisis-ridden, super-body Schwarzenegger (and his chosen genre) promoted physical solutions and unalloyed masculinity. At a time when men were more uncertain than ever about their role in the family—wedded to work, yet newly required to be at-home hands-on fathers—he made movies in which he was a beleaguered father (*Jingle All the Way*), an ambivalent father-figure (*Terminator 2, Kindergarten Cop*), the father of a lost child (*End of Days, Kindergarten Cop*), a male-mother/birthing father (*Junior*), and an oversized odd-couple sibling searching for his mother (*Twins*). At a time when postmodern uncertainties around identity and the real were becoming the stuff of popular discourse, he made movies playing with his own simulated star identity that attempted to resolve questions into apple-pie conclusions (*Total Recall*, *True Lies*, *Last Action Hero*).

Schwarzenegger became a star first through physical performance, turning to bodybuilding for reasons of masculinity and individualism. Team sports disappointed him because they lacked individual rewards, he writes (Schwarzenegger and Hall 14). But more than this, bodybuilding shored up Schwarzenegger's sense of what a real man ought to be. As he rather disarmingly reports on his first sight of men lifting weights, bodybuilders are individual, and very male: "Those guys were huge and brutal. I found myself walking around them, staring at muscles I couldn't even name, muscles I'd never even seen before. The weight lifters shone with sweat; they were powerful looking, Herculean" (14). This remarkable moment of homosocial if not avowedly homosexual spectatorship seals his desire to become the spectacle he sees, only better—the best. On first encountering a picture of his hero Reg Park, he writes, with no apparent sense of self-irony: "I responded immediately to Reg Park's rough, massive look. The man was an animal. That's the way I wanted to be—ultimately: big. I wanted to be a big guy. I didn't want to be delicate. I dreamed of big deltoids, big pecs, big thighs, big calves; I wanted every muscle to explode and be huge. I dreamed about being gigantic"(17). Bodybuilding was Schwarzenegger's passport out of European obscurity and into U.S. celebrity: he was the youngest ever Mr. Olympia (in 1970), a title he won a record seven times; the most lucrative event in bodybuilding changed its name to the Arnold Classic in his honor. Sports stardom is not the same as film stardom, but it gave Schwarzenegger a taste of stardom per se: he describes the "feeling of magnificence" he got when pumped-up and posing (74), and viewed signing an autograph (writing the self in a celebrity context) as a stardom rite of passage. Schwarzenegger's drive to stardom is bound up not just with the desire for money but with some power-exuding charismatic effect that the trappings of success seem to give off. Of his idol Reg Parks's house he writes, "It had an aura about it: it was the house of a star. That quality was unmistakable. In the dining room, for instance, you pressed a button and servants appeared" (82).

Of course, there is a long tradition of sports-stars-turned-actors, which Schwarzenegger joins—Johnny Weissmuller, Esther Williams, O. J. Simpson, and Chuck Norris. Weissmuller is perhaps the nearest comparator: hailing from central Europe and bearing a foreign name throughout his Hollywood career, he was a record-breaking swimming star and sometime bodybuilder himself. He became famous globally, primarily for the iconic role of Tarzan, the most powerful commodification of the Weissmuller-branded sports merchandise. Throughout the 1990s when he was at his film-starriest, Schwarzenegger also maintained his sports star persona for merchandising purposes. Perhaps in his focus on the body he turned film stardom into an extension of sports stardom. Yet more than swimming or martial arts, bodybuilding might be seen as perfect training for male spectacle.

Doubts have been raised over its status as a bona fide sport, and Schwarzenegger himself admits that the posing of bodybuilding is "pure theatre": "I'd see where they did slow poses, and figure out how I could put in three poses for their one, and thus be able to show many more body parts to the judges" (Schwarzenegger and Hall 69). Showier than the track, field, or water events other sportsmen used as star-springboards, arguably this made bodybuilding an easier route for segueing into other "showy" arenas (film stardom) but a problem when it came to establishing the cast-iron credentials of masculinity. Both Tasker (*Spectacular Bodies*) and Dyer ("Don't Look") have reflected on the ambivalence of the bodybuilder's body as feminized by virtue of its showiness, and as a masquerade object. As feminized spectacle—however über-masculine it might in itself be—Schwarzenegger's body has been used to challenge male gaze theories. As a costume formation, albeit a costume-as-flesh fused to the frame of its wearer, it has been read as a form of masquerade, a building block in arguments for new kinds of identity politics. The meanings it seems to bear out speak for the wider culture, and so his stardom, hooked onto that fleshly frame, is recognized as a prime symptom of that culture.

Even if, during the 1990s, he worked down from the excessive musculature of the champion bodybuilder's form and presented a relatively lithe, flexible frame more suited to the mobility of action roles rather than the static posing of bodybuilding performance, his visible body was still his primary asset, closely followed by his aural body—that voice, with its heavy European accent and limited monotone pitch. His movies make much of his magnitude despite the fact that he's only 6'1" (or 6'2", depending on which source you trust)—not excessively tall by any means. Low-angle shots are used in *Kindergarten Cop* to emphasize his gigantic size relative to his six-year-old charges, while both *Junior* and *Twins* make much of the difference between Schwarzenegger and his diminutive co-star, Danny DeVito (the high-concept formulation that underpins *Twins*—that these unlikely beings are twins—effectively presold it to distributors; see Wyatt 55).

Of course, Schwarzenegger was not the only muscled-up male on the Hollywood A-list. The battle of the action hero giants was fought in the late

"You're the best celebrity look-alike I've ever seen!" Arnie is doubled as star and character meet in *The Last Action Hero* (John McTiernan, Columbia, 1993). Digital frame enlargement.

1980s on two fronts. On the one hand, A-list action stars vied for domination, in terms of a whole range of qualities. Schwarzenegger's colleagues in the establishment of the Planet Hollywood restaurant chain in 1991—Bruce Willis, Sylvester Stallone—were pitted against him and each other in a struggle that was not just for box office supremacy. Willis had a history in other genres, particularly through the romantic comedy-thriller TV show "Moonlighting," and he was willing to tackle more indie-minded character roles such as in *Mortal Thoughts* (1991), *Pulp Fiction* (1994), and *12 Monkeys* (1995), so he had a versatility built into his career that Arnie could not match. Stallone was a writer-director who continued to demonstrate his thespian chops with titles from *F.I.S.T* (1978) to *Cop Land* (1997). Schwarzenegger, on the other hand, has his biceps, confidently comparing them to Stallone's on a *Rambo* poster he passes in *Twins*. *Last Action Hero* presents us with a curious "George Bailey" moment:[3] as Jack Slater (Schwarzenegger's character-within-a-character), he comments on a *Terminator 2* poster featuring Stallone, not Schwarzenegger as the cyborg icon. Curiously, this only goes to shore up his world dominance: Arnie is first choice; Stallone is there—in action terms—only if Schwarzenegger is not. On another front, a key star battle was fought with two other thick-accented Europeans—Jean-Claude Van Damme (from Belgium) and Dolph Lundgren (from Sweden). Lundgren and Van Damme parlayed martial arts skill into cinematic action ability. They were, as Christine Cornea points out, far more mobile actors than Schwarzenegger, whose performances are "remarkably inactive . . . his bodily movements frequently appear considered, posed and held for inspection" (285–86)—an inactive action star, then. Despite the fact that Schwarzenegger never really threw off the impression that English was a foreign language to him (an insurmountable problem in Hollywood since the coming of sound), his stardom went stratospheric relative to that of his European compatriots. Though Van Damme and Lundgren appeared primarily in action films in the 1990s, Schwarzenegger became the genre's charismatic patron saint.

★★★★★ Family, Collaboration, Action

Charisma is also, for some critics, generated through the "perfect fit" of role with star and body genre. John O. Thompson's commutation test focuses on the semiotic "rightness" of casting: "One asks oneself if a change in the signifier would make a difference, and the answer can surprise one" (185). Could the Terminator be performed by anyone else? Would Schwarzenegger be the same without the Terminator? What traces of charisma exude from that cyborg body? The character/star motifs of leather jacket, heavy armaments, motorcycle, flat ironic dialogue delivery, and, most iconically, sunshades shadowed his roles forevermore. Yet Schwarzenegger wasn't Cameron's first choice for the role, and they met with a view to his playing heroic Kyle Reese (Leamer 158–59). Sean French answers the commutation test with reference to the simple fact of stardom: "The main difference . . . between Arnold Schwarzenegger and Michael Biehn (who played Reese) is that Schwarzenegger is a star in a way that Biehn could never hope to be" (46). What "fits" between Schwarzenegger and the Terminator is also what fits the star for his career in action films generally, though the move from villain to hero is not the only tone shift Schwarzenegger makes within the genre. Action-adventure is a slippery and amoebic genre, and Schwarzenegger has ranged across its hybrid forms, playing heroes and villains in action sci-fi, action war films, action swashbucklers, action comedies, and postmodern action parody. Through each of these forms runs a myth of relentlessness that takes its cue from the star's biographical PR messages, and in turn informs the way in which his films are received. Like the Terminator, Schwarzenegger is often read as driven, focused, and, in Kyle Reese's words, one who "absolutely will not stop." George Butler, who directed him in *Pumping Iron* (1977), has said, "He is a man of bottomless ambition. . . . He sees himself as almost mystically sent to America" (qtd. in Indiana 33–34). Of course the Terminator, circa 1984, "will not stop" for deeply negative reasons, a motivation with which a star hoping to win family audiences in the global marketplace would not wish perpetually to be identified. Jeffords reads the move from the first (1984) to the second (1991) Terminators as symptomatic of a shift in preferred masculinities between the 1980s and the 1990s ("Masculinity"); for her, "1991 was the year of the transformed U.S. man" ("Big Switch" 197). Fred Pfeil reads 1991 as "The Year of Living Sensitively," including *Terminator 2* in a discussion of New Man images, because here the Terminator is "simultaneously softened and sensitized into a man who can both kill *and* care" (53). The shift from Reese's view of the bad Terminator's relentlessness ("It can't be bargained with. It can't be reasoned with. It doesn't feel pity, or remorse, or fear. And it absolutely will not stop, ever, until you are dead") is echoed in Sarah Connor's reflection on the good Terminator's credentials as a perfect father: "The Terminator would never stop. It would never leave him and it would never hurt him, never shout at him or get drunk and hurt him or say it was too busy to spend time with him. It would always be there, and it would die to protect him. Of all the would-be fathers who came and went over the years this thing, this machine, was the only one who measured up" (*Terminator 2*). None of this would work quite so well if Schwarzenegger did not present an extra-curricular air of inexorable will, and if his starriness weren't indelibly marked as driven, ambitious, calculating. It is, then, not so much his massive physical form as it is his powerful compulsion to achieve his goal that makes Schwarzenegger and the Terminator so right for each other. A limited actorly range need not be a problem if star heft can be wielded to make the performance more convincing. Schwarzenegger "was a star whose own persona was his only capital," says his biographer Laurence Leamer, who generally takes the most favorable view of his subject. "Arnold was not an actor as much as he was a performer who played various versions of his idealized self on-screen" (158). Verhoeven thought of him as a "total film star" for this reason (qtd. in Cornea 164). Reports of audiences shouting, "Watch out, Arnold. Behind you!" at a screening of *Total Recall* bear out the sense that, by 1990, he was simply Arnold: "In the eyes of his public, Arnold Schwarzenegger was no longer an actor; he had become a persona. . . . He walked through his films as Arnold, independent of the story, and in the shadow of his own persona he lugged along the character he was supposed to play" (Van Scheers 207).

Of his bodybuilding wins he has said, "The energy and momentum around me was unbelievable. I was insatiable, unstoppable. . . . And naturally I won. It could not have been otherwise" (Schwarzenegger and Hall 91). This statement could do service for other phases of his career as well.

Yet Schwarzenegger could not afford to be only Terminator-certain or Arnold-fixed if he was to demonstrate versatility. By the early to mid-1990s while his career continued in this unstoppable mode, his roles played out as something other, as elements of failure or compromise were confronted onscreen and incorporated more widely into the star image, but these elements also provided the best opportunity for diversification. Domestic concerns posed the biggest challenge to the triumph of the action star's will. As the 1990s progressed Schwarzenegger repeatedly took on roles that set him up as father, failing father, family outsider, at just the time he was publicly establishing an image of real-life doting husband and dad. These films suggest that men achieved the dream (*feminism*'s dream) of "having it all" way before women ever did (*if* they ever did): action and family, hard bodies and soft emotions, work and home, without consequences. Gallagher focuses on the incorporation into action in the 1990s "of formal elements associated with the 'female' genre of melodrama" (45), though in Schwarzenegger's hands, familial action is more often than not comedic.

Bringing lumpen or simple solutions to bear on complex family situations conservatively refigures those problems as failure of individual power. Or, as Gallagher puts it, "What a traditional melodrama might present as a problem of capitalism or family structure, an action film presents as a matter of action and inaction." This is entirely in keeping with the master narrative of Schwarzenegger's stardom itself. His biography—as told by himself and by both authorized and non-authorized writers—is essentially a series of moments of mastery, over his origins, his body, and his personal weaknesses. The Schwarzenegger self-made-man myth is that nothing will hold him back: "What I had more than anyone else was drive. I was hungrier than anybody. I wanted it so badly it hurt. . . . The meaning of life is not simply to exist, to survive, but to move ahead, to go up, to achieve, to conquer" (Schwarzenegger and Hall 53, 112). Pfeil notes *Time* magazine's identification of this sentiment as specifically American, linking a story of Arnold's steady, self-willed rise to stardom—emphasizing his old-fashioned industriousness, tractability, strong will, and good cheer—to its ensuing story, also slotted in the "Business" section, on American dominance in the global "Leisure Empire" (31).

Gallagher goes on to argue that the action/inaction response (or failure to respond) also characterizes family narratives: "By incorporating family into cinematic narratives of ritualized heroism and combat, action films sustain the illusion that viewers may attend to pressing social concerns . . . within the conventional terrain of a master narrative that puts a premium on individual autonomy and dominance" (49). Of course part of

Tooled-up masculinity in *Eraser* (Chuck Russell, Kopelson/Warner Bros., 1996). Digital frame enlargement.

Schwarzenegger's narrative journey in his family-actioners is to discover that not all problems can be overcome with a Magnum Desert Eagle. Gallagher concludes that action and family are not happy bedfellows: "*True Lies* demonstrates the fallacy of omnipotent masculinity, observing that men of action make unreliable husbands and fathers" (72). This is not characteristic of the message of Schwarzenegger's films of the period, and I would argue that *True Lies* concludes that you make a better father if you can kick ass as well as care. As twelve-year-old Danny says to Jack in *Last Action Hero*, "We're perfect buddy movie material. I'll teach you to be vulnerable, you'll teach me to be brave." Emotional unpredictability and childish or female intuition or irrationality challenge the discourse of individual autonomy, a challenge the 1990s Schwarzenegger was welcoming. There's also a distinction in Schwarzenegger's 1990s *oeuvre* between texts rated at fifteen or higher (in the United Kingdom) that confront family crises and those rated lower and marketed at family audiences; those among the latter tend to provide comedic resolutions through an action spectacle (I turn to these in the final section of this essay). Some of his films eschew firepower altogether—John Connor bans him from killing people in *Terminator 2* (he maims them instead), while Jules, the innocent genius Schwarzenegger plays against type in *Twins*, declares, "Actually I hate violence" (to which Danny DeVito's Vincent retorts, "But you're so good at it!"). Both *Terminator 2* and *End of Days* see individual will expressed through martyrdom: at each film's conclusion Schwarzenegger's character self-destructs to save the world.

A further qualification to the individual self-fashioning myth is the extent to which his most celebrated star vehicles were the products of serendipitous partnerships. For such a self-promoted, self-made man, Schwarzenegger has relied heavily on collaborators to lubricate his path to success. *Total Recall* was a characteristic Paul Verhoeven film—a tongue-in-cheek celebration/satire of U.S. genre cinema by another European émigré to Hollywood. If Verhoeven and James Cameron mentored Schwarzenegger's dominance in sci-fi action, Ivan Reitman mentored his parallel-track comedic career. By 1994 Cameron and Reitman had both directed three Schwarzenegger films, one each in the eighties (*The Terminator* and *Twins*, respectively) and two each in the nineties (action films *Terminator 2* and *True Lies* for Cameron; comedies *Junior* and *Kindergarten Cop* for Reitman). The fruitful collaboration with Cameron exemplifies a certain strain of nineties cinema—what Larry Gross in 1995 has called the "Big, Loud Action Movie"—huge budget spectacles in which every cent can be seen onscreen, and which are critically defined through hyperbole and superlatives. Excess and exaggeration usher the Big Loud Action Film's entrance into the marketplace, and they follow its record-breaking achievements at the box office. A lot of Cameron's cents went into Arnie's salary—an unprecedented $14 million, following his previous paycheck of $10 million plus a percentage for *Total Recall* (Prince 147–48). As some of the essays in Tasker's 2004 collection *Action and Adventure Cinema* argue, there is a publicly perceived correlation between the huge success of action films and their paltry critical status. In this sense the genre exemplifies the popular low-culture, high-revenue modality. All the figures circulating around Schwarzenegger products of this period are wrought in superlatives: *Terminator 2* was one of the first of a spate of "ultra high budget films," made for $100 million (then a record), grossing $204 million domestically and $310 million in foreign revenue (Balio 59). Schwarzenegger is the corporeal embodiment of this negative relationship between high commercial and low aesthetic achievement. He is brawn, quantity, and substance rather than talent, quality, and subtlety, and success is judged in quantities of dollars rather than quality of reviews.

Cameron's third film with Schwarzenegger developed this correlation. *True Lies* was bigger and brasher, but it still hung on a domestic conundrum, as might be expected from a director who has specialized in melodramatic affect embedded in action such as *Titanic*. Harry Tasker is a secret agent who masquerades to his wife, Helen (Jamie Lee Curtis), and daughter as a computer salesman. He lets them down repeatedly, and Helen nearly strays. When she finally discovers his true role, she quips, "I married Rambo" and joins him as a secret agent. The action concludes in a ludicrous sequence of stunts set in the Florida Keys, with Harry saving their imperiled daughter (and saving the world from terrorists) in an AV8B Harrier borrowed from the marines. According to the IMDb.com "Trivia" section for the film, seventy-one people die in *True Lies* (IMDb often includes a body count as a crucial statistic for Schwarzenegger pics). In *Last Action Hero* the character Arnold Schwarzenegger—played by Schwarzenegger—makes good publicity of diminishing body counts, saying to a red-carpet interviewer about his film-within-a-film, "In this movie we only kill 48 people compared to the last one where we killed 119."

Cameron has no such qualms, sculpting Schwarzenegger into a more acrobatic action hero than Cornea credits him for—he dances through flames firing with both hands, dangles from helicopters, and rides a horse between skyscrapers. The packaging of star, spectacle, and domestic peril makes *True Lies* a *prêt-à-porter* action vehicle following—by 1994—a familiar familial recipe. But it also develops another interesting strain in the Schwarzenegger profile, that of concealment and qualified identities, which has been read as indicative of a postmodern bent in his characterizations. *Total Recall*—the second in Paul Verhoeven's "psychosis trilogy" (Van Scheers 234)—might have initiated this. After the script had made the rounds for several years, Verhoeven was finally commissioned to develop it as a Schwarzenegger vehicle. As Van Scheers put it, "The businessman Schwarzenegger gave Paul Verhoeven the task of delivering the product Arnold to the public in the most effective way" (208). The story of a man who literally loses his mind, Schwarzenegger's character(s) resolve(s) his/their divided internal narrative through action strategies. In this Philip K. Dick–inspired tale of recreational psychosis, Schwarzenegger's buff blue-collar worker Douglas Quaid is given a mental holiday by having a memory implant that gives him the experience of being Hauser, a spy who ends up helping a group of underground mutant dissidents on Mars, and he frees the planet in godlike fashion. Here he gives the Martians back the very air they breathe. We are never sure if the story is an internal fantasy or if he is participating in a mental double-bluff conspiracy (he might really be the heroic Hauser who, through enforced brain-reprogramming, was inadvertently masquerading as Quaid), and in the end he neither knows nor cares.

Action spectacle—he kicks ass, displays muscles, and gets the girl—is predicated on profound psychological uncertainty. Thomas Elsaesser sees *Terminator 2* and *Total Recall* as typical of a tendency in post-classical Hollywood to present character as indeterminate if not downright inconsistent (200). And for an ostensibly non-cerebral and monolithically straight performer, Schwarzenegger took on a surprising number of roles dealing with masquerading, fractured, or self-deceiving selves, selves that are not themselves. The premise of *Eraser* is that he is a government agent who special-izes in disappearing people, erasing their identities for security purposes and placing them in safe havens if they are good, or killing them outright if they are not. Even though the disappeared identity story is all but subordi-nated to a sequence of elaborate action-by-numbers set pieces, nevertheless the action takes place in various shadow-locations populated by people who have lost all anchors to their previous lives. Elsewhere Schwarze-negger does at least two turns as a woman—a robotic disguise in *Total Recall*, and a drag turn he deploys in order to attend the women-only antenatal camp in *Junior*.

In *True Lies* Harry is "truly" a spy who plays at/lies in his role as father and husband, and most of his concealment devices are directed not at the enemy but at his family. His partner has to supply him with the props of marriage—the wedding ring, and a backstory sufficient to ease his path back into the home after the first excessive Bond-esque sequence. Mean-while, Helen is being wooed by a loser (Bill Paxton) who pretends that he is a spy for seduction purposes, and unwittingly tells Harry that he thinks of it "as playing a role—it's fantasy. You gotta work on their dreams." Harry conceals himself behind shadows and a taped voice when he watches his wife do a striptease, and he interrogates her through a two-way mirror using voice-distortion techniques. All this makes for uncomfortable view-ing for feminists, but its relationship to other Schwarzenegger masquerad-ing moments is interesting. While few of his post–*Total Recall* films show Schwarzenegger in quite such a self-forgetting role, these are resonant examples. I now turn to more overt images of self-parody or masquerade—the cartoonesque Mr. Freeze in *Batman & Robin* (1997) and Jack Slater in *Last Action Hero*—and the career drive that led him to more ambitious, world-conquering excesses.

☆☆☆☆☆ Humor, Postmodernism, and Bolted-On Stardom

Schwarzenegger's move into comedy was well planned and effectively executed, the most overt portfolio shift during an era when A-list stars of both genders were busy demonstrating that they could take on any role, however apparently against type. Despite his lunking obviousness, Schwarzenegger is identified with a popular postmodern turn in Hollywood cinema of the 1990s (postmodernism as overt commercial strategy, not covert cultural code), when complex and self-referring narratives, self-reflective characterization, and pastiche became the bread-and-butter of mainstream culture. Nineties-vintage Schwarzenegger plays with earlier iconographies of authority (including his own) and embraces ambivalent characterization. Fred Pfeil calls him "a monstrous mutation of the dead-pan, dead-souled lineage of Bronson, Eastwood, and Chuck Norris" (31), while Stephen Prince sees Schwarzenegger's films as a series of winks at the audience "to say that he knew what everyone else knew, namely, that the films were live-action cartoons" (184). David Tetzlaff reads *Commando*, one of Schwarzenegger's films of the 1980s, as subversive by virtue of its comedic critique of the action genre. Bordering on slapstick and laced with verbal burlesque, Schwarzenegger's "strong-man star-persona is actually subverted by inflating it to the point where any reasonably intelligent viewer can see that much of the action is faked" (275).

While developing action into a genre that confronts serious familial concerns, he was also simultaneously engaging in a series of pastiches of his own persona. Gallagher reads the against-type roles as comic because they are disabling: *Twins*, *Kindergarten Cop*, and *Junior* "gain their primary comedic value from placing the action star in situations that deny his trade-mark physique the opportunity to fend off enemy hordes" (163).

This sense of irony separated Schwarzenegger from Stallone, who, although a far more accomplished actor, did not so successfully branch out into non-action roles. Schwarzenegger's trademark one-line "zingers" or "Arnie-isms" were frequently inserted into working screenplays by hand-picked writers to provide the star with value-added pizzazz and, as Paul Verhoeven's biographer puts it, to make "the excessive violence of his per-sona digestible" (Van Scheers 208). ("Hasta la vista, baby" from *Terminator 2*; "I'm the party pooper" in *Kindergarten Cop*; "Consider that a divorce," on shooting his wife in *Total Recall*; and "You're luggage," to an unfortunate alligator in *Eraser*). Like parody or impersonation, linguistic catchphrases that infiltrate the wider culture are one sign that a star has become an icon. "I'll be back" is Schwarzenegger's career phrase, following its use in the *Terminator* franchise and its export to almost every other film he has made. For Murray Pomerance, Schwarzenegger exceeds his action frame (he "becomes mythic by outperforming his context") while simultaneously ironizing it: "What makes his performance ironic is the veneer of civility and civilization lying just beneath the violent surface; his ability to utter a poignant one-liner, in James Bond fashion; his gemütlich Austrian accent; the charming twinkle in his eye; his friendliness to women and children (particularly children); the sense in which he seems generally and adorably clueless" ("Hitchcock" 45). This makes Schwarzenegger an even stranger star icon, simultaneously clueless and relentless (though surely Pomer-ance's texts are selective).

Masquerading as merchandise: Arnie as Turboman cannot help himself from shouting, "I could get into this!!" in *Jingle All the Way* (Brian Levant, 1492 Pictures/Twentieth Century–Fox, 1996). Digital frame enlargement.

But friendliness to children soon became the currency of friendliness *for* children; Schwarzenegger's turn to comedy was increasingly family-audience-oriented as the 1990s progressed: both *Kindergarten Cop* and *Last Action Hero* were classified for teen or older audiences, while later in the decade *Jingle All the Way* (1996) and *Batman & Robin* were more squarely directed at younger audiences.[4] Both films featured Schwarzenegger in overt superhero/supervillain mode. For much of *Jingle All the Way*, Schwarzenegger plays another failing father: thwarted in his desperate Christmas Eve search to secure a Turboman, the must-have toy desired by his son, he more than compensates at the eleventh hour by inadvertently (cluelessly?) *becoming* a live-action Turboman in a Christmas Eve parade. Though arguably one of the most misanthropic films of the nineties (every character is repulsive; Christmas is repulsive; consumer culture is repulsive), the cartoonesque impulse of Turboman seems to possess and overcome the father's ineffectual qualities, transforming him into a villain-vanquishing powerhouse, and Schwarzenegger only really comes into his own when he dons the Turboman disguise. Verhoeven refocused *Total Recall* around Schwarzenegger as comic book star, "partly forced by having a superhero, bodybuilding/total film star in the movie, which led me to apply a more comic-book style" (Cornea 135). He does gesture and posing rather better than realist delivery (perhaps a hangover from his bodybuilding days), making his cartoon characters more credible than his regular humans (dads, husbands, working men).

The same might be said for *Batman and Robin*. When Jules in *Twins* asks, "Do I look cool now?" Vincent replies, "Mr. Ice!" as if Schwarzenegger were already lining himself up for Mr. Freeze, the DC Comics villain he was to play in 1997 for a close-to-record-breaking fee of $25 million for just six weeks' work (Leamer 246). Despite or perhaps because of his relatively limited screen time, Mr. Freeze plays to the star's strengths. He is relentless and monolithic, and practically every line he speaks is a zinger, much of it reflecting on his character ("Ice to see you!"; "Cool party!"; "Let's kick some ice!"; "The ice man cometh"). As a comic-inspired (if not comedic) figure, he is required to do little more than pantomimic gesture and quip.

Last Action Hero, on the other hand, takes its audience into a labyrinth of layered identities with no externally verifiable referent, for Schwarzenegger at least. Danny is a twelve-year-old film fan who enters the movie world of his favorite star, Jack Slater, courtesy of a magic ticket. At first Slater has no notion that he is a fictional character played by Arnold Schwarzenegger, inhabiting a movie-rendered Hollywood of pneumatic women and screen cops. Danny, however, knows the rules and slots in as Schwarzenegger's sidekick. When the pair breaks back into Danny's "real" world pursuing two screen villains, Slater saves "Arnold Schwarzenegger," who is at the New York premiere of the new Jack Slater film. Both, of course, are performed by the real actor Schwarzenegger, but in the playoff between the three of them the configuration of actor and roles begins to challenge the star referent upon which it is predicated. The fictional Arnold Schwarzenegger even has a red-carpet ticking off from Maria Shriver (played, of course, by the real Maria Shriver) about plugging "the restaurants or the gyms. It's so tacky." Slater says to the character Schwarzenegger, "I don't really like you. You've brought me nothing but pain," as if he were a self-realizing *Toy Story* (1995) figure looking in the mirror, or one of the many Malkoviches in Spike Jonze's more highly acclaimed smart film *Being John Malkovich* (1999). In the end Slater has the self-awareness to say to Danny, "I'm just an imaginary character"—perhaps this is why it was a relative failure on theatrical release.

These cartoonesque texts seem to be the overt, self-conscious manifestation of one truism of stardom as articulated by star studies. *Last Action Hero*, *Batman & Robin*, and *Jingle All the Way* seem to *reveal* that Arnold Schwarzenegger does not actually exist (manifestly fleshly though he is) except as brand or the celluloid ghost of genre. Charisma, then, seems to ooze from a film body quite separated from the real sweat of the gym. Perhaps postmodern is too broad a term or is not as interesting as what is actu-ally happening here. The genius of these schlocky movies is that they grasp the essential form that stardom takes in new Hollywood—stars are em-bodied ciphers upon which the most lucrative new identity might tem-porarily hang, until a more lucrative one takes its place. Of course it is hard to see the massive corporeal form of Schwarzenegger as cipher, but it is equally hard to see what else he might be, which might explain why so many critics have never gone beyond the muscles. Stardom is the smoke and mirrors masking the real person behind the persona (some actors even talk about their star brand in the third person—"Marilyn Monroe," "Sharon Stone"), but the fluctuations of this product's appeal to which a star brand is attached have intensified.

This is most striking with Schwarzenegger because he embarked on such deliberate rebranding strategy, and in a direction—comedy—that was apparently not his forte. It might be simpler, then, to think of him as a kind of bolted-together star, created, Frankenstein-fashion, through the addition of whatever missing parts (role opportunities or identity elements) are required to give the impression of a complete person. Proved your action chops? Now you need something comic. Done family-friendly? Now show that you don't take yourself too seriously with a knowing movie-nod to the audience. If and when all the parts slot together into the semblance of a fully rounded character, the Californians might even elect you governor (this is the subject of Gary Indiana's savage polemic *Schwarzenegger Syndrome* [2005], which reads voting for Arnold as a form of brand loyalty and sees the star's shape-shifting as the "Epitome of Arnold").

Schwarzenegger's "personal brand" is a "compilation of re-inventions, an advertisement for itself, a personality remarkable for its periodic shedding of layers" (Indiana 26). Unlike Willis, Schwarzenegger didn't tackle comedy because he had a natural talent for it, or because it stretched him artistically, but because the ongoing juggernaut of his career dictated that he must. Comedy is derived from the incongruity of his form, accent, and wooden delivery in the situations in which he is cast—Goliath to his minuscule twin, pregnant man masquerading as a woman, action cop melted by kindergarten kids. These are perfect formula films, the formula key being both that which will develop Schwarzenegger's career in desirable direc-tions and that which drives a hybrid genre to commercial success.

But what bolted-on need drove or pushed him to messianic aspira-tions? Schwarzenegger's postmodern forays go further than his signature self-ironization and cartoonesque role-play. Fredric Jameson famously lamented the political failures of the postmodern era, in which we can better imagine the end of the world than the end of capitalism. The 1990s are bookended by two significant end-of-the-world films, both of which feature the star in plainly Christ-like poses—one dystopic sci-fi, the other religious horror. *Terminator 2* actively visualizes nuclear apocalypse, then, through manipulation of its time-loop paradox, fends it off by opting for the Terminator's self-sacrifice. *End of Days* has Schwarzenegger battling with the devil, who is intent on bringing about a satanic apocalypse. Both films, though earnestly positing their preposterous narratives, also feature those knowing quips and ironic looks. Both flirt with anticapitalist discourses, suggesting that apocalypse and capitalism cannot be separated. *Terminator 2*'s conclusion is that corporate America in the specific form of the arms industry needs to self-immolate if the future is to be safe, while in *End of Days* the devil chooses a Wall Street banker as his human host.

Not that *End of Days* fails to offer multiple action cinema thrills, showing off Schwarzenegger's assets to their best advantage. This is a diversification vehicle up to a point—now aged fifty-two, Schwarzenegger here attempts a more varied characterization. Jericho Cane is a bereaved alcoholic ex-cop who pursues the devil through a millennial tale timed nicely for its late-1999 release date. It is Schwarzenegger's last film of the decade, and a return to action after two years away from movies. Here he is rougher-looking than before, and press materials stress the chance to show off a wider range of performance skills. With uncharacteristically noirish visuals, Jericho squints through Venetian blinds or is obscurely figured through chiaroscuro lighting setups that emphasize his unshaven and lined visage. Nevertheless, the star himself admits in a DVD special feature that *End of Days* was his message to fans, reassuring them that the heart surgery he had undergone in 1997 hadn't held him back, that he was still capable of the physical rigors of action. Co-star Kevin Pollack said that he expected the job to be like working with a live action figure (interview in "Spotlight on Location" documentary, *End of Days* DVD). Jericho dangles from a helicopter, shoots multiple bad guys, leaps from crashing subway trains, runs, jumps, and tools up. The devil is threatened—though not defeated—with a wide array of firepower ("Between your faith and my Glock 9mm, I take my Glock," Jericho says to a priest). But, as before, action also involves destruction of the male body, and along with a glimpse of biceps one of the first things we see in this film is Jericho putting a gun to his forehead in a contemplative suicidal gesture.

The film's diegesis subjects him to ample physical abuse, as is true in all his actioners, but perhaps most extraordinarily it provides a crucifixion sequence: the satanists tie him to a cross of metal girders and suspend him aloft in a gesture that recalls the good Terminator's self-sacrifice. Finally, when the devil possesses him after the Wall Street banker's body becomes unusable, he throws himself onto the protruding sword of an angel statue. "The message itself is extraordinary, I think," Schwarzenegger said, "especially for someone like myself who has always solved every problem with a weapon" (interview, "Spotlight on Location" documentary). If stardom, as Morin would have it, is a version of god made flesh, Schwarzenegger's 1990s forays into Christ-iconography are both the ultimate star gesture and suggestive of higher ambitions than simple political office.

Those ambitions are (at least) global, and his success is underpinned by a recognition that, as the 1990s progressed, the rest of the world increasingly mattered more than the United States. Will Smith reports that Schwarzenegger told him, "No matter how big your movies are in America, you are not a movie star until your movies are big around the world" (*Variety*, 15 December 2008). Language—or its lack—might be the key to action cinema's global success, as was the case with pre-sound cinema, which might also account for the relative unimportance of the accent issue in Schwarzenegger's case. "People don't need to understand English to know something is exploding and to enjoy that spectacle," lamented Meryl Streep in 1990 (qtd. in Prince 175). If stars continue to be read as contradictory entities, the paradox of Schwarzenegger is this: though he has striven to present himself as the exemplary individualist, a self-made man entirely in charge of his own destiny, he has developed iconic characters and made choices that speak to the period's zeitgeist. What he risked, or reveled in, was that he would be branded by those characters; and in becoming so identified with his characters, he became emblematic of his moment. In 1990 *Time* named the symbol of U.S. dominance in the global marketplace as "an overgrown Austrian man with a face and body out of a superhero comic" (qtd. in Pfeil 31). This makes Schwarzenegger a curious if familiar American icon—an immigrant whose success lies in his films' ability to sell worldwide.

NOTES

1. Schwarzenegger means "black field," though the ignorant have used the similarity—to an Anglophone ear—of "negger" to "nigger" as a way of reinforcing rumors about Arnie's racial backstory. Hack biographers in particular make much of the name—"swarthy acre" is another translation, wedding the fleshly Arnie ever more firmly to his old world Fatherland. One hilarious web discussion compares "Schwarzenegger" to "Heidegger"; see maverick-philosopher.powerblogs.com/posts/1169772973.shtml, accessed 15 January 2009.

2. Schwarzenegger used the term "Girly Man" twice when campaigning for George H. W. Bush, including it as an insult to Democrats during the 1992 presidential campaign, but—to the horror of gay activists—it has become a regular part of his political vocabulary.

3. The scene faintly echoes Frank Capra's *It's a Wonderful Life* (1946), in which George Bailey (James Stewart) is allowed the experience of seeing the world as if he had never lived.

4. *Kindergarten Cop* and *Last Action Hero* were rated PG-13 in the United States and 15 in the United Kingdom (no one under fifteen years of age could see the films in the theater or rent the videos); *Jingle All the Way* was PG in both countries; *Batman & Robin* was PG in the United Kingdom but PG-13 in the United States, partly because of its sexual innuendoes. Danny in *Last Action Hero* mocks Slater by challenging him to read out a presumably obscene line written on paper. "You can't possibly say it," he concludes, "because this movie is PG-13."

2 ☆☆☆☆☆☆☆☆☆☆

Jodie Foster
Feminist Hero?

KAREN HOLLINGER

What the career of Jodie Foster shows more than anything else is the difficulty involved in making female Hollywood stars into iconic feminist figures. In the early nineties, Foster built on her Oscar-winning performances in two films that were taken up as feminist texts and on her well-publicized move into directing to become widely celebrated as a feminist star. One might call it an act of desperation by feminist critics, like B. Ruby Rich in her influential essay on Foster entitled "Nobody's Handmaid," to seize on Foster as the poster girl for a new mainstream feminist heroics. Foster was, and probably still is, the only major Hollywood actress who consistently plays strong female characters and refuses to run away from the feminist label, yet Foster's screen personality and public image are far from consistent. In fact, her career in the nineties is a study in contradictions and a convoluted trajectory rather than a map of feminist triumph.

★★★★★ Feminist Texts

The 1990s should have been the decade of Jodie Foster, and judging from her publicity early in the decade, she was on her way to establishing herself as a new type of female Hollywood star. But that did not exactly happen, and why it did not is the subject of this essay. In the early nineties, Foster was riding high. It was the beginning of the adult phase in her long career, and her two Best Actress Oscars put that career into high gear. In 1991, Foster was also the darling of the critical establishment—both popular and academic. In fact, she was discussed in almost mythic terms. Her early career, which realistically can be seen as uneven at best, was spun into a story of epic dimensions. Told and retold in profiles of Foster in newspapers and magazines are accounts of her precocious childhood: talking at nine months, acting at age three, analyzing scripts at five, "mauled"—actually just bitten—by a lion while shooting her first film (De Angelis 33), nominated for an Oscar at thirteen for her controversial performance as a child prostitute in *Taxi Driver* (1976), and named valedictorian of her elite private school, the Lycée Français, where she excelled academically and learned to speak French fluently. From these auspicious beginnings she went on to pause her career temporarily so that she could graduate magna cum laude from Yale. Then, she quickly reignited her career by winning an Oscar for her highly praised portrayal of a rape victim in what was widely considered a feminist-inspired drama, *The Accused* (1988). To follow that up, three years later she collected a second Oscar for another role labeled by feminists and nonfeminists alike as the most heroic female character ever to be portrayed in a Hollywood film, Clarice Starling in *The Silence of the Lambs*. One is tempted to just cheer! But this isn't all. After winning her second Oscar, she announced that she wanted to direct, and quickly landed a multimillion-dollar deal with Polygram Entertainment to open her own production company, Egg Pictures. Looking at this résumé, who can blame B. Ruby Rich for hailing Foster as an entirely new type of Hollywood actress who was set to initiate a feminist revolution in the way women were portrayed onscreen? It is also easy to see why popular journalists presented her as a "Wunderkind" in the mold of Orson Welles, destined to follow up her near-mythic childhood and remarkable early career by becoming the first great feminist actress/director in the history of Hollywood.

Absent from this idyllic story are the bumps in Foster's supposed road to glory. Her career actually began in a seemingly troubled childhood with a stage mother who, struggling as a single parent to support her family, initiated two of her children, Jodie and her older brother Buddy, into show business at tender ages and later placed the adolescent Jodie into highly sexualized roles in order to promote her transition to adult stardom. Foster's Yale days were also plagued by scandal as her sexualized teen image provoked John Hinckley Jr., a demented stalker, to harass her and then to try to assassinate President Ronald Reagan, in what Hinckley later claimed was an attempt to gain Foster's attention. This traumatic experience, combined with a career that seemed to be going downhill, led Foster to fall into a deep depression after her graduation (Hal Hinson, "Jodie Foster, Down-to-Earth Star," *Washington Post*, 14 February 1993). No longer considered a desirable property, she was required to audition twice to get the lead role in *The Accused* (Christa D'Souza, "The Prime of Jodie Foster," *Tatler*, June 1994), the film that would rekindle her career.

B. Ruby Rich's 1991 canonization of Foster is representative of the exuberant praise lavished on the young star after her second Oscar win for *The Silence of the Lambs*. Rich originally wrote her laudatory piece, "Nobody's Handmaid" (first titled "Jodie Foster: Growing Up on Screen"), for the program of the Minneapolis Walker Art Center's retrospective of Foster's work—a retrospective for an actress who was not yet even thirty years old. Rich lauds Foster as "the stuff of legend" (7), presaging a new type of female screen hero who is "never submissive, but always fights back, defends herself, gets even" and refuses to adopt the "damsel-in-distress" pose or to "trade intelligence or strength for sex appeal" (8). Rich considers *The Silence of the Lambs* to be even better than *The Accused*, offering "a new kind of female hero, one whose vulnerability and emotion were seen as aid rather than impediment, one who could avenge an entire decade's genre sins in a single act" (9). According to Rich, Foster elevated the working-class female character to a new level, that of "the spunky proletariat gal who can take on anyone from a posse of rapists to a psycho killer to a manipulative genius" (8). In other words, Foster was the Feminist Wonder Woman of nineties Hollywood.

But in truth, early reviews of *The Accused* and *Silence* were mixed, and subsequent critical responses have called both films' unqualified feminist credentials into question. Although reviews of Foster's creation of Sarah Tobias, the working-class rape victim who sets out to get her day in court in *The Accused*, were and continue to be generally positive, I would question the stereotyped character of this portrayal. Foster seems too obviously a highly educated, sophisticated Hollywood star playing down to create a spunky "white trash" waitress whose attempt to be sexy leads her to engage in behavior that seems cheap and tawdry. Foster herself has said that she felt after shooting was completed that her performance "stunk" and her career was over (D'Souza, "The Prime of Jodie Foster"). However, reviewers overwhelmingly disagreed and described her acting in superlatives, calling her portrayal "mesmerizing" (Chris Hicks, *Desert News*, 14 October 1988) and "vibrant" with "a gutsy eloquence" that perfectly combines "dignity with defenselessness" (Rita Kempley, *Washington Post*, 14 October 1988).

The Silence of the Lambs also fails as the unqualifiedly progressive text that Rich would have it seem. It was indeed praised by many early reviewers for its progressive representation of Foster's character, Clarice Starling, who provides the film with a strong, intelligent, and heroic female protagonist. Clarice was a career-making role for Foster, one she has always championed in glowing terms as "such an incredibly strong and beautiful feminist hero" (qtd. in Mizejewski 176), "a mythic hero in the same way that great Greek tragedies have these great mythic heroes who go on this very long quest that usually takes them through psychically understanding themselves in ways that they hadn't wanted to before" ("Larry King Live," 17 July 1997). Foster has listed Clarice as one of her three favorite roles because she says this was the first time she was allowed to play a character who was "more me—someone whose destiny is to save those girls and to redeem their honor in a strange way" (qtd. in Sean M. Smith, "Jodie Foster: The Kid Stays in the Picture," *Premiere*, September 2005, 116). Critics have followed suit, largely agreeing with Rich and Foster that Clarice is a figure with whom women can identify, a "rare heroine" who without losing her femininity goes about her job as men do (Staiger 149). She provides "the two-hour spectacle of a woman solving the perverse riddle of patriarchy— all by herself" (Amy Taubin, qtd. in "Writers on the Lamb," *Village Voice*, 5 March 1991, 57).

Others have seen *The Silence of the Lambs* as deeply flawed in its feminism. Early reviewers began to question the film's depiction of graphic violence, its villains, and even its female hero. Jonathan Rosenbaum led a notorious early attack on the movie as an "upscale slasher film" that is "not merely stupid, repulsive, sickening, and hateful. It is worse. I think it is evil." He argues that the film really is just "exploiting, with pornographic relish, a sicko fascination with serial killers who cut up women" ("The Evil Movies Do," *Mademoiselle*, February 1991, 72). It is "soft-core gore porn," a "snuff film—that subgenre of porn that focuses on the simulation of naked women being tortured and murdered," with a female protagonist who is not heroic at all, just a psychological victim of the cannibalistic psycho-killer Hannibal Lecter (74). For many, the film's presentation of its villains represents its most serious flaw. Both Lecter and Jame Gumb, the film's other psycho-killer who is murdering young women in order to peel off their skin

to make himself a body suit, have been labeled, especially by gay male critics, as homophobic representations of gay men that play on heterosexual
hatred and a perception of homosexuals as sick (Peter Krämer, qtd. in
Kennedy 49).

Attacks on the film as homophobic took an unusual turn when the gay
press pointed to Foster as a closeted lesbian who was not averse to participating in the creation of a homophobic film (see Crimp 11–17; Brown
234; Staiger 142–43; Phillips). Rumors of Foster's lesbianism had circulated
from the time of her adolescence, and became a major part of her extra-
filmic image, especially as she adamantly refused to address them. Foster
would go on to become an icon for lesbian viewers and reputedly to enter
a serious lesbian relationship with Cydney Bernard, whom she is said to
have met on the set of *Sommersby* in 1993 and whom she refused throughout the nineties to acknowledge openly as her partner. In the latter part of
the decade, she also gave birth to two children whose method of conception she would not discuss. Michael Musto, in an April 2007 article in *Out*
magazine, labeled Foster the most prominent inhabitant of Hollywood's
"glass closet" (*Out*, April 2007). It was not until December 2007 that Foster finally acknowledged Bernard as her partner. Even the character of
Clarice, championed as a paragon of feminist heroics by some, was characterized by others as a lesbian portrayal. Still others saw her as neither
feminist nor lesbian, but rather as just another female character who is the
pawn of male father figures, the object of the gaze of the film's male characters, and even the victim of "symbolic rape" when another prisoner
throws his semen in her face as she leaves one of her interviews with
Lecter in his cell (Mizejewski 181). Drawing together all these various
strains of criticism in an insightful early analysis of the film in a 1991 issue
of *Camera Obscura*, Elizabeth Young argues that the film's "feminist critique
of male violence and power" ends finally in "incoherence rather than
innovation." According to Young, the film's "homophobic anxiety over
masculinity" prevents it from evoking a "utopian transcendence of sexual
difference" and results instead in the "confused displacement of gender difference onto the axis of sexuality" (17).

If *The Accused* and *The Silence of the Lambs* do not exactly live up to Rich's
conception of them as feminist texts that position Foster as a new type of
feminist Hollywood star, what about her subsequent career in the nineties?
Like Rich, Christina Lane in an important 1995 essay, "The Liminal Iconography of Jodie Foster," saw Foster's screen image as about "to fuse an active
female sexuality with an equally active female authority" (Rich 10). Lane
proposed that Foster embodied "a certain strategic sexual liminality" that

In this publicity still for *The Silence of the Lambs* (Jonathan Demme, Orion, 1991), Jodie Foster poses in her career-making role as Clarice Starling with Anthony Hopkins as the evil Hannibal Lecter glaring from behind. Foster characterized Clarice as a mythic feminist heroine.

allowed her to refuse the polarizing binary of masculine/feminine and attain a transcendent "mobility as an icon—her ability to slide up and down the registers of masculine and feminine" (151). Lane quotes Foster in 1991 as anticipating a new direction for her career: "Most movies use sexuality as a symbol. It's all about poses and postures, and that's not what my generation is about. I'm waiting to see a movie that explores the dynamics of why that other person completes you, why you're together. I'd like to explore female sexuality in a way that people don't get to see on screen" (153). Lane takes from this the idea that Foster was poised to develop a Hollywood cinema that is "women-centered, and even borders on the latest developments in feminist film theory." For Lane, Foster was set to "radical-ize the current masculinist and heterosexist symbolism of women's sexual-ity in mainstream texts" and to "define sexuality as a fluid category—not merely a rigid and confining projection of what men want, but instead as an orchestration of female fantasy and desire" (153).

But Lane herself points out that Foster's idea of how to accomplish this task is simply to put two people in a room together and "see what they do when no one else is around. . . . I mean people do the weirdest things when they're alone" (qtd. in Lane 153). Lane rather grandiloquently pronounces this statement an indication that Foster frames her thinking in line with the feminist conception of the public/private split in social conceptions of mas-culinity and femininity, but one might argue instead—and I certainly would, given the future trajectory of Foster's career—that it represents her naiveté and lack of a real vision for an alternative direction in which to take her por-trayals of female characters. Indeed, Foster's subsequent films in the decade and the alteration of her extra-filmic image after *The Silence of the Lambs* indicate much less radical aims on her part than Lane envisioned. After completing *Silence*, Foster did make one rather radical career decision—her move into directing. She said she always wanted to direct because she wanted to know that "the entire vision of the film is in your hands, that every decision is yours and in some way reflects the experiences that you have had in your life" ("Larry King Live," 17 July 1997). Rejecting profes-sional advice to exploit her Oscar notoriety to secure lucrative acting roles (Fred Schruers, "A Kind of Redemption," *Premiere*, March 1991), Foster decided to direct a small feature film, *Little Man Tate* (1991), based on a script she resurrected from a "slush pile at Orion Pictures" (Cameron). She seemed, extra-filmically at least, to be living up to her heroic reputation.

☆☆☆☆★ Behind the Camera

The hype that greeted Foster's assumption of the director's chair is perhaps best expressed visually in her cover photo on *Time* maga-zine's issue of 14 October 1991, under the banner "A Director Is Born." Richard Corliss, who wrote the accompanying article, "A Screen Gem Turns Director," fell all over himself with superlatives, comparing her to the renowned French director Louis Malle and describing *Little Man Tate* as having a "French film sense" that does not resort to "spoon-feeding the audience, not forcing easy moral judgments." Corliss describes Foster as having "her own confident style" and glowingly concludes that "*Little Man Tate* for all its acuity of craft and gallantry toward its characters, could be simply the first step: the Coppertone commercial of filmmaker Foster [referring to Foster's debut as a child actress in a Coppertone suntan lotion ad]. If this is the larva, imagine the butterflies to come." Other promotional articles generally followed suit, calling the film "a terrifically self-assured debut" (Vincent Canby, *New York Times*, 9 October 1991) by a director who "radiates a capable professionalism" combined with a "crisp intelligence" and a strong "technical grounding" (Horton 38). Foster was even compared to French New Wave directors like François Truffaut and Claude Chabrol (Arion Berger, "Wunderkind," *Harper's Bazaar*, November 1991, 169) and said to be creating a film that resembles a "sunny French comedy of truth . . . where laughs are built on insights" (Roger Ebert, *Chicago Sun-Times*, 18 October 1991). Like the films of French New Wave directors, *Little Man Tate* was also promoted as a very personal project for Foster. At first, she resisted this characterization, saying initially that "it's not an autobiographical movie at all, it doesn't have anything to do with my life" (Lawrence Grobel, "Anything Is Possible," *Movieline*, October 1991, 31), but eventually she welcomed this personalization as somehow supporting the auteurism of her directorial ambitions. She proposed that she identified immediately upon reading the script with the child protagonist's feelings of being different because she herself had felt different as a child actress (Jon Stevens, "Jodie Foster Goes 'Home' for her Second Feature," *DGA Magazine*, January 1996). She also says she related easily to the struggle of emotion, intuition, and normalcy versus intellect, planning, and giftedness reflected in the conflict between the two major female characters (Horton 39).

Not everyone partook of the celebratory mood, and a number of early reviewers tempered their praise with the suggestion that, after all the hype that surrounded its release, the film was really a bit of a disappointment. Some pointed out that Foster lacked a "discernable personal style," that the film kept "veering damagingly into soap opera" (Peter Travers, *Rolling Stone*, 13 October 1991) or into "TV-mawkish fable" (*Washington Post*, 18 October 1991), and that it was really rather "plain stuff, efficiently delivered. Far from Eisensteinian reach, *Little Man Tate* turns out to be *Home Alone* for geniuses. Trouble is, eggheads aren't adorable" (*Washington Post*, 18 October 1991). Even a great Foster admirer like B. Ruby Rich had to admit that the film was merely "a modest and competent movie . . . less adventurous than many films in which Foster had starred" (10). Most problematic for a director praised for her feminist sensibilities is Foster's presentation of her two central female characters, Dede Tate, a working-class single mother played by Foster herself in yet another of her stereotyped portraits of working-class women, and Jane Grierson (Dianne Wiest), the equally stereotyped wealthy proprietress of a school for gifted children. The two women are engaged in a protracted struggle over the future of Dede's young son Fred (Adam Hann-Byrd), who is a budding genius. Sandra Moffat has pointed to some of the problems created by the film pitting these two female characters against each other, with the prize being young Fred. As Moffat suggests, the film sets up a simplistic dichotomy between "fun, nurturing, loving Dede" and "hard-working, organized, intelligent Jane," and its denouement, with the traumatized Fred demonstrating his need for his mother, which suggests that it is "more important for a woman to be caring than to pursue intellectual work; a notion which perpetuates the traditional female roles of wife and mother that many women are expected to follow" (95). There is "no representation in *Little Man Tate* of a woman who can have financial stability and a child without drastically compromising one or the other" (96).

☆☆☆☆★ Conventional Performances

Like Foster's directorial debut, which neither established her as a Wellesian cinematic genius nor exhibited her feminist sensibilities, her choice of acting roles in the mid-nineties failed to achieve a radical refashioning of the representation of women onscreen. Foster's motivations for selecting her roles following *The Silence of the Lambs* seem based not on feminist ideals but on a conscious strategy to take more conventionally feminine parts. As Terry Brown points out, after *Silence*, Foster's publicity photos, which had earlier presented her as rather androgynous, began to make her look more feminine. As Brown puts it, she was transformed into the "smiling femme that the mainstream media has gone to lengths to construct" (233). This movement into mainstream femmedom can also be seen in Foster's choice of her next three film roles: *Sommersby* (1993), *Maverick* (1994), and *Nell* (1994). Each was a departure for Foster, but not at all in the ways her adulators had predicted.

Sommersby, *Maverick*, and *Nell* were all promoted as distinctly different roles for Foster. For instance, promotion for *Sommersby* reported that Hollywood was "abuzz" about the film's romantic pairing of Foster with Richard Gere and described their love scenes in the picture as "raunchy" (Kate Muir,

"Jodie Foster Exposed," *Elle*, April 1993)—which they were certainly not, at least in the final print. The film's producer was quoted as saying, "A lot of people questioned us about this coupling. And it was a gamble, because there are the obvious romantic leading females, and Jodie really is not one of them. Also, I don't think anyone had even seen Jodie in a period costume" (qtd. in Hal Hinson, "Jodie Foster, Down-to-Earth Star," *Washington Post*, 14 February 1993). The film seems to represent the beginning of a strategy Foster developed after *Silence* to soften her screen persona and refashion it to fit more closely with mainstream notions of femininity without entirely sacrificing her tough heroic side. In fact, when she took the part in *Sommersby*, Foster reputedly insisted that the script undergo extensive revision to transform her character from "a naive, very weepy woman" into a stronger female figure (Mark Harris, *Entertainment Weekly*, March 1993). It is this type of auteurist acting—which involved going after roles that she wanted to play and engineering changes in them—that really sets Foster apart from other actresses in the decade, not her role choice itself, which became more and more conventional.

After *Sommersby*, Foster changed directions again by moving into a light comedic mode opposite Mel Gibson and James Garner in *Maverick*. The film, promoted as "an experiment" and "a departure" for Foster (Martha Sherill, "The Rein of Jodie Foster," *Washington Post*, 23 December 1994), cast her as a southern belle con-woman and Gibson's love interest, as she was Gere's in *Sommersby*. All this was quite out of character for Foster, and promotional articles for the film described Hollywood as surprised that, widely regarded as an actress who "turns down everything," she jumped at the chance (reputedly accepting the role in one day) to play third fiddle to Gibson and Garner in what was described as "a frothy, $40 million remake of the 1950's television Western" (Michael Shnayerson, "Jodie Rules," *Vanity Fair*, May 1994). Foster claimed she took the role because she had been wanting to do a comedy for a long time and felt director Richard Donner and the male leads could teach her the techniques of comedic performance; indeed they did, or at least they acquainted her with one style of comedic acting. It was a style that Foster said made her somewhat ill at ease on the set because the acting was extremely improvisational (Foster xv). One big attraction of the role may have been that Foster, at least according to rumor, was to have been paid $5 million for her performance, more than double her salary in any previous film (Shnayerson). An additional benefit was that the character of Annabelle Bransford acted yet again to feminize Foster's screen image, and her next film, *Nell*, released the same year, did the same.

Nell is a landmark film in Foster's career in a number of ways, and not many of them good. It was the first film of her fledgling independent production company, Egg Pictures, which she opened as part of her $100 million vanity deal with Polygram Filmed Entertainment. According to this agreement, Foster was supposed to make up to six films in three years in the $10 to $25 million range. She could act, direct, or just produce the films (Schnayerson). Foster's motivations for entering into the realm of producing seem clear. In interviews, she said she believed producing would allow her to get worthy movies made that expressed their directors' personal vision, and to gain more control over the films she directed herself ("Larry King Live," 27 December 1999). The task proved more difficult than she imagined, however. She opened Egg in 1992, and it took two years until *Nell*, a co-production with Fox Pictures, was released. As with her assumption of the reins of director, Foster's decision to become a producer was another move greeted by huge fanfare. Publicity described her as "a born CEO" (Mark Harris, "Jodie Foster: Meet the New Boss," *Entertainment Weekly*, March 1993) who now "helms her own production company" (Williams), has other executives "in awe of her" (Harris), and is primed to be "a major player in the business" (Shnayerson). Egg's future, beginning with *Nell*, was considerably less stellar than this hype predicted, and, three years after it moved from Polygram to Paramount in 1998, Foster closed the company. In doing so, she proclaimed that rather than finding herself to be "a born CEO," she had discovered producing to be "just a really thankless, bad job" (Bambara Vancheri, "Foster Again Plays on Parental Fear," *Pittsburgh Post-Gazette*, 23 September 2005). She lamented, "Producing other people's movies is just hard on your soul" (Sean M. Smith, "Jodie's Choice," *Premiere*, February 2002). The company's record of successful film releases was limited to small films like *Home for the Holidays* (1995, of which more below), *The Baby Dance* (1998, for Showtime TV), *Waking the Dead* (2000), and *The Dangerous Lives of Altar Boys* (2002).

The critical and box office failure of *Nell*, an obvious star vehicle for Foster, can be seen to presage future problems with Egg. Even though Foster did not direct, insisting that she was disappointed with her performance in *Little Man Tate* and would not want to both act in and direct a film again (Stevens), *Nell* was clearly Foster's picture. Foster has said she produced and developed the film, hired and worked with the writers, and constructed her character almost entirely on her own, even to the extent of creating Nell's idiosyncratic language ("Inside the Actors Studio," 25 September 2005). Again, the role was regarded as a departure for Foster and one she confessed to finding a particular challenge. She describes Nell as "this extraordinarily vulnerable innocent" (Shnayerson) who was so extremely fragile because her emotions were entirely on the outside (qtd. in "Yahoo Chat," *Bigstar.com*, 20 April 2000). Foster confessed that she took the role because she wanted to "open up more" (Sherill) and felt the performance was her best ("Actors Studio"). Critics, however, overwhelmingly disagreed, and Foster acknowledged that the critical reaction to the film disappointed her greatly. Playing Nell was "the most out there I've ever been—the most naked I could possibly be—and people thought I was just foolish . . . that I was Oscar-pandering, that the performance was somehow dishonest" (qtd. in Smith, "Jodie's Choice").

Not just *Nell* but each of Foster's repeated attempts to take her career in a new direction was greeted with a mixed response from reviewers. *Sommersby* is significant in this regard because it represents the beginning of a tendency for reviewers to see Foster's performances as lacking "romantic chemistry" with her male love interests. This criticism, perhaps influenced more by rumors of her real-life lesbianism than by her acting ability, plagued and possibly doomed each of her attempts to move into more traditionally feminine romantic roles. In *Sommersby*, although her performance was largely praised as "memorably courageous and attention getting" (*Washington Post*, 5 February 1993), she and Gere were said to have "no sparks or chemistry in their passion" (*Austin Chronicle*, 13 February 1993). The same criticism would later be made of Foster in *Maverick*, *Contact*, and *Anna and the King*. Overall, reviewers saw *Sommersby* as a languidly paced remake of the French film *Le Retour de Martin Guerre* [*The Return of Martin Guerre*] (1982) that was less interesting and believable than its predecessor. *Maverick* received some of the same criticisms, seen as enjoyable in parts but overly long (Roger Ebert, *Chicago Sun-Times*, 20 May 1994), a series of comic scenes without much of a coherent plot (Rita Kempley, *Washington Post*, 20 May 1994), and a Mel Gibson star vehicle stolen by James Garner (Katrine Ames, "Pass the Milk Duds," *Newsweek*, 30 May 1994, 64). Foster seems to fall into the background in almost every review, with her role described as "underwritten" (*Washington Post*, 5 May 1994). Strangely, given its lack of real substance, this is one of the few roles that Foster accepted without requesting changes in her character (Shnayerson). In a part originally offered to Meg Ryan, Foster was said to "throw herself into this flirty role" (Kempley), but to end up looking "slightly squirmy in this burlesque" (Ames). *Nell*, however, got the worst reception of all of Foster's attempts to soften and feminize her image. It was "universally dismissed as an exercise in self-indulgence and a desperate bid for a third Oscar" (Michael Zilberman, *American Photo*, November 1995). Reviewers attacked it as "Forrest

Jodie Foster with Liam Neeson in *Nell* (Michael Apted, Egg/Polygram/Twentieth Century–Fox, 1994), a critical and box office failure intended as a star vehicle for Foster and the first release of Egg, her fledgling production company.

Gump in the forest" (Richard Corliss, *Time*, 12 December 1994, 92), a star vehicle that Foster lacked the star quality to pull off (Stanley Kauffmann, *New Republic*, 23 January 1995, 30), and a "showboat" role that "approaches narcissism" (*Austin Chronicle*, 6 January 1995). Reviews were not all bad, and some critics, who generally did not like the film as a whole, still lauded Foster's performance as "fearless, fierce, beautifully attuned" (Corliss) and labeled her "transcendent in the bravura role . . . far grander than the film itself" (*Washington Post*, 25 December 1994).

After what can be seen as the embarrassment of *Nell*'s reception and its general recognition as a serious misstep in her career, Foster turned again to directing. Her sophomore effort, *Home for the Holidays* (1995), was slated to be the film that would allow her to realize the promise many reviewers felt she had shown in *Little Man Tate*. It was not to be so. *Home for the Holidays*, billed as a zany family comedy, was an odd choice for Foster, who made it clear in discussing her experience in making *Maverick* that comedy was a genre in which she felt she had little expertise. That lack of expertise would show in her direction of this second feature. As in *Little Man Tate*, Foster worked closely with writers to make the film her own, and it was promoted as having a personal connection to her life (Roger Ebert, *Chicago Sun-Times*, 3 November 1995), although the exact nature of that connection was never specified. In fact, in discussing her work as a director, Foster has said that all her movies will inevitably be "personal films" because one should only direct a film if the screenplay "speaks to you in a personal way" ("Jodie on AOL," 16 October 1995). She describes every film she directs as "completely personal, totally me. They're my sense of humor, my voice, what I believe, what I've lived" (Tom Allen, "Becoming Jodie Foster," *In Style*, November 1995).

Rather than providing convincing proof of Foster's directorial abilities, *Home for the Holidays* instead received an even less favorable critical reception than *Little Man Tate*. Critics felt Foster's lack of a comedic sense caused the film to suffer from awkward shifts in tone ranging from frenzied humor to depressing pathos (Janet Maslin, *New York Times*, 3 November 1995). Foster was also criticized for an "inability to judge the emotional impact [that] characters are having on viewers" (Kenneth Turan, *Los Angeles Times*, 3 November 1995). For instance, in interviews Foster repeatedly complimented Robert Downey Jr. on what reviewers—and I must say this viewer as well—overwhelmingly felt was an annoyingly over-the-top performance that seemed intended to show his character Tommy to be a "loveable scamp" but actually rendered him "an immature jerk" (Turan). While a smattering of critics found the film funny, most felt that Foster's direction only demonstrated that she could not "differentiate between reproducing the insanity of a Thanksgiving run amuck and making that nightmare amusing" so that the film ended up "muddled and wearying" (Turan). The only, rather self-pitying, response Foster could offer was that in spite of its spotty reception the film was still one of her favorites because it is "true to everything I think and feel. They really can't take the satisfaction of it away" (Karen Breslow, "Jodie Foster at East," *More.com*, October 2006).

☆☆☆☆★ **New Directions**

Foster's next two films, *Contact* (1997) and *Anna and the King* (1999), represent the two different directions that her career took in the late nineties. With *Contact* she returned with limited success to the Clarice-like role of the solitary female hero fighting to establish herself in a masculine world, but with the epic romance *Anna and the King* she attempted much less successfully to pair this heroic stature with traditional femininity. Promoted as a "serious science-fiction epic set on a world stage and packed with cosmic meditations on the duel between science and God," "the most unabashedly esoteric film about aliens," and a "$90 million Event Movie for intellectuals" (Benjamin Svetsky, *Entertainment Weekly*, July 1997), *Contact* foreshadowed the types of gender-bending films that Foster would turn to in the early 2000s. In it she was the marquee star playing a heroic female figure loosely based on male writer-astronomer Carl Sagan. Ellie Arroway was a character who could easily have been played by a man. Although Matthew McConaughey was Foster's nominal love interest, the heart of the film involved the attempts of her character, a female astronomer, to make contact with beings she believes exist in outer space. It was not just a science-fiction adventure, however, but a film with intellectual pretensions. Central to its plot is an ongoing debate about the relative merits of technology/rationality versus spirituality/faith. Reviews were mixed; the film was generally seen as too long with a hokey, spiritually uplifting ending that "deteriorates into inert exposition, earnest platitudinizing, exclamatory jargon, hit-and-miss social commentary, and pompous sententiousness" (Peter Keough, "Losing Contact," *Boston Phoenix*, 10 July 1997). Foster's performance was either praised as intelligent and effective (Richard Schickel, *Time*, 21 July 1997, 71) or reviled as a portrait of a too noble "astro-nun" who is neither sympathetic nor believably human (*Washington Post*, 11 July 1997). Nevertheless, the film seemed to indicate that Foster had perhaps given up her strategy of feminizing her screen persona and had decided to return to portrayals of female heroes.

Jodie Foster's portrayal of the astronomer and would-be astronaut Ellie Arroway in *Contact* (Robert Zemeckis, Warner Bros., 1997) allowed her to return to playing strong female heroes and presaged the type of gender-bending roles she would take up when the decade was over.

This movement away from conventional romantic leads may also have been influenced by an odd turn in Foster's personal life that again brought to the forefront rumors of her lesbianism. In 1997, her estranged brother Buddy published the tell-all unauthorized star biography *Foster Child: An Intimate Biography of Jodie Foster by Her Brother*, in which he revealed sordid details of their childhood family life. According to *Foster Child*, their estranged father abandoned his pregnant wife and their four small children, only begrudgingly and infrequently paying child support (Foster and Wagener 22). According to Buddy, their mother, Brandy, whom Jodie always presented in the most favorable light as totally devoted and caring, had actually precipitated her husband's desertion by having an affair with another woman (18). Buddy describes Brandy as so unstable that she was given to hysterical fits and verbal abuse toward her children (58–59). He characterizes Jodie as a spoiled child always favored by their mother and implies that she was taught at an early age to hate men (56–57). He claims that he found his sister to be a cold, uncaring person and that he always believed she was bisexual (181). When asked for her response to the book, Foster's reaction was brief, but pointed: "This unauthorized biography consists simply of hazy recollections, fantasies, and borrowed press excerpts." She went on to say that she considered her brother to be a distant acquaintance whom she had seen as few as fifteen times in the past twenty years and who knew nothing about her personal life (Laurin Sydney, "Foster Angry over Brother's Tell-All," www.cnn.com/showbiz, 15 May 1997). Foster's position as a lesbian icon was also openly discussed in British independent filmmaker Pratibha Parmar's *Jodie: An Icon* (1996). The film presents excerpts from Foster's early films up to and including *The Silence of the Lambs*, interspersed with interviews with lesbian viewers and critics commenting on how these film moments opened up Foster's screen image to lesbian readings.

Anna and the King represents a regression to yet another romantic period piece, and it became the biggest critical failure of Foster's career. Foster seems to have seen the film as a progressive text that would tell the story of her character Anna Leonowens's experiences in nineteenth-century Siam "from an Asian perspective" (David Cohen, "Movies and Motherhood," *South China Morning Post*, December 1999) and with more verisimilitude than had earlier cinematic adaptations of Leonowens's "memoirs," most notably *The King and I* (1956). *Anna and the King* was, indeed, promoted as offering the story of Leonowens's experiences in the court of Siam's King Mongkut with respect for both historical accuracy and the dignity of the king. Foster seems to have naively accepted this characterization of the film. In interviews, she described it as telling a story that "was very—was quite true. . . . Everything about King Mongkut I think was very—was quite true" ("Larry King Live," 27 December 1999). The hesitation from "very" to "quite" suggests perhaps that her faith in the film's verisimilitude was really rather shaky, yet in the same interview she proposed that the Tuptim story, which makes up a significant part of the film, was definitely true, and that the film's portrayal of the love affair between Anna and the king, while not entirely accurate, was based on the "affection" Anna had for him and the "great respect" he showed for her ("Larry King Live"). The Thai government certainly did not agree with this assessment and refused to allow the film to be shot there; instead, it was filmed in Malaysia (Jory 201). The film's revisionist historical stance amounts to doing three things differently from its predecessors. First, it shows the king courageously struggling against Western powers (who were taking over neighboring states) and at the same time against internal enemies who threatened his reign, his life, and his family from within his kingdom. Second, it portrays Anna as flawed and as making serious mistakes in her dealings with the Siamese court. Finally, it accentuates the beauty of the Asian setting. In spite of these positive elements, the filmmakers and Foster failed to recognize inherent problems with the film's story—problems that scholars have traced back to its source in Leonowens's books.

Leonowens wrote two semi-autobiographical "memoirs," *The English Governess at the Siamese Court* (1870) and *The Romance of the Herem* (1873), which purportedly describe her five-year stay in Siam from 1862 to 1867, during which time she served as governess to the king's children. These books were then used as a source for a 1943 novel, *Anna and the King of Siam*, written by Margaret Landon. Landon's novel in turn provided the basis for a 1946 non-musical film version *Anna and the King of Siam* (1946), starring Irene Dunne and Rex Harrison; the 1951 Rodgers and Hammerstein Broadway musical *The King and I*, starring Gertrude Lawrence and Yul Brynner; and *The King and I* film adaptation in 1956, starring Deborah Kerr and Brynner, reprising his Broadway role. Andy Tennant's 1999 non-musical *Anna and the King*, on the other hand, claimed greater authenticity than its predecessors because it was purportedly based directly on Leonowens's "diaries," but the problem is that scholars have seriously called into question the veracity of her account. They have uncovered information that Leonowens was, in fact, a troubled woman, who, fleeing childhood sexual abuse, concocted a life story at odds with the facts (Kepner 9).

Anna Leonowens was Indian-born and probably of half-Indian ancestry, although she never acknowledged that heritage; she was married to a poverty-stricken hotel manager in Singapore, Tom Owen, who died and left her the single mother of two children. She would later claim to be the widow of Major Thomas Leonowens, who apparently never existed (Kepner 2). Leaving her daughter with her dead husband's relatives, she took her son with her to Siam, where she did indeed spend five years as governess to

King Mongkut's children (Kepner 12). That she had the sort of close relationship with the king that she describes, however, is very questionable. Court documents indicate that while she did have some contact with the king, Anna actually saw him infrequently and was considered "something of a prig and a nuisance" at court (Kepner 13–14). Scholars now largely see her account of her experiences as a mixture of true-to-life events with factual inaccuracies, a nineteenth-century Western imperialist ethos, and prejudiced portrayals of Siamese culture all shaped by the tendencies to fabrication and distortion that dominate her portrayals of herself and her experiences throughout her life.

Anna and the King does make a considerable attempt to reshape the Leonowens narrative in accord with a more favorable view of King Mongkut and Siamese culture. With Chow Yun-Fat in mind from the beginning to be the first Asian actor to play the king, the filmmakers transformed Yul Brynner's somewhat clownish monarch from *The King and I* into a "dignified and courageous" figure (Cohen). This dignified and courageous king, however, is a complete departure from Leonowens's portrayal, which is very conflicted: she praises him for "his scholarship and keenness of mind, devotion to his people and zeal for reform," but also presents him as given to infantile behavior characterized by "cruelty, angry rages, and unrestrained lust" (Griswold 4). As A. B. Griswold points out, Leonowens's characterization of King Mongkut is all the worse because she presents it as if it were "an impartial and carefully balanced assessment of a complex personality" (4). According to Thai historians, King Mongkut was "a pious Buddhist, a modernizer and a national hero who successfully negotiated Thailand's earliest encounter with a predatory West" (Jory 206). Leonowens's books were largely ignored in Thailand until *The King and I* came out on Broadway and was adapted to film. Both the very popular Broadway musical and its equally successful film adaptation accentuate the negative aspects of Leonowens's characterization of Thai culture and its king (Jory 205). In particular, they present the king as an arbitrary Eastern despot, a man who desperately sought to learn more about "civilized" Western ways and looked to the brilliant European teacher Anna to turn him from a childish, barbaric tyrant into a mature, rational, modern monarch. As Bruce A. McConachie has argued, *The King and I* in both its Broadway and film incarnations was influential in shaping American public opinion to support U.S. policies in Southeast Asia in the 1960s by "Americanizing Asian cultures, naturalizing imperialist economics, reducing countries in Southeast Asia to dominoes, urging their rapid modernization, and when that failed, justifying the use of force to save them from Communist 'others'"

(398). It is small wonder, then, that the Thai government refused to take the chance on allowing another version of Leonowens's story to be filmed in their country.

Given this background, *Anna and the King* seems a very risky project for Foster. While the filmmakers' revisionist stance was admirable, their reliance on such questionable source material seemed to doom their project to failure even before it began. It was really impossible to retain almost any episodes from Leonowens's account, in which most historians have concluded there is "not a single statement that can be accepted without confirmation from elsewhere" (Griswold 31), yet *Anna and the King* does keep much of Leonowens's story, albeit attempting to refashion it with revisionist aims. A case in point is the Tuptim episode, which Foster, as noted above, singled out as unquestionably true. Foster seems to have seen it as having feminist implications, but unfortunately historians question both the message to be taken from the episode and its factual accuracy. They have pointed out that central to Leonowens's justification for Western imperialism is her story detailing the king's brutal torture and execution of one of his wives, a woman who had been forced to marry the king and eventually ran away with her former lover. In Leonowens's telling of this episode, Tuptim and her lover are captured, tortured, and burned at the stake in spite of Anna's attempts to intervene with the king on their behalf. In every version of the Tuptim story, which varies slightly in the length and severity of her torture and execution, the king is presented as a cruel despot and Tuptim is seen as a martyr for true love and individual freedom.

The meaning suggested by the episode seems not so much the feminist message that women need freedom of choice in marriage, but rather the imperialist notion that this tragedy of Eastern despotism could only be prevented by Western modernization (Kaplan 44). In addition, historians have seriously questioned the factual possibility of the events Leonowens describes. No other accounts of King Mongkut's reign even mention this incident; the Siamese had a particular horror of death by fire; and King Mongkut, known as a humane monarch, would be unlikely to have used it as a form of punishment for one of his wives. Additionally, Mongkut generally allowed his wives to resign at will, and it is a matter of record that one was abducted by a boatman who was only made to pay a fine when they were apprehended (Griswold 30). The scholarly consensus seems to be that Leonowens fabricated the whole Tuptim episode to support her argument that Siamese society remained uncivilized in spite of the king's desire for modernization. *Anna and the King*'s presentation of the episode does temper earlier portrayals by having King Mongkut wishing to grant Tuptim a pardon. He is only prevented from doing so by his fear that a pardon-would make him look weak in the eyes of his internal enemies given Anna's public support for her. Even with this change, and even if it is presented in a way somewhat less condemnatory of the king, retaining an episode that most likely never occurred hardly seems effective revisionism.

Another effect of the film's attempt to make Mongkut a more attractive figure is to make Anna much less so. This is, unfortunately, accentuated by Foster's performance, which received a more harshly negative critical response than any of her work in this decade. Promotional articles for the film describe Foster as determined to play Anna differently from how she had been played in earlier versions. She was to begin as a flawed woman, rigid, opinionated, judgmental, and unlikable, but to become more understanding and open by the film's end (Cohen). Reviewers saw the unlikeable Anna, but not the changed one. Overwhelmingly, they described Foster, who seemed to be trying to give Anna an air of strength, as looking "drawn and oddly inexpressive" (David Ansen, *Newsweek*, 20 December 1999) while creating an unsympathetic character who comes across as a "chauvinistic and testy know-it-all" (*Los Angeles Times*, 17 December 1999). They branded the film as too long, too slow, stodgy, and flat, and saw the role of Anna as an "uncomfortable fit" for Foster (Ansen) as well as a serious "misstep" in her career (Stephen Holden, *New York Times*, 17 December 1999).

☆☆☆☆☆ Conclusion

It is, indeed, a sad story I have told. Foster began the decade so promisingly with her great success in *The Silence of the Lambs*, a film that was hailed by many as a progressive text. Critics even designated her the feminist star of the future, but as this close examination of her film performances and image shows, by the end of the decade her career trajectory seemed far from progressive. She had accumulated two rather lackluster directorial outings, and her attempts to shape her acting career did not really take the feminist direction that many critics in the early nineties predicted; instead, she moved into conventional roles that positioned her rather uncomfortably as a romantic leading lady. At the same time, however, it seems reductive to see the development of Foster's image in the decade completely as a study in failure. To even the more conventional heroines that she played in *Sommersby*, *Maverick*, and *Anna and the King*, she brought a sense of female strength and authority.

In the early 2000s, Foster took her career in yet another direction, reshaping traditional woman-in-jeopardy roles into action heroines in *Panic*

Room (2002), *Flightplan* (2005), and *The Brave One* (2007). While these performances have not gained her overwhelming critical praise, they have taken her in more progressive directions as she returned to characters who seem to have come from the same mold as Clarice Starling in *The Silence of the Lambs*. Her directorial efforts, while not yet establishing her as a major director, do hold promise that she can still attain that status in the future. One problem she has had as a director is moving her projects from development to completion. Two films that she has been developing for some time now, *Flora Plum*, reputedly an *All About Eve*–like drama set in a circus, and a biopic of the notorious Nazi filmmaker Leni Riefenstahl, might just furnish Foster with the opportunity to finally prove herself as a director.

Finally, although her extra-cinematic image has been marked negatively for some by rumors of her lesbianism and for others by her timidity about making public her sexual orientation, she has still distinguished herself by building her image around acting talent, female strength, and intelligence, rather than merely glamour and beauty. The lesson to be taken from Foster's career is not that she should be condemned as a failed Hollywood feminist, but rather that such a designation seems almost impossible for even the most progressive star to attain within the existing Hollywood system.

3 ☆☆☆☆☆☆☆☆☆☆☆

Denzel Washington
A Revisionist Black Masculinity

MELVIN DONALSON

Beyond the ability to command top billing and top dollar, Denzel Washington's trajectory to stardom emerged as a bellwether for Hollywood's changing racial discourse on black masculinity and sexuality outside the familiar extremes of hypersexuality and asexuality, super criminal or super human, and predator or saint. This modification became significant during the 1990s, a decade when issues of multiculturalism, revisionist history, and masculinity studies influenced American cinematic themes. In particular, books such as *Iron John* (1990), *To Be a Man: In Search of the Deep Masculine* (1991), *The Masculine Mystique: The Politics of Masculinity* (1995), and *Manhood in America: A Cultural History* (1996) assessed manhood in society at large. In a similar manner, books such as *Cool Pose: The Dilemma of Black Manhood in America* (1992), *Makes Me Wanna Holler: A Young Black Man in America* (1995), and *The Assassination of the Black Male Image* (1996) explored the challenges and dynamics specifically affecting African American men.

Benefiting from these discussions and texts, Denzel Washington's power-ful screen presence and his mainstream popularity sanctioned the variety of images of black male characters previously absent from Hollywood films. Critically, Washington's durability and his sustained box office appeal were markers that America's politics of race were beginning to progress in a measurable way. Collectively, Washington's cinematic roles revised the depiction of black men and liberated black male images from the shackles of ghettocentricity and neominstrelsy that were historically associated with black masculinity.

During the 1990s, Washington appeared in eighteen feature films, portraying the lead male character in all but two. His 1989 Academy Award–winning performance as Tripp, former slave turned Union soldier in *Glory*, opened opportunities in his film career for the following decade. However, despite the prestige and marketing value of the award, stardom in Hollywood is a rare status for most actors, with a particular challenge for black actors attempting to break through the traditional limitations effected by a combination of white studio decision makers and fickle white audiences. For Washington, or other talented black actors such as Louis Gossett Jr., whose career declined in the years following his Oscar for a supporting role in *An Officer and a Gentleman* (1982), to become a star in Hollywood has meant the attainment of a rather subjective measure of "crossover" talent.

To wear that crossover crown usually requires that the black talent in question be a comedian, as it was for Richard Pryor in the 1970s and Eddie Murphy in the 1980s, or that it be a specific racial symbol, as with the unique career of Sidney Poitier. For despite Poitier's singular position as the most successful dramatic black actor during the modern civil rights era, his career was limited by deliberately circumscribed roles based on his race. Therefore, questions surface as to why Washington became more of a crossover success than any of his predecessors. What were his personal qualities and those external dynamics that contributed to his breaking through the rigidity of the existing system of stardom for black actors? These important questions can be addressed through a reflection upon seven hallmark films of Washington's career in this decade: *Malcolm X* (1992), *The Pelican Brief* (1993), *Philadelphia* (1993), *Virtuosity* (1995), *Crimson Tide* (1995), *Devil in a Blue Dress* (1995), and *The Hurricane* (1997). These seven films reveal the culmination of a decade of films that collec-tively anointed Washington the crown prince of black male stardom who found immense popularity among black and non-black audiences alike. As film historian Donald Bogle affirms: "Certainly no African American actor proved more successful during this period than Denzel Washington. In Hollywood, his credentials were impeccable. Not only did he project the requisite sex appeal and glamour that Hollywood expects and admires in its stars but, lo and behold, the guy could act" (423). Those skills as an actor have kept Washington's name on the cinematic marquee, even though his looks and television stardom in the 1980s on the drama "St. Elsewhere" made him a celebrity. Director Ridley Scott (*Gladiator* [2000], *American Gangster* [2007]), one of many filmmakers who admire Washington's acting capacity, stated that Washington is "constantly searching . . . to know everything about the character. . . . He's a kind of method actor—the real thing, not pseudo-method, which really means that you become the character" (qtd. in Troy Patterson, "Killer Instincts," *Men's Vogue*, November 2007, 128). Scott's assessment of Washington as an artist who excels at his craft has been shared by other filmmakers and critics, but being a gifted actor does not automatically translate into stardom in American cinema.

By the late 1990s, academic studies acknowledged both the significance and the complexity of a concept of stardom, seeking to reconcile commercial cinema and artistic achievements onscreen. That significance and complexity of a "star" was best underscored with a recognition that "in a commercial cinema such as Hollywood, stars are important to the processes of production (making films) but also distribution (selling and marketing films) and exhibition (showing films to paying audiences). . . . The star therefore becomes a form of capital, that is to say a form of asset deployed with the intention of gaining advantage in the entertainment market and making profits" (McDonald 5). Yet for the attribution of star status to a black actor, such as Washington, the difficulty increases due to the necessity for Washington to be approved and accepted by both white and African American viewers who, according to critic Ester Iverem, "make up at least 25 percent of the movie going audience, spending $2 billion annually" (Iverem xxviii). Beyond the box office marketing, that particular black audience—in its many configurations of gender, class, age, and geography—needed to connect with Washington in two significant ways in the 1990s: first as a screen persona that reflected ethnic authenticity to that particular ethnic community; and second as an offscreen personality who reflected a combination of racial pride and individual integrity. Washington managed to embody these characteristics during a decade in which race, gender, and celebrity status intersected, and at a time when the emerging star came under the increasing scrutiny of both academic critics and pop culture authorities.

While portraying diverse screen characters and serving as the subject of magazine interviews and feature stories, Washington showed himself to be a dedicated professional, a loyal family man, a proud spiritual man, and an effective racial spokesperson. In short, Denzel Washington appeared to be a complex figure who was both accessible and mysterious at the same time. This combination of qualities transcends race and encourages viewers across racial lines to become, if not loyal fans, then admiring observers. Many viewers would agree with the assessment provided by one critic: "One of the prime pleasures of watching Washington . . . has been marveling at his self-possession. The key to his superstardom, more important than his exactitude or his send-the-ladies-swooning looks, is his restraint in revealing only the subtlest shades of what's on a character's mind" (Patterson 124); one could add to this his "stride too: an unstoppable swagger with a hint of military bearing and nothing to prove" (126). Washington's facility at capturing women viewers while at the same time connecting with male viewers were ingredients that further enhanced his male star status, since he attracted more viewers than he alienated. For the purposes of this study, Washington's stardom surfaces conspicuously when examining the aforementioned seven films through these three telling categories: the professional image, the good guy image, and the biographical image.

☆☆☆☆★ Denzel the Professional

The black urban professional, or "buppie," found an array of depictions by the late nineties and early twenty-first century as the thirtysomething hip-hop generation maintained its passion for hip-hop culture while pursuing the white collar jobs that promised the security and health benefits extolled by the old school generation. Films such as *Waiting to Exhale* (1995), *Love Jones* (1997), *The Best Man* (1999), *The Brothers* (2001), *Two Can Play That Game* (2001), *Brown Sugar* (2002), *Breakin' All the Rules* (2004), and *Something New* (2006), to mention some, brought the buppie to levels of mainstream or crossover audiences unseen before, where black characters balanced their ethnicity and their professions successfully. To his credit, Washington's black urban professionals in this decade enabled those later images, serving as a transition from the earlier Poitieresque perfect professionals of the sixties. These ranged from Poitier as the doctor in *Guess Who's Coming to Dinner* (1967), the teacher in *To Sir with Love* (1967), and the Philadelphia detective in *In the Heat of the Night* (1967), to Washington's more realistic and even flawed professionals such as the journalists, professional athletes, real estate agents, and lawyers seen in the later films. As that transitional image, Washington portrayed characters who were obviously black males of intelligence, articulation, and professional confidence without being "ghettoized" as was the trend in the 'hood films earlier in the decade, films such as *Boyz N the Hood* (1991) and *Menace II Society* (1993). In particular, as Gray Grantham in *The Pelican Brief* (1993) and Joe Miller in *Philadelphia* (1993), Washington embodies black male leads who find success in their given fields, without militancy or a sustained rancor toward white America. As black author Ellis Cose observes: "To be born a black male in America is to be put into shackles and then challenged to escape. . . . But just as the handcuffs, the prison cells, even the coffins that confined Houdini eventually bent to his will, the chains that bind us [black men] will yield as well, provided that we attack them shrewdly" (148). Washington's professionals in these two films are complex black males who rely less on their physical prowess and race sensitivity than their mental sharpness, tenacious commitment to just causes, and moral principles.

Interestingly, *The Pelican Brief* and *Philadelphia* "were eventually released within two weeks of one another during the 1993 winter holiday season" (Brode 163), demonstrating the belief of distributors that saturating theaters with Washington's presence was a profitable move—another clear indicator of his star quality. Additionally, each film paired Washington with an established American star—Julia Roberts in the former and Tom Hanks in the latter. Washington understood the significance of appearing in big-budget films with his A-list co-stars: "I don't know if it was because of *Philadelphia* or *The Pelican Brief* or both, but I can see the difference in my career as a result of those two films. There's a lot of people who would never go see *Malcolm X* or *Cry Freedom* or *A Soldier's Story*, but they'll go see Julia Roberts and Tom Hanks. And they see me and say 'Well, he's good, too.' Then all of a sudden you're there [mainstream stardom]" (qtd. in Brode 163). Based on a white character in John Grisham's novel *The Pelican Brief* (1992), Washington portrays investigative journalist Gray Grantham, the tenacious but savvy professional who commits to discerning the reasons behind the murders of two Supreme Court justices. The catalyst for Gray's committed investigation of the crimes is Darby Shaw (Roberts), the law student who researched and penned her project "The Pelican Brief," which connected bribery, oil drilling rights on protected marshlands, high-powered lawyers, the White House chief of staff, and the president of the United States. Darby's plight takes most of the screen time during the first third of the film, but once she reaches out to Gray, the film transforms into a buddy film as Gray and Darby bond.

In the suspense-thriller *The Pelican Brief* (Alan J. Pakula, Warner Bros., 1993), law student Darby Shaw (Julia Roberts) finds protection with heroic journalist Gray Grantham (Denzel Washington). Collection Melvin Donalson.

Together, Gray and Darby survive threatening goons, foot chases, prolonged gunfire, a car explosion, and a controlling FBI director. Washington's Gray Grantham is a consummate investigative reporter for the *Washington Herald*, and with no family and personal relationship, Gray's work is his life. Obviously in his element, Washington gives Gray matinee-idol good looks, charm, and a personable demeanor. With a smooth verbal style and relaxed body movements that ooze confidence, Washington plays Gray as a skilled professional who can easily shift from a fact-finding newsperson to a sympathetic companion. The role permits Washington to utilize his screen presence to delineate the good guy who wants to discover the truth. Once aligned with Darby, Gray serves as a hero who protects the innocent woman in distress. Gray becomes Darby's confidant, the only person she trusts with her information and her life. When she fears the chasing thugs and asks him to sleep in her hotel room on the sofa, Gray concurs, watching over her in his steadfast and unselfish manner. As they follow and analyze leads in the case, he protects her, even suggesting that she leave the country as the danger increases.

Their bond is quick and deep, but not romantically expressed beyond a tight embrace at the film's end. Notably, this anomaly of a platonic relationship between the two leading characters defied the expectation of the suspense-action genre elements shaping the film. Instead, the asexual residue of the Poitier era sneaks into Gray's character, undermining his believability and connoting racial messages heretofore absent from the film. This lack of a screen romance appears to have ruffled reviewers more than the convoluted plot, as numerous articles targeted the lack of the obligatory bedroom scene so pervasive in American cinema. In a *Time* magazine online comment, Washington argued that such a physical romance would have been inappropriate to the story, reasoning that "in *The Pelican Brief*, in the script that I read, it wasn't there, and I also felt that since [the boyfriend of Roberts's character] had died three days ago, it didn't seem right to me that . . . she falls in love with another guy" (Jeffrey Ressner and Christopher J. Farley, "Pride and Place," *Time*, 2 October 1995).

However, the inquisition involving Washington's star status and lack of cinematic sexuality and romance continued in the media. In an interview about the lack of such scenes in his films during the decade, Washington responded with his usual public aplomb: "Is [romance] being kept from me? I don't know. I can say that a love story within a film has never been a reason for my doing or not doing a film" (qtd. in Brode xxx). In fairness to Washington, in the film *Mo' Better Blues* (1990), his first with black director Spike Lee, Washington's protagonist enjoyed generous bed-hopping as a musician torn between his love for two women and his music. Still, with such a dearth of black male sex symbols on the big screen, the issue persisted throughout the decade, as out of his eighteen films, only one—*Mississippi Masala* (1991)—included romance as a focus. With Washington's handsomeness and sexiness emphasized as main attributes of his stardom, it is not surprising that attention tilts back to this subject. As Brode emphasizes, "For millions of adoring fans . . . there is no question at all: Denzel Washington is a sex symbol," the kind of man "who manages to be both supple and brittle . . . perhaps the first black man to be taken seriously as an earthy and sexual presence on-screen" (xxix).

For the most part, *The Pelican Brief* is the type of mainstream film critics and scholars may dismiss, but one that finds a connection with a large audience. In its first four weeks of release, the film earned over $91 million (Parish 362). Displaying the attributes required for cinematic heroic figures, Washington demonstrates care and concern for those in need, while showing courage and resistance to the sources of evil. With a direct and amiable disposition, Gray's positive values make him likeable, and Washington shapes his performance to fulfill the obligatory contours of the good-guy image.

Turning to *Philadelphia*, the "first mainstream Hollywood film to deal with the subject of AIDS and one of the few to feature gay characters in a serious, dramatic context" (McDonagh 210), Washington again takes on the role of a lawyer, one quite different from the manipulating character in his earlier comedy, *Heart Condition* (1990). Playing Joe Miller, a lawyer intent on taking cases that can bring him a substantial pay day, Washington also portrays the essential role as the average guy confronting his homophobia and anxiety about AIDS. Biographer Douglas Brode has concluded: "The casting of Denzel as Joe was as effective as, in a previous era, the casting of Henry Fonda might have been. There are certain stars who, owing to something special (quite apart from performance talent) in their nature, automatically serve as audience surrogates. Simply, such actors are always *us*, or more correctly, a collective representation of us. . . . Denzel, then, is the first black movie star to ever convey such a quality, doing so not only for black audiences . . . but virtually everyone" (171–72). As mainstream stars at the time, Washington and Hanks made a bold move in taking on roles in a film that focused on a homosexual AIDS victim. Janet Maslin noted in a *New York Times* review that "Mr. Hanks gives a brave, stirring performance as a man slowly wasting away. But Mr. Washington, who is also very fine as the small-minded shyster who becomes a crusading hero, has the better role" (*New York Times*, 22 December 1993). Most reviews carried similar observations about Washington and Hanks, confirming both an equal billing in the film and an equal popularity with audiences.

As Miller, Washington's character was the one that typified the prejudices and consternation among those who had little, if any, ongoing contact with the gay community. Miller initially meets Andrew Beckett (Hanks) as they present their court arguments regarding a restraining order on a construction company. On a similar level as lawyers, they acknowledge each other's efforts at winning a decision that ultimately goes to Beckett. Later, Beckett arrives at Miller's office, seeking legal representation against his law firm that has recently fired him due to his illness—AIDS. For the remainder of the film, Miller undergoes a transformation in his attitude and behavior toward gays, and Beckett prepares himself to succumb to his ailing condition.

In the early sequences, Washington presents Miller as that everyman who rejects any tolerance for homosexuality, insisting that "manhood" remains synonymous with heterosexuality. Miller reduces all gay men into one single stereotype, removing any possibility of masculinity from a man identified as gay. Washington delivers these discriminatory lines with a tone and physical gestures that confirm his character's conservative and unflinching position. Miller's private declarations of anti-gay feelings are spiteful, but they remain couched within a likeable family man personality. He is never the raging bigot who would aggressively attack a homosexual, but he's blinded by stereotypes that prevent him from seeing gays as individuals.

Washington effectively pulls off a formidable task in embodying Miller. As in earlier films, he balances his dialogue, pauses in speech, body movements, and reaction shots in a way that suggests complexity, keeping Miller from seeming one-dimensional in his interaction with Beckett. Consequently, this allows for Miller's growth. He now exhibits an understanding and openness toward Beckett, delivering a powerful payoff for the character's developmental arc. At the same time, Washington's acting receives a star burnishing particularly in the manner of essential scenes shared equally with Hanks. The screen time given to each actor suggests their equal footing in the film, and the generous close-ups of each and the editing between them accentuates their corresponding significance to the story and for the audience.

☆☆☆☆★ Denzel the Good Guy

What Washington's professional images in *The Pelican Brief* and *Philadelphia* accomplish is a welcome counterbalance to the pervasive black ghetto male images in the 'hood films of the early 1990s. Moreover, his traditional role of "the good guy" also embellished Washington's star status during the decade. Washington depicted the good guy image in numerous films where his roles as police detectives placed him on the side of the law and morality, specifically in *Ricochet* (1991), *Virtuosity* (1995), *Fallen* (1998), and *The Bone Collector* (1999). However, beyond carrying credentials as a cop and as a good guy, two additional films in 1995—*Crimson Tide* and *Devil in a Blue Dress*—sustained his good-guy persona, as he mesmerized audiences with performances that surpassed the weaknesses in the content of the movies.

In *Virtuosity*, for example, Washington carries a badge, but with a slight twist. He portrays Lt. Parker Barnes, imprisoned for killing the psychopath who murdered his wife and daughter. In order to gain his freedom, Barnes must hunt down the nihilistic SID 6.7 (Russell Crowe), described by a scientist as a "nanotech synthetic organism" that crosses over from cyberspace into the real world. In a technoculture film that possesses a cinematic similitude to *The Terminator* (1984), *The Matrix* (1999), and even

Avatar (2009), *Virtuosity* submerges the viewer in a world of computer advancement, inter-dimensional transport, and special effects. One part science fiction, one part action-cop thriller, and one part cautionary story about scientific irresponsibility, the film centers Washington's character. Given that he dominates the frame in the plurality of the scenes, *Virtuosity* is Washington's film, and when he is sharing sequences with Russell Crowe's villainous SID 6.7, Washington's good-guy commitment to capturing this vicious killer ignites our interest in watching the film through all its cacophony of shattering glass, gunfire, screams, and explosions. Commenting on Washington's role, critic Kevin Thomas declares: "Forget all the technical stuff, however, for the film's real inspiration is in casting Denzel Washington as its star. He brings humanity to the carnage. . . . Washington has the kind of stature and star presence to hold together an often highly improbable chain of events" (*Los Angeles Times*, 4 August 1995, F12).

Indeed, Washington's Barnes invokes sympathy as a wrongly imprisoned man, while his sarcasm, physical and mental strength, intelligence, and sexiness layer a character that could have easily been a paint-by-numbers action protagonist. The action is certainly evident with the obligatory fight scenes, gun battles, car and foot chases, and bloody violence, and Washington delivers the heroic elements expected of the genre. His physical fitness is tapped carefully to provide a more virile figure than presented two years earlier in *The Pelican Brief*. In an early sequence, Barnes must stand nude in a scanning chamber before reentering the prison, and as laser scans move vertically along his body, the camera lingers closely on his chiseled muscles, cutting away just at the most revealing moment to be provocative. Additionally, the character of Dr. Madison Carter (Kelly Lynch), a criminal psychologist, is carefully scripted as his watchdog, allowing her lustful gazes and physical attraction to Barnes to function as a measurement of his irresistibility.

Significantly in this film, the physical dimensions of Washington's character serve as an announcement to his heightening star status. In this action film, he emerges as both the action star with outstanding physical prowess and the sex symbol with an undeniable attractiveness. In a further testimony to this appeal, Washington appeared on the cover of the 29 July 1996 issue of *People* magazine as the "sexiest man alive," a distinction that at the very least measured the actor's mass popularity and his position as the model for mainstream audiences' fantasies. This proclamation, via a national periodical, confirmed Washington's unique qualities and challenged the traditional racial norms and aesthetics about manliness, handsomeness, and physical magnetism. The cover story exuded the giddy praise for Washington's allure from various women; as the author Pam Lambert put it, "There's something heroic about the open visage of this actor who has embodied such giants as Malcolm X and South African activist Steven Biko. . . . Washington's noble bearing, combined with the mostly up-standing, smart characters he has chosen to play, make him a thinking-woman's heartthrob. The kind of guy who can get you into trouble just by being on your mind" ("Heat from a Cool Source," *People*, 29 July 1996). An amazing quality possessed by Washington has been his ability to project an edgy sexiness, which stirs his women fans while maintaining a masculine persona that does not repel his male fans.

In *Crimson Tide*, Washington dons a military uniform in an alternative embodiment of the good-guy image. His Lieutenant Commander Ron Hunter is first shown taking pictures at his little girl's birthday party, where his family unit is completed with a wife and son. This image of the family man is quickly juxtaposed against the acerbic Captain Frank Ramsey (Gene Hackman), who reveals in an interview that Hunter attended Annapolis and Harvard, there gaining important knowledge of, and experience in, riding horses. Needing an executive officer, Ramsey approves of Hunter for the upcoming mission to police the waters around Russia where one rebel leader threatens nuclear aggression against the United States.

Beginning with the interview and later during the voyage at sea, Hunter and Ramsey clash, often over ethical and philosophical perspectives. Ramsey's direct, by-the-book, follow-the-rules approach to commanding and to war contrast to Hunter's more rational, thoughtful perspectives. Washington gives Hunter an intelligence that is held in check by his naval respect for the chain of command. Without being haughty or arrogant, Hunter is a man who states his mind carefully, attempting to avoid any aggressiveness with a commanding officer who is not his intellectual equal. In the face of Ramsey's traditional hardline about war, Hunter states: "The purpose of war is to serve a political end, but the true nature of war is to serve itself. . . . In my humble opinion, in the nuclear world, the true enemy is war itself."

A crucial eruption occurs between the characters when Ramsey plans to follow a radio message to launch nuclear missiles at Russia while Hunter demands that the complete details of a second partial message be obtained. This sets into motion the ultimate battle between Hunter and Ramsey as each man's military style, personality, and leadership strategies are laid bare. Hunter's cool insistence on logic and unflinching commitment to making the smart decision elevates the moral scope of his character. His verbal toughness is matched by his physical presence as he refuses to adhere to a reckless rush into nuclear war. He emerges as the hero, the leader who places the immediate welfare of his men and the future survival of the world before himself. When Ramsey punches Hunter twice in the face to force a surrender of a key to unlock the submarine's missiles, Hunter stands tall to the assault without hitting back, responding with his courage to treat war only as a last resort.

The issue of race as a subtext in *Crimson Tide* comes through selected areas of the dialogue and through the obvious pitting of a black senior officer against a white senior officer. Serving on a submarine proudly named the *Alabama* (consequently, the *Crimson Tide* moniker), Hunter, as second-in-command, marks his distinction as a black officer of power and achievement. Ramsey understands this distinction, and his smirks and verbal challenges consistently underscore that race is not mentioned but serves as a source of measurement of characters' mettle. It is significant, then, that toward the finale Ramsey verbally engages Hunter, remarking that Lipizzaner stallions from Portugal—all white in color—are the most highly trained horses in the world. The analogy of color, training, and superiority are not lost upon Hunter, who clarifies the issue: "Yes, sir, I'm aware that they're all white. But they're not from Portugal, they're from Spain. And at birth, they're not white . . . they're black." Soon thereafter, Hunter is proven correct about the horses, and, more important to the narrative, about that crucial second message, which in its totality instructed a termination of the missile launch. Hunter's correct call on this crucial mission attests to his leadership skills, and Washington's stalwart demeanor as a black officer under fire is not insignificant.

In this film's ongoing battle of wills, Washington is more than capable of matching the intensity of Gene Hackman. Their scenes together become more engrossing than the plot points about nuclear disaster: both characters fill the cramped space of the submarine with their passions and commitments. Washington's performance of inward strength and outward leadership makes it difficult to imagine another actor surpassing him in the role.

In this regard Hunter bears a close good-guy resemblance to another Washington role, private detective Easy Rawlins in *Devil in a Blue Dress*, for which he also received praise. "Washington's performance," wrote one critic, "is alert and subtle, as he mixes a simmering desperation over his deepening involvement in nasty doings with a laid-back quality that communicates his awareness of his wisdom of keeping his own counsel" (Todd McCarthy, *Variety*, 18 September 1995, 93).

In *Devil in a Blue Dress* (Carl Franklin, TriStar, 1995), Washington plays Easy Rawlins, a working-class man pulled into a world of corruption in 1940s Los Angeles. Collection Melvin Donalson.

Based upon the first in a series of sleuth novels by black author Walter Mosley, the film follows Rawlins, a war veteran and working-class guy in 1948 Los Angeles who faces losing his job and consequently losing the thing he loves most—his house. With few options, he takes a job for quick money, which requires him to find a white woman socializing and hiding in the black neighborhoods of the city. Rawlins must consequently deal with corrupt politicians, dead bodies, racist police detectives, pedophilia, racial passing, segregated Los Angeles settings, and an uncontrollable friend, Raymond "Mouse" Alexander (Don Cheadle), who is addicted to violence. Although continually confronting corruption, Rawlins rises above the chaos to remain true to his goal of the American dream of home ownership— admirable and understandable across the racial and class lines of any audi- ence. True to the good guy characters Washington convincingly enacts, it is not surprising that Rawlins possesses a moral code that functions as the cornerstone of cinematic heroes, and as a working-class man the character represents the majority of men who long for simple lives, good jobs, and fair treatment in their daily routines.

Rawlins's voiceover musing and hard-boiled dialogue are tellingly amusing for a black character in this detective genre: "Everybody was peeing on my head and telling me it was rain. Guess they figured I was some new kind of fool." However, Washington's portrayal of Rawlins never suggests him to be a fool. He is an average guy who deals with life-and-death situations with a calculated calm. Washington also plays Rawlins as a sensible black man of the 1940s era. He knows and measures the repercussions of being in white neighborhoods after dark, of being beaten in an interrogation room by white cops, and of negotiating with wealthy and powerful white men. Played with Washington's familiar subtlety, Rawlins is not a fast-talking, slick black male but a wise black man who comprehends the limitations of social and political lines.

From the opposite end of Rawlins's calculated calm emerges the nihilism of Mouse, Rawlins's best friend, who arrives to provide protection and support. Washington's mellow shading of Rawlins contrasts strikingly with the wild volatility that Cheadle gives to Mouse. The juxtaposition of their black masculinities underscores the problem of placing a monolithic tag on all black men. Washington once again gives depth to a black male character, one at the other extreme in education from the characters of Gray Grantham and Joe Miller.

When considering the good guys Washington embodies, it is notable that his star presence conveys perceptible codes of ethical behavior. His characters in these films are usually grounded in the foundation of ordinariness, people who step forward to take a stand when necessary. Rather than an over-the-top superhero, Washington's good guys are cloaked in realistic probability, the kind of men who avoid the spotlight but demand our attention.

☆☆☆☆☆ Denzel and Biopics

We now shift to the third category of Washington's star text in this period: that of biographical images, roles based upon real-life people. Biopics bring a particular degree of scrutiny from both viewers and critics. On one hand, the dearth of dramatic renderings of heroic black males undermines the scores of true-life people who affected and shaped the history of the black communities and the society at large. On the other hand, one black actor can't carry the burden of portraying them all. Yet in taking on roles such as South African activist Steven Biko (*Cry Freedom*), Malcolm X, and boxer Rubin Carter (*The Hurricane*), Washington "has arguably done more than even [Sidney] Poitier to redefine black masculinity on screen. So what does it mean that Washington would rather bat away direct questions about his own cultural importance? Probably that

The title role in *Malcolm X* earned Washington wide acclaim for his portrayal of the slain leader as well as an Academy Award nomination for Best Actor. (Spike Lee, Largo International, 1992). Collection Melvin Donalson.

he's too smart to get caught burnishing his own aura and too savvy to box himself into any corners" (Patterson 129). Washington, however, proved his durability to withstand examination, his commitment to research, and his acting skills in portraying Biko, a substantial role that brought him an Academy Award nomination. Five years later, he received another Academy Award nomination for his performance in the title role of Spike Lee's *Malcolm X* (1992).

Because Malcolm was a sacred legend for many, one author notes, "Lee knew it was impossible to make a movie that would satisfy everyone; the necessary inclusion of inflammatory speeches in his film would upset entrenched conservatives, while an honest depiction of infighting among black nationalists would not sit well with true believers, who wanted propaganda that would portray all blacks as brothers" (Brode 142). Washington likewise understood this dilemma and prepared himself accordingly, as he would later for *The Hurricane*. He committed himself to a demanding regimen of research into Malcolm's life, reading biographical materials, watching videotapes, studying mannerisms, speaking to Malcolm's relatives and friends, reading FBI files, and taking classes in the Black Muslim religion (146).

Malcolm X was Washington's second film with Lee, and it became more ambitious, especially in historical scope, than any film either had been involved with before. Running more than three hours, the film covers the leader's life in four notable sections: his street-thug phase in Boston and New York, his prison life and transition into the Black Muslim religion, his work as a minister and community organizer under the leadership of Elijah Muhammad, and his final year when he established his separate mosque and his racially inclusive leadership agenda. With this complex character, Washington again constructed a man undergoing a physical and attitudinal metamorphosis. In the early years Malcolm calls himself "Red" and inhabits the streets and clubs with his friend Shorty (Spike Lee). For this Washington dons zoot suits, adopts a stylish strut, and has his hair chemically straightened, exuding a reckless, selfish exuberance where his physical prowess and flashing smile take his character far in living the hedonistic life. In the dance hall choreography, we witness Washington's energetic and striking dance moves, his affected cool attitude and banter. Washington thus emphasizes the youthfulness and devil-may-care attitude so crucial to understanding the charisma of the young Malcolm. Importantly, this persona is contextualized by flashbacks that show Malcolm's difficult childhood, visualized under the more mature voiceover of an older Malcolm.

Dealing with the anxiety of discovering his racial heritage from the perspectives of the Black Muslim polarities of black and white, Malcolm slowly loses the buoyancy and abandon of his days as "Red." A key feature of the Malcolm mythos is his transition from hedonist to virtuous leader, one capable of subscribing to a demanding religious philosophy rooted in Afrocentricity. As such, the role presents a particular challenge for an actor intent on conveying the arc of Malcolm's journey. Having studied Malcolm's gestures and mannerisms from extant footage, Washington delivers a performance that goes beyond mimicry, utilizing his body and voice to capture the finest details. In so doing he limns the contours of both a public man with the responsibilities of spiritual and political leadership and a private man attempting to maintain a marriage and family.

Later, when Malcolm becomes a speaker and organizer for the Black Muslims, Washington shapes his character into a zealot who draws attention through his blazing rhetoric and undeniable charisma. Resolute and without fear, Washington's Malcolm is magnetic, stating principles and beliefs in a fast-paced voice unclouded by doubts. Whether speaking to a black person at a rally or dealing unflinchingly with white police officers, Washington gives Malcolm a commanding presence that fills the screen with the powerful influence of the legendary figure. In this part of the film, Washington's fiery characterization of this complex leader demonstrates his skills in becoming the character he portrays. Working on an epic canvas, Washington paints a comprehensive portrait of an international figure that strengthens the actor's appeal as a consummate screen star. In a generous measurement of the actor's accomplishment, one critic concludes: "Much of the film's strength lay in the performance of Denzel Washington, who enabled us to see Malcolm *think*, making his conversion and straight-arrow drive altogether convincing and heroic. . . . Washington's quick and ready smile, smooth handsome face, and indisputable charm make it hard *not* to like him or to agree with his politics" (Bogle 355).

Like *Malcolm X*, *The Hurricane* was a controversial film due to the discrepancies between historical events and story demands, with Washington delivering another Academy Award–nominated performance. *The Hurricane* approaches its protagonist, Rubin Carter, as a complicated and physically gifted boxer, who from his youth was targeted by an obsessed, racist white police detective, and as a young black male maligned by an equally racist legal system that stripped Carter of his professional success and incarcerated him based on the testimonies of dubious witnesses. Championed by celebrities of various races, but befriended by a core of believers—a black youth and his Canadian caretakers—Carter's screen depiction suggested a man of incredible strength and self-sufficiency who struggles and succeeds in gaining his freedom.

Amid all the rancorous voices clashing in the media about the movie's version of the truth of Carter's life experiences, the consensus of most sources was the remarkable performance of Denzel Washington. One critic wrote: "Taking his character from impetuous youth to middle-aged prison guru, Washington makes Carter a heroic figure, but one that is recognizably human. We sense the precarious balance of his life between anger and acceptance and between love and hatred" (Kirk Honeycutt, *Hollywood Reporter*, 20 December 1999, 15). Playing both the emotional and physical demands of the film, Washington "dropped a whopping 44 pounds from his frame in preparation for the film. He trained for six months, two hours per day, learning to throw more than a punch a second" (Brent Simon, "Hurricane Denzel," *Entertainment Today*, 31 December 2000, 6). Washington's transformation from a boxer in his prime to a middle-aged inmate is seamless, delivering the emotional layers that provide a three-dimensional rendering to the character. The portrayal resonates so hypnotically that, as *Los Angeles Times* reviewer Kenneth Turan observed, "Nothing really prepares us for what he does in 'The Hurricane.' With power, intensity, remarkable range and an ability to disturb that is both unnerving and electric, it is more than Washington's most impressive part, it sums up his career as well, encapsulating why he's one of the best actors working in film today" (*Los Angeles Times*, 29 December 1999).

The Hurricane reunited Washington and white director Norman Jewison, who had worked together on *A Soldier's Story* (1984). *The Hurricane* reveals the demanding physical and emotional aspects of Washington's role from the opening credits. Beginning in a 1960s boxing match in which Carter defeats the welterweight champion, Washington's toned, muscular body shows his ability to authenticate the visceral, brutal pounding of man against man in the ring. Then, cutting to 1973, the incarcerated Carter waits in his cell, the same fury boiling over as he yells out and shadow boxes, calling forth his challenge to anyone daring to enter and search his cell. He declares to prison guard Lieutenant Williams (Clancy Brown) that he will kill anyone who attempts to confiscate his autobiographical manuscript, his source of freedom and survival. That juxtaposition between the physical and emotional sustains itself to varying degrees of intensity throughout the film, and Washington manages to make each scene resonate magnificently.

Throughout the film, Washington's onscreen appearance is complemented by his intriguing voiceover narration. From his character's truncated childhood to his stint in the army to his submersion in boxing, Washington develops Carter powerfully as a man who seeks affirmation through violence and confrontation, portraying the character's agitation and impatience through erratic body movements, a hard-nosed attitude, and aggressive glances. When Carter lands in prison, he maintains control by turning his body into a survival tool. In his voiceover, Washington's hoarse and stern voice states: "I gave up all the worthless luxuries that most inmates crave. . . . I hated them. In fact, I hated everyone. I didn't even speak English. I spoke hate and its verbs were fists. I made up my mind to turn my body into a weapon that would eventually set me free." This descent into the bowels of the legal system suspends all semblance of a normal life, as Carter endures sixteen years of incarceration and physical aging. Washington molds his facial reactions and posture to serve his character effectively: his expressions of disgust, anger, and horror at his condition weigh upon him and are palpable to the viewer. According to one critic, "Denzel's knockout performance (pun intended) amounts to a veritable gamut that includes boxing in the ring, struggling for a shred of dignity as defiant prisoner, and becoming emotionally available to those who try to help him" (Mapp 99).

These biopics displayed Washington's highly believable portrayal of dignified, complicated black men who, when confronted with racism, respond with strength and perseverance. Malcolm X and Rubin Carter are black male figures who demonstrated survival over adversity. Both men, having endured the penal system's ongoing hunger for black men, rose above their incarceration and metaphorical shackles to succeed in life and to become models of success for the larger black community. By portraying such black male characters, Washington contributed to the A-list of films that, in Edward Guerrero's fitting terms, "endeavored to define, portray, or diagnose those vital aspects of black male humanity so often subordinated or missing in dominant cinema" (274). Washington's effective portrayals of these real-life individuals emphasized his skills at assuming their larger-than-life personalities and breathing life into figures that accentuate the complexity of black masculinity in films.

By the end of the 1990s, Washington had reconstructed key dimensions of black masculinity, revealing the narrowness of earlier images and disturbing the sacrosanct white male dominance of his contemporary times. With consistently impressive performances, carefully selected screen roles, and a carefully guarded private life, Washington became a bankable star and a secretive celebrity. This combination connected to a decade shaped by multiculturalism, dominating pop culture appetites, revisionist historical texts, and the burgeoning masculinities studies in both academic and popular books. Washington was certainly the antithesis of the prevalent gangsta rap masculinity of young male hip-hop celebrities, and he was more confident and virile than the older, stoic, conservative male figures of earlier media constructions. As a result, he surfaced as the decade's answer to the questionable black male images of the past, while offering the many possibilities as to where the representation of black males could go in the future. As underscored in the 1995 *Time* article by Ressner and Farley,

> Denzel Washington stands apart . . . playing a variety of challenging and not race-specific roles. For every *Malcolm X*, in which he starred as the slain Muslim leader, there was a *Philadelphia*, in which he played a homophobic lawyer who just happened to be black. He has shown a facility for Shakespearean comedy (*Much Ado About Nothing*), as well as for Spike Lee's drama (*Mo' Better Blues*). . . . Other black actors—Wesley Snipes, Samuel L. Jackson, Laurence Fishburne—have drawn deserved critical acclaim, but none has achieved Washington's mix of box-office clout and acting craft. He is a black actor—proudly, fiercely so—who has succeeded in making that term merely descriptive, not professionally limiting.

The gains that Washington made personally as an artist invigorated the complexity of available roles featuring black masculinity, achieving normality, depth, and humanity too often excised from earlier decades of extreme representations. Although one person—one star—cannot be expected to alter an entire medium or to represent an entire group of people, Washington's contributions to and effect upon the images of black men have been crucial, significant, and historic.

4 ☆☆☆☆☆☆☆☆☆☆☆

Julia Roberts
Cultural Phenomenon

R. BARTON PALMER

First achieving prominence in the industry with the surprising mega-hit *Pretty Woman* (1990), by the end of the decade Julia Roberts had become Hollywood's most bankable performer, with her agreement to participate in a project a guarantee that pre-production financing could readily be obtained. Against the odds (for she made a number of career miscalculations, some rather serious, during the middle 1990s), Roberts had also emerged as one of the few actors whose name on the marquee could "open" a film, that is, make sure that the first weekend was a solid financial success so that attendance momentum (and significant box office) could be generated for the weeks immediately following. As a result, her upfront fee rose steadily during the decade until it reached a rumored $17 million (according to numerous sources, but these are only reasonable guesses), a stratospheric compensation level that few, if any, of her fellow actresses at that time could even come close to matching (only in the 2000s were Reese Witherspoon and Cameron Diaz reported to be receiving similar upfront compensation, which for all three is now substantially in excess of $20 million). As of this writing, Box Office Mojo calculates that Roberts's films through 2009 have earned a staggering box office total of $2.3 billion, making her by far the highest producing female star in world cinema history.

It is perhaps unusual that her growing appeal was in large part due to a turbulent personal life that, hyped by the media, generated huge, sustained interest around the world. She became not only a star but also a celebrity. At the beginning of the new millennium, in fact, Roberts had become one of global culture's best known and most widely admired public personalities even though marriage and the birth of several children had considerably restricted the number of projects she has been able to complete in the last decade. In one sense, Roberts at the end of the 1990s was a cultural phenomenon, not only a star who could profitably perform in major films, but also a figure whose professional and personal life had become an irresistible subject, constituting a narrative whose anticipated conclusion (marriage to a Mr. Right and the establishment of some sort of satisfying domesticity) generated its own twists, turns, reversals, and suspense.

Some critics have suggested that this press coverage, and its intrusive nosiness (which many, perhaps most, would find obnoxious), has turned Roberts into a near-tragic figure whose psychological health has survived only because of her inner resolve and self-confidence. ("Roberts is certainly not the first Hollywood star to find the pressure of fame overwhelming. Comparisons were quickly made with the likes of Marilyn Monroe and Elizabeth Taylor—sometimes with sympathy, and sometimes not" ["Julia Roberts"]). Even more so than the steely Taylor, however, Hollywood's ultimate survivor, Roberts appears undamaged and undaunted by the attention, which, favorable or not, has only boosted her visibility and professional viability, a calculation she is certainly shrewd enough to have made for herself.

In any case, that she became first a star and then a cultural phenomenon was only indirectly the effect of the success—somewhat checkered and marked by significant absences from profitability and, then, from the public eye—that Roberts had as an actress *tout court* during the first full decade of her career in the 1990s. A number of her films made a great deal of money (romantic comedy eventually emerged as her most dependably profitable genre, as is the case for both Witherspoon and Diaz as well), but many did not, especially those in which she played a serious rather than romantic role. Though certainly she is a competent actress, it would be incorrect to label any of her performances compelling, affecting, or bravura (and this is true even of her Academy Award–winning role in Steven Soderbergh's

Erin Brockovich [2000], an appealing, but certainly unnuanced, imperson-ation of an uneducated but feisty and dedicated legal assistant). Roberts's essential screen qualities—which might be summed up in the words "attractive" and "sympathetic," with her gorgeous and toothy smile a con-siderable asset—have been on display from the beginning. It cannot be said that she has matured significantly in terms of technique or range during the two decades of her career. Her unimpressive attempts to do quirky sup-porting roles in both Stephen Frears's gothic thriller *Mary Reilly* (1996) and Neil Jordan's grim political biopic *Michael Collins* (1996) did nothing to advance her career. Roberts has subsequently avoided projects of this kind, though she has been successful playing serious dramatic roles, at least to a degree, in independent films such as Steven Soderbergh's *Full Frontal* (2002) and Mike Nichols's *Closer* (2004).

The 1990s, if not a period of artistic triumph, proved to be a phenome-nally successful decade for Roberts in every other way. In her role as the sympathetic young prostitute in *Pretty Woman*, lacking sleaziness but with an emerging sense of self-worth and few bad habits (no drug use and no manager mister on the scene), Roberts became the ideal wish-fulfillment figure for female viewers less interested in building a respectable career and more taken with the romantic fantasy of being swept away by a rich (and also handsome) man (Richard Gere), whose sole pleasure in life, beyond a bit of discreet sex, soon becomes buying her the expensive accoutrements and funding the customary pleasures of upper-middle-class life. The more interest he shows, the less professional their relationship becomes, until she finally signals a different kind of bargain by kissing him on the mouth, a demonstration that she no longer considers him a john. The film's most important secondary character, the manager of the hotel where she is stay-ing, with some reluctance takes on the burden of instructing this Eliza Doolittle in what are for her the unfamiliar refinements of life at the top, teaching her about such matters as the proper use of silverware and what is regarded as acceptable dress in high society. Roberts's role demanded little more than being the charming, beautiful, and appealingly vulnerable pupil as well as an object of desire, since the only fully developed character arc in the film belongs to Gere's Pygmalion figure, who becomes increas-ingly interested in the young woman he has first hired to do a job and whom he gradually finds himself remaking in ever more personal and per-manent ways.

The narrative completely lacks plausibility, of course, as, aiming for a romantic connection, it abandons even the dubiously credible motivation of its ultimate source in the George Bernard Shaw play. Why would any good-looking rich man, despite an unfortunate marital past, have any interest in engaging a prostitute, and not a very high-class one at that, to satisfy desires that are absolutely conventional and might easily be catered to by companions not practicing the world's oldest profession? But this is perhaps too much to ask of a bit of screen fluff. Roberts functions admirably as the grateful yet feisty object of his desire who is then, as recipient of his unexpected generosity, lifted up and away from a life of penury and degradation to a future of shopping in Beverly Hills' swankiest boutiques and dining in its toniest eateries, with an upscale home in the Valley as perhaps her ultimate reward. In *Pretty Woman* (the film's title is very suggestive about the ultimate basis of her screen career), Roberts showed she made an ideal object of romantic fantasy, but the role was actually less challenging than her performance in *Steel Magnolias* (1989), where she was called upon not only to produce a credible facsimile of diabetic shock, but also to suddenly lapse into irreversible kidney failure, even though in this earlier release as well she did not otherwise have any memorable performance moments.

☆☆☆☆★ Mostly a Pretty Appealing Woman

In the wake of *Pretty Woman*'s surprising success, Hollywood professionals, who are not stupid about the use of actors who possess the *je ne sais quoi* that marks out the budding star, clearly saw that Roberts was a valuable property needing careful and appropriate handling. Even so, her career during the next ten years suffered from sudden ups and downs. It seems no accident that the most successful films in which she starred during the 1990s have tended to follow the same pattern as *Pretty Woman*, casting her as a beautiful and charismatic young woman in a narrative where she is supported by at least one but more often an ensemble of other, more experienced or talented professionals, who do most of the heavy lifting acting-wise. In *Flatliners* (1990) Roberts plays one bright medical student among a similar group of high-achieving and daring others (Kevin Bacon, Kiefer Sutherland, and William Baldwin chief among them) in a narrative whose focus constantly shifts, offering no main character; Roberts held up her end very nicely in a production that never quite came off as expected and was a box office disappointment. In mega-director Steven Spielberg's *Hook* (1991), her Tinkerbell is a reduced presence in every sense; the film belongs rather to its hero (Robin Williams's Peter Pan) and, perhaps more so, appealing villain (Dustin Hoffman's Captain Hook). *Dying Young* (1991) is a gloomy drama, featuring another cross-class romance, this time between an angry rich man, struck with a terminal illness, played by the

Garry Marshall's *Runaway Bride* (Paramount, 1999) attempted with some success to re-capture the magic of *Pretty Woman*, with its tale of altar-shy Maggie Carpenter (Roberts) and persistent suitor Ike Graham (Richard Gere). Courtesy Photofest New York.

very talented Campbell Scott, who had all the major scenes, and the down-on-her-luck young woman (Roberts) who agrees to serve as his in-house assistant. The film was marred by many problems (including its unappealing title), but an important one seems to have been that Scott lacked the charisma and star appeal for a romantic lead (he has gone on after this flop to have a very successful career, mostly in off-beat roles). He could not carry the picture, with its flawed script, and Roberts, therefore, could fade attractively into the background. Also significant, Scott and Roberts struck no sparks (he holds the dubious distinction of being one of the few Roberts leading men in the decade with whom she conducted no offscreen romance).

Sleeping with the Enemy (1991) further exemplifies the problem. The film's first half, in which Laura Burney (Roberts) placates and then escapes from her psychopathic abusive husband, Martin, works fine as Patrick Bergin turns in a compelling, if at times over-the-top, performance as a man obsessed with a woman he would rather kill than let escape his grasp. The film's second half, concerned mostly with the life that Roberts tries to reconstruct on her own, falls flat for the most part as Roberts's new love interest is a relative unknown (Kevin Anderson), picking up momentum only when Martin reappears hungry for either repossession or vengeance. *I Love Trouble* (1994) offered Roberts better support, but she could not get along with a very badly behaving Nick Nolte, though the concept seemed a winner, considering the established appeal of Nolte as a rough-edged romantic lead (he and Roberts are reporters, teamed together to cover a big case in what seems an attempt to repeat the magic of Nolte's other buddy films like *48 Hours* [1982]). Similar problems marred the box office possibilities of Robert Altman's *Ready to Wear* (1994) and Lasse Hallström's *Something to Talk About* (1995), in the latter of which Roberts, embroiled in a difficult marriage with Dennis Quaid, is outshone and out-acted by Kyra Sedgwick playing her sister; that Sedgwick garnered an Oscar for the supporting role was an unfortunate punctuation mark.

But when Roberts was good, she was very good indeed, turning herself, especially as the decade ended, into box office magic. *The Pelican Brief* (1993) saw Roberts reemerge to prominence after a two-year absence from filmmaking occasioned by the failures of *Dying Young* and *Sleeping with the Enemy*, along with the inevitable personal difficulties, including her last-minute abandonment of marriage to Kiefer Sutherland, scheduled for 14 June 1991 and promising to be the celebrity celebration of the year. This sudden change of plans seemed to reveal an instability and fickleness that are subsequently provided with appealing (meta)fictional form in both *My Best Friend's Wedding* (1997) and *Runaway Bride* (1999), films that boldly dissolve the borders between star biography and fabulation. Steven Spielberg, in a candid comment to a "60 Minutes" reporter, declared that, after all the trouble she had raised during the production of *Hook*, he would not work with her again, and the reputation of being a temperamental star was not one Roberts was interested in acquiring (qtd. in Sanello 140). *Pelican* offered her an excellent script, based on John Grisham's fast-paced novel, and excellent leads to work with (Denzel Washington and Sam Shepard), turning her into a main character about one-third of the way into the narrative, and with well-directed suspenseful action supporting her performance as a dogged law student turned unofficial CIA agent who has discovered a serious scandal at the highest levels of government. Four years later Roberts found herself playing a similar role in *Conspiracy Theory* (1997), a thriller that seems little more than one continuous chase in which Roberts plays the sane, accidental sidekick and love interest to the quirky but sympathetic paranoid played by Mel Gibson, who carries the picture. *Conspiracy Theory* was a great success, earning more than $137 million in

In the romantic comedy *My Best Friend's Wedding* (P. J. Hogan, TriStar, 1997) Julianne Potter (Roberts) plots to steal the affections of her erstwhile best friend (played by Dermot Mulroney) from Kimberly Wallace (Cameron Diaz, right). Courtesy Photofest New York.

worldwide distribution, about double its production costs, and this was very good news indeed for its producers. But it was Roberts's starring presence in two mega-hits, the romantic comedy *My Best Friend's Wedding* and the dramedy *Stepmom* (1998), that firmly established her as Hollywood's most dependable big earner. Significantly, in both projects Roberts worked with attractive ensembles (Dermot Mulroney, Cameron Diaz, and Rupert Everett in *Wedding*, and Ed Harris and Susan Sarandon in *Stepmom*) that effectively exploited her appeal. She had finally arrived at a position of unquestioned dominance in the industry.

☆☆☆☆★ Depicting a Life in Pictures in *Notting Hill*

Roberts appears to have recognized the career-boosting potential of this shift in her position within Hollywood. At decade's end she agreed to participate, and at what was reported to be only a fraction of her usual asking price, in what was essentially a comparatively low-budget British project whose appeal was that it would offer an attractive version of the "Julia Roberts" story. *Notting Hill* (1999) would be produced by Duncan Kenworthy (who had achieved considerable success with the ensemble dramedy *Four Weddings and a Funeral* [1994]) and directed by Roger Michell, whose sleek BBC TV production of Jane Austen's *Persuasion* (1995) had met with similar critical and popular approval. Her interest in the proposed film, and her willingness to take a substantial pay cut, was surprising for other reasons. Though Roberts would be the film's star, she would by no means be the main character, a role that would fall to British actor Hugh Grant, who would reprise his role as a charmingly bumbling romantic lead, a characterization he had played to perfection in *Four Weddings* and a number of other mildly successful releases such as *Nine Months* (1995). Roberts would play the same role played by Andie McDowell in *Four Weddings*, a somewhat distant and infrequently glimpsed object of erotic longing. The film, in other words, would offer Roberts very little in the way of big scenes, and the script by Richard Curtis (who had also written *Four Weddings*), which she read with great approval, placed a good deal of emphasis on intriguingly grotesque or comic secondary characters, a significant feature also obviously recycled from *Four Weddings*. *Notting Hill* would not provide her with the screen prominence she had enjoyed in her recent screen box office successes such as *The Pelican Brief* and *Stepmom*. If *Four Weddings* was essentially Grant's film in terms of his character's narrative centrality, *Notting Hill* would be as well, but *Notting Hill* offers an appealing and attractive version of the offscreen life of Roberts's glittering star presence, replete with a wish-fulfillment conclusion.

Roberts had been reluctant at first to sign up for a project in which she was to play a famous, eminently bankable American actress named Anna Scott who was exactly like Julia Roberts but, at least according to Roberts herself, entirely different. In fact, she seems to have hated the way in which the film, while ostensibly biographical, distorted the star persona she had carefully created ("Anna is still unsure of her own worth, whether as an actress or as a person. What is written about her concerns her a lot more than it would concern me" is what she observed to a reporter from *Vanity Fair* [qtd. in Sanello 197]). Roberts had perhaps forgotten her own desperate exasperation at the intense press coverage of her romantic life, especially the last-minute cancellation of her much-ballyhooed marriage to Sutherland and her subsequent nuptials to, and then divorce less than two years later from, singer Lyle Lovett. In any event, reading carefully through Curtis's script, Roberts quickly realized that the project showed great potential, and she was correct ("Fuck, I'm going to do this movie!" she enthused when signing on to the project [qtd. in Sanello 195]).

It is tempting to believe that Roberts eventually saw that the film's engagement with her filmmaking career and personal life would appeal to her fans and serve her career well, providing something of a capstone image of her mercurial success and well-publicized romantic difficulties. There is no better way, in fact, to approach what Julia Roberts had come to mean for Hollywood filmmaking by the end of the 1990s than to examine the ways in which this film constructs the life and meaning of Anna Scott, mega-star. Though her fans certainly saw (and were meant to see) *Notting Hill* as intriguingly biographical, Roberts is right, of course, that the film at first presents Anna Scott as lacking in self-confidence and vaguely dissatisfied with a life of stardom and the poisoned relationships it seems to engender. Because Anna is shown to be somewhat unwillingly entangled with a (tellingly) nameless lover played by Alec Baldwin, whose turbulent romantic life offscreen was at the time well known to one and all, viewers were strongly encouraged to endorse Anna's view that stardom, at least in terms of the romantic possibilities it offered, is not all that it is cracked up to be.

But if Anna starts out as a somewhat neurotic, even reticent version of a Julia Roberts famed for her brassy self-assertiveness (qualities that have been successfully exploited in a number of her film roles, including her "taking-care-of-business" reluctant heroine in *The Pelican Brief*), by film's end she has become an ideal version of the star, a woman who, because she is now loved by and loves in return a relentlessly ordinary joe, William Thacker (Hugh Grant), can fully possess herself. As biography, this ending closes out the narrative of Roberts's "life" that had been intriguing her fans since her breakout role in *Steel Magnolias*, where she surprisingly held her own in an intimidating ensemble of charismatic, experienced actresses (Sally Field, Shirley MacLaine, Dolly Parton, and Olympia Dukakis).

As displaced star biography, *Notting Hill* is not only a romantic comedy but also a woman's picture—and on both its fictional and metafictional levels. The film traces a pattern of maturing self-awareness that is connected not only to romantic fulfillment, but also, and arguably more important, to the full acceptance of the responsibilities and discontents of cinematic stardom. Like Julia Roberts, Anna is not forced to choose between a husband and happy domesticity, on the one hand, and a satisfying career, on the other. Quite the contrary. *Notting Hill* makes it quite clear that the relationship with a man who comes without the baggage of his own career completes rather than replaces Anna's professional life, promoting the notion of a woman liberated and empowered rather than entrapped by romance, with her drive for success at least as important as what personal happiness her glamour and charm might win for her. It is no accident that the film repeats the narrative pattern of the nineteenth-century *Bildungsroman*, as Scott follows what, culturally speaking, had been an exclusively masculine trajectory toward maturity, with Thacker imagined as her peace-of-mind-conferring secondary attachment.

☆☆☆☆★ The Stranger Known to One and All

The intriguing doubleness of a woman fully in control of her acting career yet unable to sustain a satisfying romantic relationship had been an important element of the particular star fantasy that Roberts came to embody in the course of the 1990s. Mr. Right always seemed to be lurking just around the next corner in her life; there was never a lack of contenders, as one relationship ended only just before (or, sometimes, after) another began. Julia Roberts seemed destined to have her cake and eat it too—the only question was when this would happen. Like Anna Scott, she confessed even early in her career to a desire for a fulfilling family life in addition to success as a performer. Speaking to an interviewer from *Rolling Stone* in 1990, Roberts said: "Movies will come and go, but family is a real kind of rich consistency. . . . When you have family, friends, and there's love in your life, and you give in to that, you can see instant gratification. . . . And it's easier to give that way than it is to just be giving to this . . . black machinery" (qtd. in *Newsmakers*). Feature pieces published throughout the decade routinely praise Roberts's onscreen successes while pointing out that she has yet to settle into a relationship that will provide her with a long-wished-for domestic happiness. A newsweekly article from early 1999, for example, observed that, despite her unique professional accomplishments, "Roberts seems to have sought—often impulsively, just as often

unsuccessfully—a single gift, peace of mind. . . . Roberts and long-term relationships are not the safest bets." Though the handsome and accomplished
Benjamin Bratt seemed at that time a dependable companion and a viable
contender for the hand of the star, the writer of the piece—correctly as it
turned out, for the romance soon afterward tanked—expressed doubts that
this particular coupling, however promising it seemed, might be the one to
provide peace of mind: "Yes, we've heard that story before" (*People Weekly*,
11 January 1999, 94).

If Anna Scott, according to the actress who came to embody her, initially lacks the self-confidence and immunity from criticism that Julia possessed aplenty, the film's narrative seemed carefully calculated to reproduce
the substantially hyped version of Roberts's life that the media had been
promoting since the release of *Pretty Woman*. As James Spada, one of her
biographers, has observed with just a bit of hyperbole, "It is her personal
life and the press and public's almost inordinate fascination with it that has
elevated Julia Roberts from movie star to one of the cultural phenomena
of the last twenty-five years. . . . Her love life . . . provides enough juice
for a Jackie Collins miniseries" (Spada 8). Roberts's offscreen life was not
only, as it has been for many stars, a supplement to the attractive self displayed over a series of performances. It was itself a story, a sensational
story, in fact, of the kind that the best-selling novelist, especially in the
behind-the-scenes show-biz tell-all *Hollywood Wives* (1983), had been entertaining readers with for decades. In fictionalizing that life, *Notting Hill* skips
over much of the "juice" Collins would have taken delight in (for example,
her version of the abusive, egocentric, but devastatingly attractive lover
played by Alec Baldwin, a compelling bad boy, would never have been
reduced to a walk-on). The film instead concentrates its wish-fulfilling
rhetoric on the kind of sentimental final act (straight out of the Jane Austen
fantasies that screenwriter Richard Curtis so admires) for which her millions
of fans had been hoping against hope, as one romantic connection after
another soured or fizzled.

The most important structural element of the film's versioning of the
Roberts narrative may be that the star is not personalized even as she
becomes the focus of the plot. In the transpersonal psychological drama
that provides the solution to her unhappiness, Anna, like Julia herself, is
seen from the outside, that is, from precisely the perspective from which
fans and filmgoers view her performances and her life. The viewer is implic-
itly asked to believe that Anna's real life (that is, the life that matters, especially to us) is not an interior one, a matter of consciousness. This form of
being belongs only to Thacker, the film's "ordinary" protagonist, who can

Hugh Grant's William Thacker may be the main character of Roger Michell's *Notting Hill* (Polygram, 1999), but Anna Scott (Roberts) is no doubt the film's star. Courtesy Photofest New York.

be imagined as a voice narrating his own story, unlike Anna, who must remain an objectified image. Anna does not lead the narrative, but, rather, provides it with forward motion, with both its motive and goal. And yet she is the star around whom the film is built; Grant's Thacker, attractive and appealing as he might be, is the stand-in for the viewer and fan, not really a protagonist in the classic sense. Anna is literally the stranger known to

one and all who wanders accidentally into his life and in so doing transforms it, lifting this male Cinderella out of the dull sameness of his everyday life. As not in the traditional romance, here the woman rather than the
man constitutes the problem that must be solved in order for their romance
to be consummated. In this way, the film models the interest of viewers in
the persona of a star like Julia Roberts, who is the passive agent of both
seduction and wooing, the one who confers value on Thacker simply by
appearing in his shop and noticing him. Anna's sudden embrace of Thacker
at first meeting (an erotic whim? an urge for connection with a seemingly
sympathetic and unthreatening man? an unplanned signaling of availability?) is a gesture that cannot be refused. Of the star's essence, in fact, is her
unrefusability. Her charisma and sex appeal, established as beyond individual taste, have bestowed upon her the right to desire as she wills. As Curtis
recognized, the film need supply no explanation why he becomes her love
object. She is Anna Scott, after all, and *cela explique tout*. The stupefied
Thacker, who will never query her motives, is shown to understand perfectly that aspect of their encounter.

What matters is that through the connection she makes with him and
that he reciprocates, Anna emerges at the end from the uncertainty and
ennui that plague her. This dissatisfaction, as it emerges, has been deep
enough to provoke her to seek out real life (or at least the commercial cinema's version of it), which she does by visiting in easily seen-through disguise a small and persistently unprofitable niche bookstore in the
charmingly funky London neighborhood of Notting Hill, there encountering owner Thacker. The shocked young man, just recovering from being
rejected by the woman he loves, is immediately smitten by the charms of a
visitor from the other, seemingly unreachable world of global celebrity, and
he is then led to think that she finds him attractive when without a word and
seemingly out of the blue she kisses him passionately (he is too surprised,
or too reticent, in the presence of secular royalty, to return the embrace, as
his hands refuse seemingly of their own volition to grasp her body).

Later, persuaded to take her out on a date, Thacker introduces her to
the lovable grotesques and relentlessly everyday folk who constitute his
circle of friends and family. Anna, who has become accustomed to being the
object of nonstop, probing attention, seems satisfied to be treated like just
another guest at an informal dinner party, though she is of course known
to one and all as a celebrity. Her being treated as "just one of the gang"
emerges as a deception, of course. Ordinariness is not a realm of being that
the star, once having transcended it, can ever reenter. Escorted out the door
by Thacker, the pair hear the other guests break out into howls of surprise

and joy, hitherto repressed, at the exalted presence that happy accident has brought into their midst. That she can be just like everyone else is shown to be merely an effect of English reticence and politeness. The true meaning of her appearance among ordinary folks is signaled earlier in the sequence when Thacker's wacky sister arrives at the party, spots Anna by her side, and explodes with a very loud "Holy fuck!" before lapsing into wordless awe. Anna Scott can only be Anna Scott. Likewise, Julia Roberts can never be an anybody, and having worked hard to become a star, why in any case would she then embrace an ordinary form of ordinariness?

☆☆☆☆☆ A Liberation from Powerless Anonymity?

Anna's real life (that is, the life she has that matters) is contained in the objectified glamour of her image; it is not inner, not a matter of consciousness. Many shots in the film capture others capturing that image, especially in montage sequences that are meant to be read as characteristic of the life she leads, which seems centered on posing for photographers. These glamour shots explain the interest of those inhabiting the world of the story about Anna Scott, but, metafictionally, they remind the viewers of *Notting Hill* why they have bought tickets to see the film (interestingly, this is an aspect of *Notting Hill* that has no equivalent in *Four Weddings*, a contrast explained by the substantial difference between Andie McDowell, a well-known supermodel, and Julia Roberts, whose position in the culture was quite different). An interior view of the character would dispel the mystique that is the star's stock in trade. An inner being, the revelation of which confers familiarity, even intimacy, can belong only to Thacker, the film's "ordinary" protagonist, even though he is reduced mostly to reacting to Anna's unexpected appearance and different expressions of interest in him.

So that he can be transformed into a simulacrum of the traditional male romantic protagonist, *Notting Hill* must in fact generate a double ending. The relationship between screen queen and commoner is actually finalized when Anna, who had seemed distant and uninterested (precisely how the unexceptional Thacker thinks she should feel because he is a nobody), tells him that she wants them to spend more time together, but then, suffering from hurt feelings and fear of further emotional injury, he is allowed an initial refusal (which, we might remark, is the conventional response of a wooed woman, unwilling to surrender too quickly to availability). Later, Thacker, counseled by his friends about the absurdity of refusing an Anna Scott, recants that refusal, rushing to convince Anna of his sincerity in the midst of a press conference that positions him not as himself but as yet another petitioner, however *faux*, from the insatiable media. But Thacker has hardly "won" her. Anna's acceptance of his recantation simply repeats in more conventional form her earlier request that they continue their relationship, transforming her from a petitioner (she had visited him in his store to reconnect with him) to a dominating injured party who is quite visibly disposing, as the center of a press conference, of the power she wields as a celebrity.

The entertainment press had been emphasizing for years in its continuing narrative of her love life that Julia Roberts had a problem; she could never manage to sustain a relationship with any of the high-powered and glamorous men (all of them in the entertainment business) to whom she had become connected. And if that problem had not yet been solved in real life, *Notting Hill* could do the trick onscreen, offering a wish fulfillment that was absolutely conventional. Girl and boy get each other in the end, triumphing over the obstacles of personality and character they themselves have in their insecurity erected to block their coupling, making the film in some sense simply an updating of *Pride and Prejudice*. Made miserable rather than happy by a succession of Alec Baldwins (his role in the film is an intriguing metonymy), Julia—I mean Anna—finds contentment this time with a man whose reticence and uncertainty mirror her own, but who is pointedly not being carried along by the ever-moving machine of a high-powered career.

Through her relationship to Thacker, which properly begins with the kiss she bestows upon him, Anna discovers an answer to the paradox of celebrity. Celebrity, like its similar states such as aristocratic birth, seems to offer freedom in conferring the unanticipated power to shape relationships, a power that is only partially charged by the wealth that celebrity customarily brings. But this liberation from the restraints of ordinary living threatens a different form of entrapment. As Leo Braudy has pointed out, "Fame promises a freedom from worry about the opinions of others, only to trap the aspirer inside an even larger audience. . . . Lurking behind every chance to be made whole by fame is the axman of further dismemberment" (Braudy 8). The film, lighthearted fantasy that it is, offers a penetrating exemplification of such dismemberment. Scott flees to the seeming protection that Thacker's absolute anonymity provides (he is literally unfamous) when she discovers that some nude photographs she had consented to pose for when poor and unknown have been unearthed and may be circulated. The photos did not matter when Scott was literally a nobody—her body would then be read as any body, as an anonymous source of arousal or interest simply because it was female and attractive. The photos, and what they may be read as implying about her moral character, could not be easily traced to her since she was, to all but those in her immediate circle, ordinary, that is, essentially unrecognizable. The photos would be known but not known; they would possess no powers of revelation and thus could circulate without doing harm to the woman they represent.

But now that same body, embodied in images whose form is only slightly different from that in which her glamour is currently promoted, belongs to a somebody, a somebody in whom there is the most intense interest (which is both the cause and result of her success). The photos mean everything because they testify to a hitherto unknown history, promising a further revelation of the star whosc knownncss is never satisfyingly complete. As such, the photos portend an embarrassment of global proportions that will never dissipate, at least as long as the public has an interest in Anna Scott. Seeking anonymity in Thacker's flat as she tries to recover from the shock of the sudden reappearance of the photos, Anna ironically makes her situation only worse by provoking yet another media sensation: reporters, fed the information that she is hiding in Notting Hill, cluster around Thacker's door, which he opens in a state hardly suitable for company. A crisis in their relationship follows as Scott, who had happily shared the young man's bed the night before, accuses him of selling her out to the press in order to acquire his own little bit of fame, a stolen portion of reflected celebrity, as he too becomes "known" to the world. If in the modern world, as Braudy points out, "fame promises a liberation from powerless anonymity," *Notting Hill* underlines the substantial discontents of that state of eminent, unbounded recognizability (7). *Notting Hill* tellingly dramatizes how the star, to quote Braudy once again, must suffer from the fact that "we applaud our heroes, and we condemn them," but this is a harsh truth from which this otherwise conventional story quickly retreats, interestingly illustrating yet another function of a star like Julia Roberts: providing viewers with a wish fulfillment whose very implausibility is the most powerful element of its affective rhetoric.

Through her connection with Thacker, Anna emerges at film's end to become a less fictionalized version of Julia Roberts. The key to professional happiness, so the film suggests, is a satisfying personal life. Here Anna learns how to be, and enjoy, "herself" and, although her relationship with Thacker goes through the required twists and turns, also how to be loved and love in return. She becomes, in her own phrase, "just a girl, standing in front of a boy, asking him to love her." But, of course, Anna Scott, however much in one sense she wishes to be understood as "just a girl," remains a star whose most important quality is shown to be a glamorous charisma (Anna is constantly flashing the noted multimillion-dollar Julia Roberts smile). The film does not disavow the attractions of a life of stardom; it only suggests that there is more to life than this kind of rare accomplishment and the resulting knownness. Thacker does not demand that she give up her career, but, on the contrary, seems eager and willing to participate in it. His sacrifice, if sacrifice it is, is to surrender an unfulfilling life of small business ownership, an occupation that, as the Cinderella (transported suddenly from daily drudgery and genteel squalor to glamour and riches), he can be imagined as readily abandoning: all of this the film shows through a succession of happy accidents. The only man with whom Anna can be happy must not be pursuing a career that competes with hers (in fact, he must be available so that she, escorted, can better promote herself). But what he has to offer is not only his compliance, but also a connection back to the ordinariness she has worked so hard to abandon.

The film's final scene, in fact, emphasizes how romantic fulfillment of the conventional kind (marriage, children, a life centered in some sense around loved ones) can be reconciled with endless, inevitably narcissistic performance and self-promotion. With poise and aplomb, Anna publicly accepts William's charmingly bumbling apology for rejecting her earlier offer to explore the possibility of a permanent connection. She agrees to cancel plans to return from London, where he lives, to Hollywood, where another project awaits, proclaiming instead for all to hear that she will stay in the U.K. so that their courting can proceed. This bargain is sealed in the unlikely venue of a press conference as the two lovers become the targets of the assembled paparazzi. Their subsequent life together is revealed in the "characteristic" scenes of a post-finale sequence. Here director Roger Michell emphasizes both how Thacker makes an appropriately presentable partner for Scott at a gala premiere and how the couple, now a part of his circle of friendship and love, make a place for themselves apart from the world of show business, whose intense pressures (as we have been given to understand through the off-again, on-again relationship between the peripatetic couple of Anna Scott and the Alec Baldwin character) can tear a relationship apart.

Life, as the cliché has it, often imitates art, or, more precisely, imitates the way in which art imitates life. This was true for Roberts shortly after the 1990s ended, with a long-expected change in her personal life recalling the fairy-tale narrative of *Notting Hill*. In the wake of her divorce from Lovett in 1995 after a brief marriage (the couple, as it turned out, were too busy with their professional lives to spend much time together), as well as a seemingly endless string of much-publicized, short-term relationships with leading men and friends from the industry (including Liam Neeson, Dylan McDermott, Matthew Perry, Jason Patric, and others, most spectacularly, perhaps, Kiefer Sutherland), *Notting Hill* proposed a fictional resolution of Julia Roberts's problem. A result of Michell's influence, perhaps, *Notting Hill*'s dramatization of a successful romance emphasizes the force of the inevitable discontents of the human condition, as these are magnified by Anna's stardom, which exposes the couple to the harsh glare of publicity and the promise that missteps, once part of the record, can never be truly expunged. Love triumphs, however, because mistrust, misunderstanding, and an unhealthy sense of vulnerability can be swept away by empathy, reason, humility, and the good offices of friends, a message about the path to human happiness that Jane Austen would likely endorse.

Soon after the film's wildly successful release, and certainly against the odds, the celluloid match with Thacker found its biographical reflex in the romance that blossomed and developed between Roberts and cameraman Daniel Moder. Very much in the mold of Thacker, Moder is a talented professional who was nevertheless absolutely, positively different from every other man with whom Julia Roberts had ever been linked. The couple were wed—at the beautiful Taos ranch owned by the star—in 2003. As of this writing, Thacker and Moder remain happily together eight years and three children later, closing out in real life the Julia Roberts narrative that largely offscreen had enthralled her fans throughout the 1990s.

5 ☆★★★★★★★★★★

Leonardo DiCaprio
King of the "World"

MURRAY POMERANCE

Chased through an apartment complex by a pack of hungry, hairy monsters in Kristine Peterson's *Critters 3* in the fall of 1991, Leonardo DiCaprio made no impression at all on either critics or the general public. It was, perhaps, a perfectly modest beginning for a career that would come to explode worldwide. By then, sixteen years old, DiCaprio had done only a few television series bit appearances and had not yet been suited with a role that could match his expansive energies and talents at mimicry. Hungry as a middle-class kid from Los Feliz could be, and eager for connections beyond what would be available to him stepping briefly into "Santa Barbara"

The portrait of Leonardo DiCaprio is reprinted courtesy of the Academy of Motion Picture Arts and Sciences.

or, twenty-two times from 20 February 1991 through 25 April 1992 (and in the shadow of Kirk Cameron), "Growing Pains." In Katt Shea Ruben's *Poison Ivy* (1992), a Drew Barrymore vehicle, he appeared as the virtually invisible "Guy," utterly generic and virtually unseen onscreen; again he was invisible to critics, even though the film raised Jonathan Rosenbaum's pique enough for him to label it, enticingly, "kiddie porn" (onfilm. chicagoreader.com/movies/capsules/7200_POISON_IVY).

It was Michael Caton-Jones's adaptation of Tobias Wolff's autobiography *This Boy's Life* that put DiCaprio in the limelight for the first time. Playing the central character (and narrator), and bravely holding his own in difficult scenes with Robert De Niro and Ellen Barkin, he brought to the surface a snappy, cocky, yet tender young masculinity that was at once well-scrubbed and unpredictable, meditative and eruptive. Writing in the *New York Times*, the sixty-seven-year-old doyen critic Vincent Canby complained that DiCaprio's Toby was "a rather vapid if eccentric kid who is never quite at home" ("An American Boyhood Memoir of the 1950's," 9 April 1993, C10), echoing, if with considerably less stridency, the attitude of Toby's resentful and bullying stepfather in the film more than offering a clearheaded appraisal of a tense and controlled, ultimately brilliant performance that had sprung out of the blue. Over four hundred young actors had gone up for the part (Looseleaf 40), and DiCaprio had won it principally by facing up to De Niro with more brazen courage than anyone else at the audition; but he was not a known quantity for the filmmaker, or a recognizable face for Canby or the rest of the critical audience. What appears to weaken DiCaprio's work is editor Jim Clark's wounded sense of pacing, which leads him to leave the camera on objects and faces far past a point of dramatic climax and to devote excessively long takes to close-ups of empty reactions. When DiCaprio is let loose—at the moment he must don an oversized Boy Scout uniform, or stealing a car by night, or waging a climactic fistfight against the tyrannical man who has been repressing him for years—he lights up the screen with his emotional plasticity, his fiery gaze, and his broken but endearing voice.

★★★★★ Allure

Already at such an early stage in his career, his persona was attracting the attention of young female groupies—a phenomenon perhaps less related to the personality or physical style of DiCaprio or any particular young actor than to young girls' need for an iconic type to daydream about; and to the conventional star-audience relationship that was routinely sold through the publicity apparatus, cultivated by the media, and, now in the post-Reagan 1990s, focused on a pliable, even girlish masculinity that could seem to be founded upon sensitivity, beauty, and equivocation. When James Dean offered the image of the beautiful boy in the mid-1950s, he was ahead of his time, after all, and Elvis Presley could capitalize upon it only by dressing it up and showing off an incendiary surface. By the time of *This Boy's Life*, however, the extended Brat Pack, as displayed prominently in Coppola's *The Outsiders* (1983) and the films of John Hughes (such as *The Breakfast Club* [1985]), had redefined what youthful males could look like: stars such as Andrew McCarthy, Rob Lowe, Ralph Macchio, and Matt Dillon were prototypes fixed more and more solidly in screen convention, and had led to the boy heroes of the 1990s, such as Jonathan Brandis, Devon Sawa, and the slightly younger Jonathan Taylor-Thomas. Thus, DiCaprio's mixture of the caustic and the sweet was predictably attractive to girl consumers. He could fight, but he wasn't a fighter; what he needed wasn't action, it was love. DiCaprio told a biographer that while he was filming *Life* in Washington, "a lot of girls from Concrete were hanging around his trailer. 'In packs'" (Looseleaf 42).

This Boy's Life did not make this boy's—or anyone else's—fortune, taking in only a little more than $4 million at the box office. Even as they marketed the film before releasing it, producers Jon Peters and Peter Guber tried hard to play up the tension between De Niro and Barkin's canny, adult performances with their surrounding drama, on one hand; and DiCaprio's startling physical presence, quite beyond his performance, on the other. "He looked like the ideal husband. He seemed like the perfect father," the poster text dissembled: on the right side of the poster, De Niro in brush cut and cardigan is sweetly sashaying with Barkin in Alberto VO-5 flip, this image underexposed and washed out; and their names get full billing. To the left, however, is a megablow-up of DiCaprio, chin to hairline, in saturated blushing color, one eye shadowed and the other staring unhesitatingly at the viewer over a pair of rosy lips. The appeal of this young actor's innocent-looking features, directness, and proximity are intended to overtake the emotionally gripping story that the older actors barely represent. It was DiCaprio's presence in the film (giving what one viewer calls "the first important performance of his career" [Looseleaf 46]), the audience's ability in scene after scene to stare at his postures and react to his reactions, that might sell the film. But 1993 was the year that beautiful male presence on the screen had been appropriated by Johnny Depp.

By the time *Life* was in distribution, DiCaprio was in Texas shooting with Depp, in fact, for Lasse Hallström's bittersweet melodrama *What's Eating*

Gilbert Grape. Depp is the title character, a lonely teenager suffocating under the pressures of family life—a dead father, a mother weighing more than five hundred pounds. As Arnie Grape, the mentally challenged younger brother, DiCaprio was playing a "role he could really stretch his acting abilities with" (Looseleaf 53), and had "the most fun I've ever had" (IMDb.com). Larry Carroll accurately observes that DiCaprio's performance in this film is "so good, in fact, that it's difficult to watch" (Rottentomatoes .com). In the *Austin Chronicle*, Marc Savlov wrote that DiCaprio is "utterly, tragically convincing as the boy who wasn't expected to make it to ten, much less eighteen years old. All tics, flailings, and full-open, drooling laughter, DiCaprio seems to have captured the damaged heart and soul of Arnie Grape" (11 March 1994). "DiCaprio's remarkable performance doesn't stint on the erratic behavior," wrote Todd McCarthy in *Variety*, "and also brings the kid alive as a human being who must be cared for and nurtured— as hopeless a task as that might be" (6 December 1993). The effusive weakness displayed by DiCaprio's Arnie, a magnet for Gilbert's sincerest care and love, is nowhere better on display than in a painful scene that plays out from Gilbert's meeting and falling for Becky (Juliette Lewis), who is passing through town but stalled for a few days until her aunt can get a replacement part for her Airstream. One of Gilbert's chores around the house is to bathe Arnie, but he has a rendezvous with Becky, so he gets his brother settled in the bathtub and skips out. Romance takes its course, and the two young lovers spend a night together. Back home the next morning, Gilbert goes to use the toilet and finds Arnie still sitting in the bathtub, now chilled to the bone. Filled with remorse, he stands the boy up and towels him warm, but DiCaprio's turn as a blue-skinned shivering waif is so earnest and precise that for a moment we fear for him—completely inhabiting Gilbert's nauseating guilt and shame. Since in the rest of the film DiCaprio is spastically monkeying around, hanging upside down from the apple tree, putting himself in danger by blithely climbing the town water tower, and so on, this moment in which his energies are frozen and his weakness is made so palpable has a resonating dramatic effect. "The film's real show-stopping turn comes from Mr. DiCaprio, who makes Arnie's many tics so startling and vivid that at first he is difficult to watch," said Janet Maslin of the *New York Times*. "The performance has a sharp, desperate intensity from beginning to end" ("Johnny Depp as a Soulful Outsider," 17 December 1993).

While some reviewers found the tone of the movie "false" (see Desson Howe, *Washington Post*, 4 March 1994), and the box office failed significantly to glow, netting a few million dollars less than the $11 million budget, DiCaprio was nominated for an Academy Award and a Golden Globe as

DiCaprio with Johnny Depp. Arnie's search for warmth after spending a chilling night in the bathtub, in *What's Eating Gilbert Grape* (Lasse Hallström, Paramount, 1993). DiCaprio wore a dental appliance beneath his upper lip to produce Arnie's characteristic embouchure. Digital frame enlargement.

Best Supporting Actor for this performance and won an Emerging Actor award from the Chicago Film Critics Association and a Best Supporting Actor award from the National Board of Review. The original American advertising art focused almost exclusively on Depp, however, framing the film as a personality story about a young man trapped by obligations: "Living in Endora is like dancing to no music." DiCaprio got no star billing. The reviews, indeed, which tended to find his performance generally galvanizing and bizarre, and thoroughly credible, failed to focus on the young actor's remarkable timing and expressive range, or on his ability to cannily reproduce minute flickers of behavior, and substituted for respectful appraisals of his skill shocked appreciation of the character he was working to create. Arnie was so thoroughly worked out he became real, and DiCaprio disappeared beneath him. At the Oscars, he was clearly out of his league as a youngster with a remarkable performance under his belt in the company of seasoned and mature actors such as Pete Postlethwaite, Ralph Fiennes, John Malkovich, and Tommy Lee Jones. Jones won.

If his work in *Gilbert Grape* was "marvelous" and "completely unselfconscious" as well as "audacious" and "technically amazing" (Looseleaf 55), if it seemed "infectious, beautifully detailed, and fully deserving of every award in sight" (Richard Alleva, *Commonweal*, 22 April 1994, 18), if in playing his scenes with Depp he was able to summon a "kind of sad magic" (Harper Barnes, *St. Louis Post-Dispatch*, 9 October 1994, 3C), still DiCaprio did not come away from this film—as one might have thought possible given *This Boy's Life*—with a fan base of adorers who would struggle to reify him as a physical or romantic type. A fan in Jackson, Missouri, summarizes what many observant admirers of the film thought:

> I was certain that the actor playing Arnie was mentally handicapped. This was the performance to end all. I have been around mentally challenged people who were the carbon copy of the character that Leonardo portrayed. I do no [*sic*] think that anyone else could have pulled this off without looking ridiculous. Our protagonist, Mr. Johnny Depp, did his usual amazing work, but it is the performance by Leo that makes this film a must see. I just saw it again tonight, and was blown away again. Acting schools must have copies of this in their files!! Will always be a Leo fan for this one film alone. ("Can you believe Leo is not brain damaged?!" registered user online comment to IMDb.com, 26 November 2004)

Another fan writes that DiCaprio outperforms Depp in this film, a fact that spurs realization of "just how talented he is, *even though sometimes it gets blurred by his good looks*" ("The movie belongs to Depp," registered user online comment to IMDb.com, 30 January 2006). *Sometimes*, which is to say, *not now*; not now, because his "good looks" are not on view. Like comments from other fans late in the 1990s or early in the twenty-first century—after DiCaprio's establishment as a heartthrob—this one struggles with an early performance that was not geared into the system of merchandising actors on the basis of their sex appeal. Similarly, another fan gasps, "Amazingly enough, you will not see leo dicaprio in the role of a hero or even a lover, this time" (12 July 2003). This was a performance that would play a signal role in bringing to the surface of American consciousness, and in meticulous detail, the quotidian trials of single parenting, obesity, poverty, mental retardation, and loneliness in a society stripped of social supports and reeling economically. It was a kind of neo-Brechtian social therapy being worked out through characterization, as well as an opportunity for emotional, hormonal, and gestural release in a boy whose desires outstripped his maturity. In a way, *as an actor*, DiCaprio was like Arnie: gangly and clumsy (his height had shot up while shooting *This Boy's Life*, so that finally he had had to stoop so as not to be taller than De Niro), reaching beyond himself, fascinated by the smallest aspects of social and natural life, and delirious at the warmth of social contact (he and Depp "often took to amusing each other [off camera] with weird facial expressions and pranks" [Looseleaf 55]).

Now Sharon Stone, who was producing *The Quick and the Dead* with Sam Raimi directing, wanted him for the part of the Kid—Gene Hackman's son—

who would have a strange quasi-romantic connection with her own character in the film, and then die pathetically near the end. Most of the principal photography was done in locations around Tucson, especially the tiny
"town" of Mescal, in which a few structures—including the residence of
Herod (Hackman)—were built around structures that have been used since
"Bonanza" (1959). In this prototypical western setting the young actor had
to find a way to be at home, notwithstanding the curious fact that the production called for him to seem, at least physically and emotionally, out of
his league with the grizzled, foul-toothed, malevolent gang of shooters who
would try to plug one another in showdown after showdown as the plot
unwound. DiCaprio's leather coat and brown cowboy hat are a little large,
his laughter and boasting a little loud, so that he gives off incessantly the
effect of being a puppy at a dog scramble. He is a very good shot—"I'm so
damned fast," he tells the Stone character, "I can wake up at the crack of
dawn and rob two banks, a train, and a stagecoach, shoot the tail feathers
off a duck's ass at three hundred feet [he slaps her thigh] and still be back
in bed before you wake up next to me"—and can polish off most of his chal-
lengers rather easily. Finally, the Kid is his own biggest fan: "Whew! Damn,
am I fast! D'you even see me, I was so damn fast!"

The logic of the story makes possible a number of onscreen turns that
assist in presenting DiCaprio to his audience in a new way. Gone is the
introspective and whining narcissism of Tobias Wolff, and gone, too, is the
spastic contortionism—phenomenal to watch, but not alluring—of Arnie
Grape. The Kid is all blue-eyed yearning, eager to grow up, eager to be in
bed with Ellen (Stone), eager to prove himself to his narcissistic father.
Thus, camera close-ups of his face as he stands ready for his shootouts can
take advantage of exquisite star portraiture lighting that models the sunset
over his cheekbones and lets the eyes shine strongly; he becomes a paradigm of the beautiful Apollonian figure. The story, further, can diegetically
feature the idea of the exceptionally good-looking and cocky boy shooter,
so scenes are possible where the girls of the shabby little community line up
to watch him parade by, cooing, "There he is!" This is a direct signal that
such a response is appropriate from the viewing audience, too, and indeed
in this film DiCaprio gets his first opportunity for this kind of dramatic setup
at a point in his life, and his character's, where sexual maturity can be
presumed. The presumption was made, at any rate, by so professional an
observer as Janet Maslin, who noted of Stone and the "immensely promising Leonardo DiCaprio" that "they wake up together, she with a bad
hangover and he claiming to have won her in a poker game. This episode
has next to nothing to do with the rest of the story. And a brash, scrawny

adolescent who is nicknamed the Kid can make even the most glamorous movie queen look like his mother" (*New York Times*, 10 February 1995). Maslin was distracted by the sexual innuendo, of course, and therefore missed the fact that this scene has a great deal to do with the rest of the story: the Kid demonstrates that his bed, in which Ellen has been sleeping semi-nude, sits on dynamite (that she will employ in the finale, when he is dead).

Most crucially, however, the film openly, brazenly markets DiCaprio to an audience that might have been expected to be familiar with him as a quirky but talented character performer and needed some guidelines for reinterpreting him in a glamorous star role. The mechanics of the sell lie directly in the story form, which posits a kind of assassination tournament. As showdowns between protagonists result in the exclusion of characters one by one, two dramatic mechanisms are put in play. First, to the degree that the Kid is presented to us as attractive and lovable, and some or most of the others involved in the shooting game are shown as hideous, immoral, malformed, malevolent, and dull, we find ourselves hoping with increasing intensity that DiCaprio will survive onscreen. As we see unfolding reports in the story itself of the betting odds on the Kid, we are seeing in effect the odds of our own disconnection or engagement with his fate. DiCaprio thus becomes more and more watchable as *The Quick and the Dead* rolls on, even though he is distinctly watchable even in the beginning, slouched back innocently in his barroom chair and carefully watching as characters introduce themselves. Secondly, because there are some sixteen protagonists to begin with, and a great number of shootouts, DiCaprio cannot be involved in all of them, and so between the scenes where he plays a key role—and in which we get especially constructed artful views of him—there are pauses in which he is absent in one way or another. His presence onscreen is therefore logically arranged through rhythmic presentations and withdrawals, and we come to appreciate every fresh presentation more fully than the last because we have been deprived in anticipation of it. The same can be said, of course, for Russell Crowe, Stone, Hackman, and any other actors whose fans take pleasure from their rhythmical presence in this film. Between the viewer and the persona of DiCaprio in this film, there is a genuine copulation.

Nevertheless, the film made just a little more than half of its $32 million cost back at the box office, and while DiCaprio was generally praised in reviews for his "strong presence" (Peter Travers, *Rolling Stone*, 9 March 1995), fans were still somewhat skeptical. "Leonardo DiCaprio sticks out as undisciplined," wrote one, a few years after the release ("The ultimate postmodern western," registered user online comment to IMDb.com, 8 December 1998), and another complained, "Leonardo DiCaprio's role was so cardboardedly acted that it was nonexistent" ("Ick," 11 September 1999). If he was irritating to some viewers, DiCaprio was at least now unimpeachably present as a major player who could hold his own onscreen with the true professionals of the business; nor are his detractors utterly objective in their assessments, since his interplay with Hackman is sensitive and believable at each moment and his romantic horseplay with Stone is at least fun to fantasize about. With River Phoenix recently dead, the door was open for a pale-haired blue-eyed young romantic type. "It's hard to see," wrote Anthony Lane in the *New Yorker*, "how he can veer away from stardom now" (Looseleaf 61). But what DiCaprio wanted at least as much as stardom was to show that he valued his characters, that he could act up a storm as he inhabited and displayed them. The career that was being shaped for him, at any rate, largely through the scripts to which he was committing himself, was one that would showcase his talents at metamorphosis, not his superficial appeal as a pretty face.

☆☆☆☆★ Marginality

Occupying and maintaining a star persona in 1990s Hollywood filmmaking required acquiescence to certain dominant and publicly displayed values, and compatibility with all the principal tenets broadcast by American film generally: for example, DiCaprio would have to show that he could be what Leslie Fiedler called a Good Bad Boy ("'Oh, Tom, you bad boy!' Becky Thatcher cries to Tom and we take it as an endearment" [Fiedler 267])—that is, that he could show popular and appealing qualities as a promising, heterosexual, sport-loving, competitive, appropriately aggressive, and yet sweet and adorable male figure. The puppy had to mature into a young dog, and, more importantly, had to be seen to have done so. Bryan Goluboff's script of Jim Carroll's autobiographical coming-of-age novel *Basketball Diaries*, purchased by Liz Heller for Scott Kalvert to direct, was in many ways an optimal vehicle for effecting the necessary transformation. The scrawny Kid, hyperawkward Arnie, and withdrawn Tobias could be replaced by someone who would confront his world, interact boldly with his peers, engage with the girls (at least in a businesslike way), and take a beating without evaporating, all the while showing himself to have a sensitive poetic spirit, a charming wit, and a thirst for adventure.

Basketball Diaries is essentially an addiction-rehabilitation saga, depicting a period in the life of a rebellious teenager in a Catholic high school in

As Norman Bates put it, "A boy's best friend is his mother." DiCaprio as Jim begging for funds in *Basketball Diaries* (Scott Kalvert, New Line Cinema, 1995). Lorraine Bracco is at left. Digital frame enlargement.

Manhattan. Jim falls into drug use and systematically deteriorates until he is doing tricks in public men's rooms and threatening his mother to get money for a fix. The film is shot with haunting purity by David Phillips, beautifully evoking the erotic solitude of New York streets at night and the questing urgency on the faces of Jim and his little gang of friends. Possible and plausible here are numerous portraits of DiCaprio looking earnest, unblemished, and meditative—a telltale signature of young male stardom— as well as plenty of action shots of DiCaprio playing basketball, both on a lonely street court with the princely Ernie Hudson and in various gyms as a member of his highly reputed school team. Jim's skill at basketball— achieved on film principally through deft editing by Dana Congdon—allows us one venue for witnessing his degradation, since he can now falter with dramatic effect: in one game late in the film DiCaprio and friends, having taken downers by accident, are literally collapsing on the court as they try to play.

Any degradation story requires for its success an initial phase in which full-bodied (including sexual) vigor, beauty, and wholesomeness can be established for viewers. Perfect for this purpose are a number of scenes DiCaprio plays with a great sense of poise and relaxation: in one, he has taken his terminally ill friend Bobby (Michael Imperioli) out of the hospital for an evening at a strip house, but the sedated sick boy cannot get excited as the stripper begins her act; behind his back, however, Jim can, and doesn't want to leave, his eyes virtually on fire as he stares at the stripper's decorated breasts. In another, a bourgeois girl who has fallen into heroin addiction (Juliette Lewis) offers to "do" Jim and his friends for a few dollars. In another, he finds himself in a swank West Side apartment with a girl who offers high-class drugs and initiates a sexual relation (that is not detailed onscreen). All these establish DiCaprio as sexually ready, excitable, and alluring in a way that no previous screen work had done, and, indeed, biographical assessment of him falls in line with this presentation of self: "Leo's short list of dates read[s] like a who's who of supermodels" (Looseleaf 66). If this film doesn't position him on the highest rung of male stardom, then, it clearly shows that he is ready to climb there. And his sexuality is clearly established as being both normal and substantial; he indicates to Bobby at one point that he masturbates as much as seven times a day, and in one scene we see him in a rapture of self-fulfillment, naked on his rooftop: "Time sure flies," says he in voiceover, "when you're young and jerkin' off." In other scenes, we see him reject the homosexual advances of his basketball coach and suffer a late-night fellatio from a stranger as a torment worse than withdrawal, all this verifying to the heterosexually dominant viewership that his credentials are in order while at the same time offering to gay spectators, who formed a significant part of the audience for this film, the fantasy of pleasurable contact.

To say critical reception was mixed for this evocative little film—it netted only about $2.5 million—is an understatement. Roger Ebert thought DiCaprio "miscast," and not tough enough by a long shot (*Chicago Sun-Times*, 21 April 1995), while Peter Travers was wholeheartedly won over: "Can an acting tour de force redeem a muddled movie? Check out Leonardo DiCaprio in *The Basketball Diaries* for a lesson in how it's done. . . . In *Diaries*, he gets his first starring role and slam-dunks the sucker to victory even when Bryan Golubuff's [*sic*] conventional script and Scott Kalvert's glossy direction threaten to turn a stinging true story into a TV-ish I Was a Teen-age Junkie. DiCaprio is electrifying in a bust-out star performance" (rollingstone.com).

It was the idea of producing an "acting tour de force" that continued to inspire DiCaprio, who, although he might have been expected to move immediately to a large-budget mainstream romantic role such as the star-crossed lover in *Romeo and Juliet* (the character dies but the actor who plays him lives on forever) chose instead to work for Agnieszka Holland in France and Belgium, playing Arthur Rimbaud against David Thewlis's Paul Verlaine in the bizarre and challenging *Total Eclipse*. It is hard to escape DiCaprio's incongruous bounciness as he moves along narrow cobblestone streets with a clay pipe rammed into his mouth, his nose in the air to suck in poetic and philosophic inspirations with a very mundane spring in his step. And his speech is thrillingly undisciplined—"I need a piss," says he, upon introduction to Verlaine's home—this quality giving yet further play to the noteworthy mouthiness, the mewling and grimacing, the drooling and tough-guy bluntness, that characterized his performances so far. Here, surprising the somewhat repressed Verlaine over roast chicken with the fact that he is only sixteen, Rimbaud betrays a high-pitched, even hysterical voice—a voice that might cause any listener, diegetic or otherwise, to hope fervently that time will soften and mellow it.

That the film plays out a certain complex homosexual passion between the two men—in love scenes with Thewlis, DiCaprio is seductive, hungry, even feminine (at one moment, mockingly reading out a note Verlaine has written his wife, he in fact puts on a female chirp)—is not its only affront to the stolid heterosexual image DiCaprio's performance had mounted in *Diaries*: he stares at Mme Verlaine (Romane Bohringer) over the dinner table and refuses to read out his poetry for her, then spits onto his plate in front of her face. Moments later, being indoctrinated to the pleasure of absinthe by Verlaine in a café, he responds to Verlaine's query, "What do you think of my wife?" with a straightforward, rather perturbing, "I dunno. What do *you* think of her?" Childishness mixed with utter frankness— "Couldn't care less about being published. The only thing that matters is the writing itself"—in a body floating somewhere between innocence and depravity. The homoeroticism was sufficiently chaste to be appealing to a female audience eager for what Elizabeth Woledge calls "intimatopia"; nor could it disappoint those who, understanding as Richard Dyer does that "the penis can never live up to the mystique implied by the phallus" (*Stars* 136), might yet be tickled by DiCaprio's flashing moment of full frontal nudity (again on a rooftop!). The performance hits entirely new extremes of jealousy, passion, tenderness, resentment, lust, and connivance, indeed becoming exactly what Verlaine labels Rimbaud's poems when he learns the astonishing youth of their writer: "unprecedented." Not all viewers found the homosexual posturing pleasurable, to be sure, a viewer from Texas vowing openly, if perhaps not with untrammeled honesty, that "this film ruined Leonardo DiCaprio films for me. Really. I have no issue with gays. I do take issue with low-life cruelty for cruelties [*sic*] sake, which this film specializes in. . . . Rimbaud would have been played by River Phoenix, had he lived. I hate that Phoenix is dead, but I am grateful that he wasn't in this horrible film" ("Thank God River Phoenix didn't star in this offal," registered user online comment to IMDb.com, 19 November 2003). Not that DiCaprio's publicity didn't work overtime to assure his heterosexual fans that no boundaries had seriously been crossed: *Eclipse* was an "even bigger challenge" than *Diaries*, given that kissing a guy, as he is reported to have said, is "difficult, because you have to act like you're really into it" (Dennis Hensley, "Lovin' Leo," *YM*, April 1997, 95). On the other hand, *Seventeen* posed DiCaprio as an archetypal Scorpio in its February 1996 issue, allusively commenting that "Scorpios tend to keep silly secrets that come crawling out from under rocks at the most inopportune times" (86).

Box office was disarmingly light, and, unsurprisingly, reviewers took the poet subjects of this film more seriously than the film itself, adjudging the central performances in terms of the fidelity of their portraiture rather than in terms of any inherent cinematic interest they might have had. The *New York Times* complained that DiCaprio "conveys all of Rimbaud's arrogance with little of his all-important acuity and charisma" (Janet Maslin, "Portrait of the Artist as a Young Boor," 3 November 1995), a fair enough assessment had the poetry itself, rather than Rimbaud's infatuation, centered the film. The *Chicago Sun-Times*' Roger Ebert called the film's portrayals generally "unpleasant, sniveling, monstrous, egotistical and annoying" (3 November 1995), picking out DiCaprio's Rimbaud as "a person who . . . had seen too many Mickey Rourke movies" and who at moments "anticipates Jim Morrison." With a backhand, Ebert compliments the young actor for "finding new ways to make obnoxiousness fresh," a comment that is intended to be deprecating but that in the context of DiCaprio's career at this point actually constitutes a stunning observation: obnoxiousness is a far cry from the signature glamour the succession of his movies had prepared the actor for, and thus signals a clear attempt by DiCaprio and his management to head away from the marquee and toward opportunities for saturating characterizations. In the *San Francisco Chronicle*, Edward Guthmann is prescient enough to see that DiCaprio is "his generation's great acting promise" but bemoans the bad match between David Thewlis's cultivated British accent and DiCaprio's Southern California twang (3 November 1995).

Having now demonstrated as clearly as any critical audience might wish that he could dance on both sides of whatever "tracks" there are that purport to define our gendered identities in the West; and having shown, too, that he could be as beautiful in moments of sadistic control as in moments of passive vulnerability; indeed, having rounded out physically and being, as Gene Kelly and Donald O'Connor happily put it in *Singin' in the Rain*, "fit as a fiddle and ready for love," DiCaprio was prepared for the film that would launch him securely into the orbit of teen girls' consciousness, *Romeo + Juliet*. Baz Luhrmann was filming a modern-dress, hipped-up, neonized,

MTV-generation version of Shakespeare's classic in Mexico, with an all-star cast including Claire Danes (who had gained a cult following with "My So-Called Life"), Pete Postlethwaite, Paul Sorvino, Brian Dennehy, Paul Rudd, Miriam Margolyes, and Diane Venora; hot guns instead of swords; hot rods, hot looks, and hot violence. If DiCaprio would be lashed to the Bard's strict meter, at the masquerade ball he could flash around Juliet's giant aquarium in gleaming knight's armor and in the rest of the film he could sprint and sing, wait for the camera to swoop into his face, and capture the screen kinetically as never before. Twentieth Century–Fox not being sold in advance on DiCaprio's strengths, Luhrmann flew him to Australia and coached him for weeks, videotaping the sessions. With this footage he could convince Fox "that his version of the classic tale would indeed draw in a young and potentially mass audience. With Leonardo on board, the production seemed to make more sense to the studios" (Looseleaf 78). In its first month, the film earned $36 million, hardly a surprise in the face of the luscious advance publicity accorded by the press. *Seventeen* laid a head shot of DiCaprio into a New York street scene next to shots of other presumably available young male stars such as Mekhi Phifer, Chris O'Donnell, Dean Cain, Jeremy London, and Devon Sawa. "Leo likes to party on the New York club circuit," ran the text, and, "Next project: *Romeo and Juliet*—you can expect him to be, uh, to die for" (June 1996, 84).

Again, the substance of the film resting ultimately in high art, the critical establishment tended toward a profoundly established reading, as though Luhrmann and his actors were more interested in being faithful to Shakespeare than marketing a vision to a generation that had shown little interest in him. To read *Romeo + Juliet* as a literary adaptation—the stodgy approach—is to come to the same conclusion as Roger Ebert, that both DiCaprio and Danes are "in over their heads" (*Chicago Sun-Times*, 1 November 1996). But to let oneself go with this film, allowing it to do its proper work, is to be open to other possibilities. *Rolling Stone* was wowed: "These babes from the TV woods . . . fill their classic roles with vital passion, speak the Elizabethan verse with unforced grace, find the spirited comedy of the play without losing its tragic fervor and keep their balance when the audacious Australian director Baz Luhrmann hurls them into a whirlwind of hardball action, rosy humor and rapturous romance. . . . DiCaprio and Danes make the bandying of words a sly, erotic game. Shakespeare has never been this sexy onscreen" (rollingstone.com). And the *New York Times* acceded that DiCaprio and Danes "have the requisite magic and speak their lines with passionate conviction" (Janet Maslin, "Soft! What Light? It's Flash, Romeo," 1 November 1996, C1). We may note that this is the first time in his career that the word "passionate" can have been applied to DiCaprio in precisely this way, as invoking not only the will and the flamboyant spirit but a distinct sense of embodiment.

With a role this hefty behind him, DiCaprio was in a position to calmly decline the role of Dirk Diggler in Paul Thomas Anderson's *Boogie Nights* (Looseleaf 85); he had "broken through to Hollywood's A list" with a "mesmerizing characterization" (84) and had helped Fox's $15 million investment, and Luhrmann's reputation, leap into profit within only days of its release. The film did over $11 million on opening in 1,276 theaters, climbing to a $46.3 million gross in the United States and over $100 million internationally. Regardless of one's critical opinion on the quality of DiCaprio's Romeo as a Shakespearean performance, it must be seen that the film established him as the target for a broader and more powerful audience of image consumers, not older viewers who might be astonished by the exceptional talent of a kid but members of his own generation, who might now unabashedly claim him as their own.

☆☆☆★★ Sailing into the Light

> They bring you in like a piece of meat, saying, "Here's the next cute kid." And it could ruin your career, you get washed up really fast. I'm looking for *longevity*.   —Leonardo DiCaprio to Robin Rauzi, 1993

That young audience would have to hold its breath, however, since DiCaprio's next move was not a more bombastic popular appearance but a retreat to serious acting. He chose to play Meryl Streep's outspoken, defensive son in Jerry Zaks's film of Scott McPherson's play *Marvin's Room*. Shot in Florida and at the Astoria studios in Queens, this bittersweet concoction is essentially a sibling conflict vehicle for Streep and Diane Keaton (the latter requiring bone marrow from her nephew [who thinks "the transplant will make him the center of attention"]); the young actor—looking slightly uncomfortable with his co-stars—would hardly occupy the center of the scene, although he would move with more sureness than ever before, with a newly mellowed voice and a body that seemed tailored to his lanky personality. Released days before Christmas 1996, the picture had a wide release in 1,153 theaters across North America and grossed $3.2 million on its opening weekend, less than half of what *The Quick and the Dead* had brought in at a comparable time.

James Cameron's *Titanic*, of course, would tell a completely different story on the ledger. Released on 2,674 screens, this blockbuster drew $28,638,121 in its first two days (boxofficemojo.com) and has continued to

More than four hundred photographic elements were composited to create the iconic "king of the world" shot for *Titanic* (James Cameron, Twentieth Century–Fox/Paramount, 1997). DiCaprio with Danny Nucci at the prow of movie history. Digital frame enlargement.

make money at an astonishing rate, amassing from its worldwide audience onscreen and in various home formats $1,843,000,000 at this writing (box-officemojo.com) and positioning itself at the prow of the luxury liner that is Hollywood film as, literally, "king of the world." The story of *Titanic* and DiCaprio's role in it (for the benefit of the handful of readers who have not seen the film more than three times) are simplistic almost to the point of absurdity, given cinema's movement, through the 1930s and in the decades that followed, away from the kind of simple romantic ditty that characterized much of early film. A working-class youth boarding the *Titanic* moments before she sails, Jack Dawson accidentally comes into contact with the aristocratic (but penniless) Rose Bukater DeWitt (Kate Winslet) when he saves her from petulantly throwing herself into the sea. Although her mother despises him at first glance, he gets invited to dine in the first-class salon and regales Rose and her oily fiancé Cal Hockley (Billy Zane) with his ineffable charm (by now the DiCaprio trademark). But Hockley resents Jack bitterly. Soon enough, our beautiful heroes are locked in a steamy sexual pretzel in the backseat of a limousine below decks, Jack trembling with what viewers can have imagined was a virgin excitement that extended to the actor beneath. In the melée after the iceberg strike, Hockley eventually manages to get Jack accused of a petty crime and locked to a steam pipe, so that it is only thanks to Fate and the youth's energetic earnestness that he manages to escape and join Rose at the stern of the ship as, turgidly, it goes down. The experience of filming the catastrophe was jarring for the actor:

We were on the sort of tilting poop deck which was on hydraulics, and we were cabled on, and below us there was like, you know, twenty stunt men on bungee cords and . . . and as the ship was going up they had to jump off and bounce off these sort of steel girders and tumble all over each other, and I looked up and there was like, you know, twenty cranes above us and Jim swooping down on an elevator crane coming up into a close-up past us to the stunt men, to a green screen, and . . . and I mean that lasted for a week and we were just, you know, pfft, shell shocked.   (*Titanic* Interview, YouTube.com)

Now Rose is aboard a little raft, Jack clinging to its side with gelid fingertips, as under the panoply of stars and in the blue-dark night the sea silently closes around the glittering satellite of post-Victorian civilization that is now gone. Jack cannot withstand the cold, and swearing his love to her he sinks away, leaving Rose forever. ("Leo's a natural," cooed Winslet, "the actor of the century" [*People*, 29 December 1997].) Viewing all of this from a present-day bathyscape, divers hunting to recover the *Titanic* come across remnants of this love; and the aged Rose, on board the recovery vessel off Newfoundland, wells up with tears as she recalls her sweet, tender, lost amour and faces the prospect of what time has done and will continue to do. As the credits roll, Céline Dion wails James Horner's sucrose "My Heart Will Go On" in a purple haze.

It is hardly sufficient to say that this film had an enormous impact on the filmgoing audience of the late 1990s, or that Leonardo DiCaprio was anointed through his participation in it as *the* absolute symbol of youthful romantic-sexual allure for years to come. Looking at his perfectly skillful performance objectively, it is possible to see that, one aspect aside, it is made up of exactly the sorts of gestures, moves, phrasings, and evocations that built all his other work to date: in short, this is the Leo audiences had every reason to expect, and whom they could instantly recognize and empathize with. The exception was the love scene, where even through the directorial gauzing of the distant camera and the masking limousine it was evident to any eye that what was taking place in the heart of the steam cloud was nothing less than full authentic penetration and thrilling climax, all this constituting foreplay for an even profounder moment not long afterward when the flank of the liner is ripped open by a mountain of ice and the esteemed monument to technology and Western civilization prepares to sink like a stone. Stepping aside from his performance in a contemporary documentary interview with Joe Leyden, DiCaprio is able to put on a serious mask, thematizing the "importance" of the film in sociocultural terms quite remote from the enthusiasms of his viewers: "It had a lot to do with our arrogance in thinking that we could have . . . with the Industrial

Revolution at that time we thought we could build the biggest and the best things and, you know, Mother Nature sort of slapped us in the face" (YouTube.com). Fascinatingly (and hilariously), when the interview is done the camera continues to roll for a few seconds and DiCaprio, fully aware, reaches down and pulls a (magnate's) cigar back into his face.

The film boasted a shocking 20 percent repeat viewing rate, some of which was produced by the kind of eccentric moviegoing Hollywood was unaccustomed to at this time:

> Zabeen Qassim is an unlikely junkie with a newly acquired habit. Every Saturday night, for the past six weeks, the 24-year-old university student kisses her husband goodbye before slipping out of their home in Mississauga, a sleepy Toronto suburb, to go get her fix. For hcr, watching James Cameron's $200-million Titanic has become a spiritual experience.
>
> "It's inspiring," she said. "It makes you believe things like love and relationships are deeper than the physical world." She plans to keep going back each week, for as long as the theatre run lasts.
>
> (Alexandra Gill, *Globe and Mail*, 11 February 1998, C1)

"Titaniacs," as these obsessed fans were sometime called, in a loving nod to the Spielbergian tenor of the film and its smash appeal, included bug-eyed observers who had seen the film more than ten times before a year was out, and tended, in large part, to be

> girls afflicted with what [Tim] Doyle [an ad copywriter who created a "Countdown to Titanic" website] calls "Japanese school-girl disease," the symptom being an incurable crush on the film's main man, 23-year-old Leonardo DiCaprio, or "Leo," to those in the know. For DiCaprio's legion of largely prepubescent followers—who have been known to talk about little else and set up shrines to the pretty heartthrob in their bedrooms—he *is* the movie experience. "I'm in love with him," 12-year-old Carly Niesen said. "He's gorgeous, and he's sweet, and he's the whole reason I loved the movie."   (Gill)

And, now that he had played an onscreen love scene, he was properly marriageable, or at least beddable, and so the fantasies of his viewers (of both genders) could expand appropriately.

It was, however, principally an "enormous pool of young female fans" that DiCaprio attached to his work in this film (Nash and Lahti 67). "Leo was the candy," said his director, and the popular press jumped for it just as quickly as the fans. Nash and Lahti report, for example, that when Claire Danes was named "Celeb Most Wanted for a Best Bud" by *Seventeen* magazine, the rag, reflecting largely on the almost tactile link between Leo's work in *Romeo + Juliet* and *Titanic*, commented, "When your main topic of conversation is Leo's love life, who knows more than this girl?" (69). Citing Janet Maslin's comment in the *New York Times* that DiCaprio's image reflects "angel-faced purity" and "reduces the camera to one more worshipful fan" ("L'Etat, It's DiCaprio: C'est le Brat-King," 13 March 1998, E14), Nash and Lahti suggest that this kind of journalism is complicit in building for the actor a persona that suits the explicit needs of his young teen audience (71). *Seventeen* for May 1998 touts a cover image of Leo with a broad, lippy smile, twinkling eyes, and tousled, slash-cut golden hair— "He avoids the Hugh Grant habit of tossing a forelock by securing it with a tiny wire headband. 'I've been wearing this for many years, since I was 18,' he says. 'It's the most masculine one I could find'" ("Leo Takes Wing," *Vanity Fair*, January 1998)—wearing a nappy, perfectly starched white camp shirt: "the Leo you don't know," teases the text—"his *Titanic* tryout, his bad boy school days, and what it's like to kiss him." Perfectly placed directly beneath is a teaser for a second, apparently unrelated, article: "Quiz: are you psychic?" In one fan letter quoted by Nash and Lahti, the writer (psychically) gushes, "Nobody could ever play Jack as well as you did. . . . I'm not just saying that because of your good looks or the fact that you['re] the world's sex symbol" (75). But such responses are, in a way, scripted themselves. Nine months before *Titanic* was released, *YM* prepared its young female audience to expect Leo playing "an artist who falls for a well-bred woman in first class" (Hensley 95), and reports that his real first kiss, according to the actor himself, "was the most disgusting thing in my life. The girl injected about a pound of saliva into my mouth, and when I walked away I had to spit it all out" (94).

In general, the world press collaborated to paint the post-*Titanic* DiCaprio as at once grown up and cuddly; at once a concoction and a professional; at once a dreamboat and an ordinary human being. "*Titanic* made a man out of me," he told fans at the Los Angeles premiere (Steven Smith, "Ship's Star Trooper," *Los Angeles Times*, 14 December 1997). The *Times* of London sympathized that "the angelic Hollywood star Leonardo DiCaprio" couldn't find a proper black tie (as, presumably, he knew he should) (Jasper Gerard, 20 November 1997, 22). In Italy, it was reported, a girl came to a small-town theater so many times to see—not Leonardo but— Jack Dawson, who is "cuter than Leo," that the management started letting her in for free; so profound was the acting, then, that the character had finally triumphed over the actor (Associated Press, 14 March 1998). For *Teen* magazine he was a "regular guy diving headfirst into the odd, sometimes rough waters of superstardom" (Maureen Basura, "Sailing to Superstardom," *Teen*, May 1998, 54). Half a year after the premiere, gossip floated that Jack Dawson would come to life again in a sequel with "the lovers meeting again on a World War I battlefield in France" (*South China Morning Post*, 27 June 1998).

France was right, the battlefield and era were wrong. He proceeded to Vaux-le-Vicomte to shoot *The Man in the Iron Mask* for Randall Wallace, playing a dual role—the vapid and corrupt Louis XIV and the noble youth Philippe who is enjoined to replace him—while such luminaries of the screen as Jeremy Irons, John Malkovich, Gérard Depardieu, and Gabriel Byrne crept around him like so many lowly attendants. This rather lengthy (172-minute) piece of "high art" opened in wide release to almost $18 million at the box office, with very large foreign grosses to predictably follow. It was being an actor again, not a movie star; losing oneself in the role—in this case the vibrant alternation between a pair of roles; and thus adamantly refusing to take the easy—and sucrose—road laid out by *Titanic*. Playing a king was hardly a challenge for DiCaprio: Louis was like "a hot young film star surrounded by sycophants" (Richard Covington, "Old Boys," *Los Angeles Times*, 8 March 1998). Passing up the lead in *American Psycho*, he also played a cameo part in Woody Allen's *Celebrity*—the snot-nosed and monstrous young star (that so many may have had reason to think he really was).

"Leo," said Claire Danes to an interviewer one day in the mid-1990s, driving up to Griffith Park, "*is* the next James Dean" (Christine Spines, "I Would Die 4 U," *Premiere*, October 1996). That Deanish spark of wildness struck in the 1990s remains present, undeniably, in every DiCaprio performance, with a strange admixture of awkwardness and poise that bespeaks authenticity. But Dean's candle burned too fast. Just as DiCaprio has always most fondly wished, his power to perform, long-lived and glowing, moves on.

ACKNOWLEDGMENTS

With thanks to Jennifer Brayton, Doreen Fumia, Lisa Goldberg, Jennifer Johnson, Evelyn Tchakarov, and Jessica Thom.

6 ☆☆☆☆☆☆☆☆☆☆☆

Antonio Banderas, Andy Garcia, and Edward James Olmos

Stardom, Masculinity, and "Latinidades"

LAURA ISABEL SERNA

On the cover of the 11 July 1988 issue of *Time*, bright yellow letters shout "*¡Magnifico*! Hispanic culture breaks out of the barrio." Beneath that cheerful proclamation, the smiling face of a man perhaps vaguely familiar to *Time* subscribers, actor Edward James Olmos, painted larger than life on a barrio-style mural, smiles out at the viewer. The swirling points of a huge silver-white star surround Olmos's face, as if to help readers understand this brown face as that of a "star." The mural painting, a form of artistic expression associated explicitly with the barrio or inner-city neighborhood, gestures toward the social space of limited opportunities, ethnic insularity, and exclusion from the mainstream of American life that *Time* asserts "Hispanic culture" is leaving behind. Olmos's public persona doubly rendered in this image as existing in the space of both mainstream mass media and Hispanic culture represents the new visibility of Hispanic actors, who, this constellation of image and text implies, are the primary vehicles and evidence for this newfound mobility.

Inside, the magazine declared that the United States was "receiving a rich current" from its growing Hispanic population (*Time*, 11 July 1988). As other scholars have noted, the rhetoric of *Time*'s special issue marked *latinidad*—defined by Frances Aparicio as "the ways in which the entertainment industry, mainstream journalism, and Hollywood have homogenized all Latinos into one undifferentiated group," foreign to the American mainstream and confined to the realm of entertainment and aesthetics in the form of "new" rhythms, "new" flavors, and "new" faces—hip and thus desirable (Aparicio 91; Newman 77). Chief among the contributions of Hispanics to American culture, *Time* suggested, were films with "Hispanic color and spirit" and "new marquee names" with a "Spanish ring." As suggested by Olmos's privileged position in the magazine's construction of the mainstreaming of Hispanic culture, Latino film stars were mobilized as highly visible representatives of a perceived sea change in American culture at large.[1]

This essay shifts our focus to three male stars who became icons of the Latino Boom in 1990s Hollywood: Spaniard Antonio Banderas, Cuban American Andy Garcia (born Andrés Arturo García Menendez), and Mexican American/Chicano Edward James Olmos. Latina stars, particularly singer-actress Jennifer Lopez, have received sustained scholarly attention in terms of the way their celebrity illuminates the "complex and contradictory discourses and social dynamics at work" in the construction of gendered and raced stars (see Beltrán, *Stars* 108–30; Aparicio). The discursive construction of each of these male star personas is borrowed from earlier models of Latino stardom, such as the Latin Lover, the *bandido*, and the social-problem film protagonist, models that confined contemporary Latino actors to stereotyped roles on- and offscreen (see Rodríguez, *Heroes*; Berg).

Although they share the experience of being read as Latino, each of these men presented a differently inflected version of socially acceptable Latino masculinity. As a foreigner, Banderas had to be incorporated into a

U.S. discourse on latinidad. His stardom reinforced longstanding ideas of Latino male sexuality and physicality, while his identity as a Spaniard allowed him to become a pliable, nonthreatening representative of Latino masculinity. In contrast, Garcia's stardom, though likewise premised on discursive constructions of Latin "passion," promoted a narrative of Latino assimilability in which cultural difference was primarily relegated to the private realms of family and the individual. Finally, Olmos's celebrity revolved around a perceived permeability between his on- and offscreen personas. Although he is presented as an ethnic star unflinchingly committed to his community, his stardom was also constructed in terms of mainstream expectations about individual exceptionalism. At the same time, throughout the decade he mobilized that ethnically coded stardom to claim cultural citizenship—a sense of cultural belonging in the United States—for Latina/os (see Silvestrini 44). In this decade, many Latina/os organized and advocated for their rights based on their sense of cultural, rather than formal, political citizenship. Tracing the contours of the stardom of Antonio Banderas, Andy Garcia, and Edward James Olmos demonstrates how contemporary Hollywood produces and commodifies ethnic masculinity in ways that, as Richard Dyer has argued in relationship to Paul Robeson's star image in the 1930s, "deactivates" the perceived threat of Latino men in society at large (Dyer, *Heavenly*). What is more, their ethnically coded stardom demonstrates how race and ethnicity, designations typically assigned to groups of people, problematize the individualist ethos that Dyer locates at the heart of star discourses.

While pundits and journalists speculated about the effect an ethnic demographic shift would have on the American political and social landscape, all, including Hollywood, agreed that Latinos were fast becoming an important economic force (see Dávila). Mainstream news articles that celebrated the various Latin(o) booms in music, sports, and literature as well as in Hollywood frequently highlighted the potential purchasing power of the growing Latina/o population believed to share an orientation toward family, linguistic practices, and a commitment to a common cultural heritage (Dávila 42). A 1999 report on Latina/os in the film industry commissioned by the Screen Actors Guild likewise forecast a "potential boom . . . among Hispanic entertainment consumers" (Melissa Grego, *Hollywood Reporter*, 5 May 1999). The report found that although Latina/os did not spend as much money as their white counterparts did on entertainment, they spent more than blacks. U.S.-born Latina/os in particular were avid moviegoers who, the study had found, were more likely to go see a film if it featured a Latina/o actor (Pachon et al.). Issued at the end of the decade, the study conducted by the Tomás Rivera Policy Institute echoed calls to pay attention to this neglected audience.

Historically, Hollywood had paid little attention to Latinos as a potential audience. Depictions of Latina/os in early cinema had been almost uniformly stereotypical or at best exoticized, indicating that studios paid little regard to the perceptions of Latina/o or Latin American audiences (see Serna; Vasey 84–99, 118–20). Under Franklin Delano Roosevelt's Good Neighbor Policy during the late 1930s and 1940s, studios softened their often disparaging representations of Latina/os in an attempt to appeal to Latin American audiences and generate hemispheric goodwill. The civil rights movement of the 1960s and early 1970s enabled Chicano and Puerto Rican activists to heighten pressure to increase the representation of Latinos both onscreen and behind the scenes (see Noriega). In the 1980s, independent Chicano and Latino film production began to blossom, though mainstream cinema continued to produce films, such as *Fort Apache the Bronx* (1981), that portrayed Latino communities as full of depraved and dangerous criminals. Intrigued by the success of specialty films aimed at Latino audiences that had achieved some crossover success, such as *La Bamba* (1987), a biopic about musician Ritchie Valens (born Ricardo Valenzuela Reyes), and *Stand and Deliver* (1988), a film set in East Los Angeles about an inspiring Latino calculus teacher and his low-achieving students who succeed despite the odds, studios began to look for bankable Latina/o stars who would appeal to Latino and mainstream audiences alike.

Changing longstanding negative representations of Latino men proved challenging. Charles Ramírez Berg identifies three dominant types of Latino stereotypes: the vicious, violent, and criminal *bandido*; the simpleminded and emotional buffoon; and the Latin lover who combines "eroticism, exoticism, tenderness tinged with violence and danger" (76). Forged in silent and classic Hollywood cinema, these stereotypes were updated in the form of drug dealers, gang members, and Lotharios. What is more, in the nineties, the "illegal alien," coded as Mexican, male, anonymous, and simultaneously disempowered and dangerous, became an established media trope. The popular imagination often equated Latino masculinity with machismo—a broad category that encompassed "negative attributes such as male dominance, patriarchy, authoritarianism, and spousal abuse" and a perception of Latinos as hypersexual and exotic (Mirandé; see also Beltrán, "Hollywood"). In the 1990s all three stars considered here were associated in varying degrees with popular understandings of machismo, an association that formed the basis of their racialized masculinity.

☆☆☆☆☆ Antonio Banderas: A Pan-Latin Star

The title of a profile in the *London Guardian* summed up the Banderas paradox succinctly: "There are millions of them in America. So why does Hollywood need to import its Hispanics?" (Sarah Gristwood, *Guardian*, 1 February 1996). In the 1980s, Antonio Banderas had established himself in Spanish cinema through his roles in edgy sex-comedies directed by Pedro Almodóvar, including *Matador* (1986), *Mujeres al bordo de un ataque de nervios* (*Women on the Verge of a Nervous Breakdown*, 1988), and *Átame* (*Tie Me Up! Tie Me Down!* 1990). As Chris Perriam argues, in Spain Banderas came to be associated with a type—"the young male whose body is used as much for violence as for sex" (Perriam 46). Although Banderas often played sexually confused characters, the Spanish media used the trope of the "young drama student from the provinces" to neutralize that association in the public's mind (46, 48).

In the early 1990s, Banderas made the move to Hollywood and became, virtually overnight, one of the most visible Latino actors in the industry. As in Spain, his personal history as the son of a policeman and a teacher who had journeyed from Malaga, a city near the Mediterranean, to Madrid and eventually to Hollywood was mobilized frequently in media profiles. But in the United States his stardom came to revolve around the ways in which his onscreen and offscreen persona conformed to ideas about Latino sexuality. Save two initial turns in gay roles in *Interview with the Vampire* (1994) and *Philadelphia* (1993), his American career was built on his "hot" heterosexuality and physicality. The oft-repeated story about his introduction to American audiences as the hot young Spanish star who rebuffed the pop star Madonna on camera during the filming of the documentary *Madonna: Truth or Dare* (1991) established him as an object of (white) American female desire.

Banderas's body as a sexualized object became the dominant register in which his stardom was articulated in the United States. Heralded as Rudolph Valentino's contemporary heir, he was expected to exude sex onscreen and off. Director Richard Donner called him "the personification of male musk" (*People*, 6 May 1996). Spanish critic Joseba Gabilondo concurred with *People*, deeming him the "sexiest man alive." Often, Banderas was reduced to a list of physical attributes: "espresso-colored eyes," "that face, those eyes, those lips, his 'naked butt'" (Rita Zekas, *Toronto Star*, 20 October 1995; Karen Schoemer, *Newsweek*, 16 November 1991). Such a fetishizing discourse reduced Banderas to a set of desirable body parts. Those physical characteristics were linked, in turn, to popular constructs of

Latino men as inherently passionate and seductive. Profiles of Banderas used adjectives that bordered on the cartoonish, such as "hot and spicy," "red-hot," and "Latin-spiced" (Zekas; Steve Persall, *St. Petersburg Times*, 6 October 1995). Perriam notes that this construction of Banderas as sex symbol was transnational, extending from his early career in Spain through his emergence onto the Hollywood scene (65).

The sexual and physical dimensions of Banderas's star persona can be seen clearly in a series of photographs published in *People*. In the first photograph, from 1992, Banderas, hair disheveled and wearing a slightly rumpled shirt open to show a tantalizing bit of chest hair, looks out seductively at the camera, his lips ever so slightly puckered. He is framed against a wrought-iron fence that invokes Spanish architectural motifs. In the second, published just two years later, Banderas again wears a rumpled shirt. His hair is tousled as if he has just gotten out of bed and he looks straight at the viewer, his head slightly cocked to the right and his lips closed in their trademark soft pout.

Finally, in 1996 when he was named one of the world's "most beautiful people," *People* featured a photo showing him crouched in an almost feline position. This pose draws attention to the former soccer player's athletic body, but the focus of the photo, as in the others, remains his seductive gaze. Each of these photos works with its accompanying text to simultaneously sexualize and racialize Banderas. For example, the short article above the 1994 photograph reinforces the photo's attention to his "bronze skin, soulful brown eyes and sensual mouth" (9 May 1994). The 1996 profile informs readers that his "glistening black hair and desperado stubble drive women wild" (6 May 1996). At the same time that they sexualized Banderas, these multimedia constructions worked to domesticate that sexuality subtly, reassuring readers that, despite the focus on his physical features and his being photographed using conventions associated with women's glamour photography, the star did not see himself as a sex symbol.

This focus on his sex appeal extended to evaluations of his onscreen characters. In *Interview with the Vampire*, where he had a small supporting role, critics called his character "dangerously sexy" (Scott Jordan, *Rolling Stone*, 14 February 2001; Janet Maslin, *New York Times*, 11 November 1994). In *House of the Spirits*, Banderas worked his "matinee-idol magic" (*New York Times*, 1 April 1994). In *Desperado*, independent director Robert Rodriguez's Hollywood remake of his independent sleeper hit *El mariachi* (1992), Banderas, playing opposite Mexican actress Salma Hayek, cut "a devastatingly attractive figure," his "cocky attitude, glistening black hair and two-day beard" making him "a *macho icon*" (Todd McCarthy, *Variety*, 25 May 1995).

El Mariachi (Antonio Banderas) wreaks destruction with sawed-off double-barreled shot-gun and pistol in hand in *Desperado* (Robert Rodriguez, Columbia, 1995). Collection Laura Isabel Serna.

In *The Mask of Zorro*, his first full-fledged U.S. hit, in which he played a Mexican rather than a Spanish Zorro, he "cut a sexy figure" (Peter Travers, *Rolling Stone*, 11 May 2001). Most of these films featured sexually charged scenes between Banderas and his leading ladies, in which the actor's physical attributes were put prominently on display. Banderas's sexuality dogged him even as he extended his range by appearing in family films at the end of the decade. One reviewer called his performance in *Spy Kids* (2001) "absurdly sexy" (Elvis Mitchell, *New York Times*, 30 March 2001).

Critical to the discourse on either his offscreen persona or his various roles was an understanding that Banderas did not *act* sexy; he *was* sexy. For example, in describing his performance in *The Mask of Zorro*, *New York Times* critic Janet Maslin asserted that Banderas had "obviously been born to play" the role of Zorro's "hot-blooded protégé" (17 July 1998). In her review of *Evita* (1996), Maslin suggested that Banderas's inherent sexuality superseded his craft. Banderas, she wrote, "shares Madonna's way of looking so good that he diverts attention away from what he's trying to convey" (*New York Times*, 25 December 1996). Similarly, media coverage of Banderas's relationship with co-star Melanie Griffith, whom he married in 1996, described their relationship as "all Latin volatility," a volatility ascribed to his cultural background (*Sunday Times*, 6 August 1995; *Toronto Sun*, 29 March 1996).

Banderas was seemingly omnipresent in 1990s Hollywood. Filmmaker Spike Lee remarked, "I don't think there is a boom in Latino cinema. It's just that Antonio Banderas is in every single film at the moment" (Sarah Gristwood, *Irish Times*, 3 February 1996). Indeed, in film after film during the decade he played a very wide range of Latin American or Latino characters: an Argentine revolutionary, a Cuban plantation owner, a Hispano swashbuckler, a gay Latino, a Mexican assassin. Unlike some of his counterparts, for whom being typecast was perceived as an obstacle to success, Banderas willingly played variations on the same role in a seemingly unending parade of films, hits and critical failures alike. As Frances Aparicio has observed about Mexican stars working in Hollywood, Banderas's high profile as a pan-Latin performer "displaces and replaces the need for the development of local, national . . . talent in the acting profession" (Aparicio 100). As a Spaniard (a cultural identity carefully cultivated in profiles that repeated his biography and informed readers that he and Griffith maintained a home in Spain), Banderas could be held at one remove from the politics of being Latino in the United States while still "representing" Latinos onscreen. Where U.S.-born Latinos might have seen restrictions in being limited to Latino roles, Banderas, admittedly limited by his accent, saw unlimited possibilities; he often expressed the sentiment that he had felt more trapped in his Spanish career (Nick Madigan, *Daily Variety*, 12 April 1999).

Banderas himself adapted to the industry and media's perception of him as "Latin(o)." In 1999, the Imagen Foundation, an organization dedicated to "encouraging and recognizing the positive portrayals of Latinos in the entertainment industry," honored Banderas with a "Lasting Image

Award" for his body of work in the United States (www.imagen.org). Upon receiving the award, Banderas said it was "special and emotional to be recognized by my own community" (Madigan). He went on to remember the "'invisible heroes' of the Spanish-speaking world, trying to make their lives and the lives of their communities better" (Madigan). Rhetorically, Banderas incorporated himself into a subset of the Latino community in the United States, the film industry, while adopting an expansive definition of latinidad based on shared linguistic heritage or practice that could encompass Spain as well as the Americas.

Intertextual constructions of Banderas as a Latino star marked him as exotic in ways that appealed to persistent popular ideas about Latin Lovers. This image appealed, as it had historically, to mainstream audiences intrigued by Latino sexuality they perceived as dangerous, exotic, and passionate. At the same time, Banderas's biography allowed him to occupy a general category "Latino" that studios hoped would appeal to the Latino audiences Hollywood hoped to capture, without addressing the issue of equity for U.S.-born Latinos in the industry. Banderas willingly adapted himself to a star system that, as film studies scholar Mary Beltrán phrases it, "celebrate[s] and objectif[ies] difference" (*Stars* 80).

☆☆☆☆☆ Crossing Over: From Havana to Hollywood

Cuban-born Andy Garcia, who had appeared in various television series and as a Latin American drug dealer in *8 Million Ways to Die* (1986), was voted Male Star of the Year in 1991 by the National Association of Theater Owners after receiving an Academy Award nomination for his performance in *The Godfather: Part III* (1990). The press predicted that Garcia was "on his way to legendary status" (Elena Kellner, *Hispanic Magazine*, 28 February 1994). As with Banderas, the mainstream media as well as the industry's publicity machine marked Garcia—who was being groomed by Paramount Studios—as a representative of the Latino Boom in Hollywood. In contrast to Banderas's rearticulation of Latin Lover stereotypes, Garcia's stardom functioned as a model of Latino assimilation. He, too, was described as attractive in racial terms. He was "tall, dark, and handsome," flirtatious ("a genetic Latin American trait"), and the possessor of "dark, smoldering good looks" (Walter Martinez, *Latin Style*, February 1999; Stephanie Mansfield, *GQ*, December 1990; James Dillon, *Hollywood Video Insider*, April 1999). But this focus on physicality was superseded by constructions of Garcia as an exile or, as one profile phrased it, part of "a generation of Cubans who are very happy to be here" (Mansfield). As he was constructed as a rising Latino star—*Hollywood Reporter* named him the Latino star of 1995—his latinidad was framed as something private, relegated to the discursive spaces of home and family, and as distinctly cultural rather than political.

A popular text that places the two stars side by side makes this comparison concrete. A 1999 Independence Day tabloid feature, "We Like to Be in America," whose title alludes to the 1960s assimilationist musical *West Side Story*, featured various "foreign" Hollywood stars such as Nicole Kidman, Salma Hayek, and Arnold Schwarzenegger talking about why they "love Americans on this Fourth of July" (*Star*, 6 July 1999). Mini-interviews with Banderas and Garcia affirmed the feature's affective structuring of the relationship between these stars and American culture. While Banderas reminded readers, "I am a visitor here. I always will be," Garcia emphasized his autobiography as a version of the American Dream. After a period of adjustment and acculturation, he "was embraced by this country and its culture. . . . In America, dreams can come true if you apply yourself and never give up." As this quote suggests, Garcia's celebrity involved framing his path to Hollywood as an immigrant success story.

Garcia's biography as circulated in the mainstream media routinely begins with his idyllic childhood in pre-revolutionary Cuba, his family's subsequent exile, and their hard work to rebuild their lives in Miami's Cuban exile community. His father, a gentleman farmer and lawyer, and his mother, an English teacher, were among the elite of the small town of Bejucal near Havana. Until the revolution intruded, Garcia and his siblings led an idyllic existence evoked by a constellation of oft-repeated images: the avocado trees his father cultivated, his grandmother's piano playing, and various details of small-town life. In the United States, Garcia's "tight-knit, hardworking, conservative Catholic" family eventually attained the American Dream in the form of a successful family business.

This story of one family echoes in microcosm a broader narrative of Cuban Americans as "good" immigrants. In contrast to the discourse on Mexican migration in the nineties, in which all Mexican migrants seemed to have come to the United States as illegal undocumented workers to wreak social and economic havoc, Cuban immigration, particularly the first wave of which Garcia's family was a part, has been portrayed as a political exile provoked by the imposition of an illegitimate, communist regime (see García). The Garcia family were members of the first waves of Cuban refugees, a profile in *GQ* informed readers, "the intelligentsia and the entrepreneurs who crowded into Miami's Freedom Tower the same way the fictional Vito Corleone passed through Ellis Island" (Mansfield). Like the paradigmatic Italian American family, this comparison suggests, Garcia's family immigrated the "right way." Garcia would subsequently find himself in Hollywood, where "like his father twenty years before him, he was a stranger in a strange land" who would have to work as hard to make it in the entertainment business as his father had worked to become a successful small business owner (see Mansfield).

Thus, for Garcia, becoming a star involved not luck, a common version of the star biography, but striving. In interviews he remembered struggling to fit in as a boy who spoke no English; eventually he "was embraced by this country and its culture" and became an average American teenager (Susan Morgan, *Interview*, February 1993). Struggle also emerges as a dominant trope in descriptions of his early acting career. Garcia worked at a series of manual and service jobs typically held by immigrants—on the docks, as a waiter—while waiting for his big break. Perhaps even more pertinent to his construction as a Latino star, in interviews Garcia spoke frequently about his "war wounds," memories of ill treatment and the racist practices of the film industry (Jennet Conant, *Redbook*, January 1993). In an interview with *Latin Style*, a now defunct glossy aimed at the coveted Latino middle-class demographic, Garcia remembered, "It was very hard for me to get an agent and auditions. . . . You have that subtle stereotype and racism that exists in all the casting process" (Martinez). Once he got work, he struggled against being typecast, turning down "dozens of opportunities to play Hispanic drug dealers" (Conant). Referring back to his immigrant heritage, his persistence in the face of rejection by casting agents is attributed to his having "learned strong work ethics from his parents" who when they came to the United States "learned English and worked hard" (see Kellner). In this way, Garcia's path to stardom was cast as a version of the immigrant's struggle to make good in a new land.

Garcia's assimilated immigrant image emerged in the roles he played throughout the nineties. Paramount Pictures cast Garcia so as to build on media predictions that he was one of the hottest young stars of the decade and on his proven ability to "cross over," by moving back and forth between ethnic and non-ethnic roles. He played an assimilated Italian, Giuseppe Petri/George Stone, in *The Untouchables* (1987), an aspiring Italian mobster, Vincent Mancini, in *The Godfather: Part III* (1990), an Irish cop in *Night Falls on Manhattan* (1996), and ethnically ambiguous but ostensibly white characters in both *Black Rain* (1989) and *When a Man Loves a Woman* (1994). These casting choices aligned Garcia with white ethnic groups that had successfully assimilated into American society while retaining the cultural markers of their ethnic identity, such as their names or an association with particular

Assistant District Attorney Sean Casey (Andy Garcia) confronts his father, police officer Liam Casey (Ian Holm, left), about corruption in the NYPD in *Night Falls on Manhattan* (Sidney Lumet, Paramount, 1996). Collection Laura Isabel Serna.

professions (see Ignatiev; Guglielmo). Another set of roles allowed Garcia to play Latino professionals whose identities were only partially defined by their ethnic background. For example, the character Raymond Avila in *Internal Affairs* (1990) is marked as ethnic by his name; by his habit of dropping Spanish into conversation, particularly at moments of emotional intensity; and by his ability to move easily in the world of Spanish-speaking Los Angeles. At the same time, he moves unfettered in the predominantly white world of the LAPD. This constellation of onscreen identities reinforced Garcia's offscreen biography as an assimilated and successful immigrant.

Despite this emphasis on assimilation, Garcia's cultural identity remained a salient feature of his celebrity that kept him from fully embracing stardom. Being Cuban American was portrayed as fueling his performance style. The media attributed his ability to convey pain, passion, and intensity to his experience of exile. "The Cuban in him" emerged, one journalist wrote, "no matter what role he finds himself playing (Irish, Italian, etc.) whenever he gets excited" (Mansfield). At the same time the family values constructed as emerging from his Cuban heritage led Garcia away from stardom as typically construed. Profiles emphasized his "reputation for being a solid family man," exemplified by his long marriage to a fellow Cuban émigré, his Catholic faith, and his refusal to do nude scenes (Kellner). Stardom had not prevented him from maintaining strong ties to

Miami and the Cuban immigrant community. Garcia asserted, "I've always maintained a home there [in Miami], in the emotional sense. My parents, my family, my roots are there" (Morgan). Thus, Garcia's refusal to fully embrace the lifestyle trappings of contemporary Hollywood stardom was cast as the natural result of his cultural background and his strong ties to the Cuban community.

Garcia's Cuban roots—his "private passions"—animated his highly publicized offscreen pursuits during the decade (Guillermo Cabrera Infante, *Harper's*, January 1996). Most noted by the press, Garcia revived the career of Israel "Cachao" Lopez, the inventor of the Mambo, who had lived in obscurity in Miami after defecting from Cuba in 1962. He produced a tribute concert film *Cachao (como su ritmo no hay dos)* (*Cachao: Like His Rhythm There's No Other*, 1993) and organized a nationwide tour featuring Cachao and other musicians. Garcia framed this project as the reclamation of the cultural traditions that had been cast aside in the chaos of the exile experience (Robert Hofler, *Miami Herald*, 24 September 1995).

This labor of love joined Garcia's star persona to broader patterns in the Cuban exile experience that emerged in the nineties. As travel and trade with Cuba became even more tightly restricted, a worldwide vogue for Cuban culture blossomed, manifesting itself most insistently in the sudden popularity of traditional Cuban music. A wave of "nostalgic fantasy" was built on the nineties Latin Boom in music that had its base in Miami and traded in images of dance clubs, cars from the 1950s, and Afro-Cuban music (Fernandes 94). This nominally depoliticized affirmation of Cuban culture celebrates pre-Castro Cuba and, by extension, pre-revolutionary Cuban politics. It also serves, in concert with the other discursive constructions of Garcia's stardom, to make nostalgia the dominant register in which his cultural difference is articulated. This focus on the past reinforced constructions of Garcia as an exile who had been forced to come to the United States, and distanced him from contemporary debates over undocumented immigrants. The positive qualities associated with latinidad, such as being hardworking and family oriented, distinguished Garcia from other stars while promoting a vision of cultural difference as belonging to a personal history, a particular family, and a singular home (albeit within an ethnic community) rather than signifying the public and political at large.

★★★★★ **Edward James Olmos: Actor Activist**

Edward James Olmos might seem an unlikely star. Unlovely, with a pockmarked face and dark skin, he has a physical appearance that stands in opposition to the exotic good looks often associated with Latino stars. Olmos, who began his career in the 1970s singing in a rock band and appearing in minor roles in television series including "Kojak," "Starsky & Hutch," and "Hawaii Five-O," garnered critical attention after appearing in the role of "El Pachuco," a prototypical macho, in the critically acclaimed play and then the film *Zoot Suit* (1981), both directed by Chicano playwright Luis Valdez. As Olmos would repeat over and over again in celebrity profiles, despite the fact that his growing family needed the money, he passed up role after role until finally he was granted creative control over the character of Lieutenant Castillo in the eighties television procedural "Miami Vice."

These two roles established the fundamental parameters of Olmos's professional persona as it manifested in the nineties: his commitment to participating in projects that brought aspects of the Chicano experience to the screen and his refusal to play what he considered stereotypical Latino characters in film or on television. With both *Zoot Suit* and "Miami Vice," Olmos sought creative control over characters and projects. *Los Angeles Times* journalist Victor Valle asserted, "Instead of trying to cross over . . . he has battled to define his screen image on his own terms. . . . He would not accept roles that portrayed Latinos or anyone else with lopsided stereotypes" (19 March 1989). Accordingly, he worked on a series of projects focused on the Latino experience, including *American Me* (1992), *A Million to Juan* (1994), *My Family* (1995), *Roosters* (1995), *Selena* (1997), and *The Disappearance of Garcia Lorca* (1997), the majority of which had only moderate success at the box office.

What, then, made Olmos a star? As Mary Beltrán observes, descriptions of his early career mobilized a discourse of "determination and talent," emphasizing that his success was the result of perseverance and his skill as an actor (*Stars* 118). Olmos's celebrity emerged, paradoxically, out of his rebellion against the star system that asks Latino stars to conform to "safe" white notions of latinidad. The same media outlets that reported his new projects and profiled the actor declared in the same breath that he had in fact failed to become a star. The mainstream press laid this failure at the feet of his social activism and his unwillingness to separate the politics of representation onscreen from larger social issues. In the words of one reporter, the very qualities that brought him to the media's attention prevented him from reaching "the top echelons of stardom . . . the level of power at which a project gets made on the strength of a name" (Lawrence Christon, *Los Angeles Times*, 1 September 1991). Ironically, although Olmos did not purportedly have the star power to get a film made on the strength of his name alone, he became the face of Latino achievement in the entertainment industry.

The conflation of his two identities, "one as an actor and the other as a spokesman for the Latino community," required that Olmos perform Latino authenticity both onscreen and off. In an interview Olmos presented his own labor as a performer as that of "express[ing] our particular experience" (Ilan Stavans, "Un actor [Chicano] se prepara: entrevista a Edward James Olmos," *Gestos*, November 1988,149). He was acutely aware of how the characters he played served as positive role models to Chicana/o audiences. "I've given you more positive [Latino] images," he said in 1992; "I gave you Jamie Escalante [the math teacher in *Stand and Deliver*]. I gave you five years of Lt. Castillo ['Miami Vice']" (Glenn Lovell, *San Jose Mercury News*, 13 March 1992). For Olmos, it was not enough merely to have Latino faces on the screen; those roles needed, from his point of view, to be true to the social experience of Latinos in the United States.

Beginning with his starring role in the inspirational education film *Stand and Deliver*, his nineties roles, including that of one member of an extended Mexican American family in *My Family*, and the stern but loving father in *Selena*, reinforced his image as an actor intimately connected to the historical and contemporary experience of Latina/os in the United States. Media coverage of Olmos focused on his origins in East Los Angeles, often subtly implying that he himself had escaped the fate that befell the all-too-familiar at-risk youth in some of his films and propping him up as a role model of inner-city success.

His multiple roles, as director, co-producer, and star, in *American Me* exemplify the way that his onscreen characters and offscreen persona participated in this discourse of authenticity. Originally conceived in the 1970s as yet another gangsploitation film, *American Me* was recast by Olmos to address the Latino community for whom he hoped the film would function as a warning about the dangers of gang activity and toxic family relationships. He played the lead role of Montoya Santana, a young Chicano who becomes the leader of a powerful prison gang. The film focuses on the warped machismo fostered on the streets and in prison, asserting through its narrative structure that violence begets violence. Reviews of Olmos's performance focused on the "low-key seething demeanor," his "mesmerizing, implacable" presence, and the "danger and electricity" in his performance (Chris Hicks, *Deseret News*, 16 March 1992; *Variety*, 1 January 1992; Lovell). Janet Maslin wrote in the *New York Times* that Olmos's direction was "awkward and dour" and that the film displayed "Mr. Olmos's familiar dolorous, chilling charm" (13 March 1992). These characterizations attributed qualities—anger, dissatisfaction, seriousness—to Olmos himself that perhaps better described his character and reinforced the image of the

Edward James Olmos (center) as gang leader Montoya Santana inside Folsom Prison with members of La Eme (the Mexican Mafia) in *American Me* (Edward James Olmos, Universal, 1992). Pepe Serna is at left, William Forsythe at right. Collection Laura Isabel Serna.

star constructed in publicity photographs, which rarely showed the actor smiling.

Primarily, however, the film was evaluated as a social message film. "Olmos is angrily taking a message back to the barrio that he claims it will not want to hear," wrote Maslin (*New York Times*, 13 March 1992). No one, in or out of the barrio, seemed to want to hear that message. Glenn Lovell of the *San Jose Mercury News* described the film as "showing the fetid underbelly of the urban experience" (13 March 1992). Others called the film "preachy" and a "sordid polemic" (Peter Travers, *Rolling Stone*, 2 April 1992; Rita Kempley, *Washington Post*, 13 March 1992). The reaction from Latino viewers was no less critical. Luis Valdez, with whom Olmos had worked on *Zoot Suit*, called the film "a diatribe against Latinos" (*San Jose Mercury News*, 29 February 1992). Cultural studies scholar Rosa Linda Fregoso critiqued the film as a dystopian, masculinist vision of the Chicana/o experience. She took issue with Olmos's assertion, both in the film and in the publicity, of the family "as the source of the cancer in our barrios" (Fregoso 123–24). Thus, both mainstream and Latino viewers expressed discomfort with the film's graphic portrayals of violence, though for different reasons.

Despite such critiques, Olmos remained committed to using the media to address social issues relevant to Latino communities. While Hollywood and the mainstream media used his image as evidence that real change had occurred in the representation of Latina/os onscreen, Olmos in turn used that publicity to advance explicitly political projects offscreen. In addition to maintaining an almost nonstop schedule of speaking engagements at juvenile detention centers, schools, and other community venues, he was connected to a long list of political and charitable causes, including serving as the head of the Hazard Education Project (a gang prevention organization). Although many contemporary stars are involved in charitable causes to varying degrees, these activities became the substance of his stardom, and they were portrayed as both the logical extension of his ethnic identity and as an obstacle to crossover success.

Comparing mainstream and Spanish-language press coverage of Olmos's activism clarifies the way it structured his star image for different audiences. Never a candidate for *People*'s list of the world's most beautiful people, Olmos appeared once in the magazine in a feature that showcased his 1996 humanitarian mission to Chiapas, Mexico. The trip, which took food and supplies to communities impacted by a recent hurricane and during which he met the media-savvy leader of the EZLN, Subcomandante Marcos, was called "his most demanding offscreen role." The feature hinted that rather than adding to his star image, at least in the mainstream his "hyperactive social conscience" threatened to turn Olmos into a "caricature of the socially aware actor" (Peter Carlin, *People*, 9 September 1996). In contrast, the Spanish-language press consistently hailed Olmos as a community hero. *La Opinión*, the greater Los Angeles area's most widely circulated Spanish-language daily, celebrated his role in calming the Los Angeles Latino community during the looting and violence that followed the Rodney King incident in 1992. His outspokenness in the face of silence from government officials and his actual presence on the streets of L.A., broom in hand, proved "his commitment to the community" (Roberto Rodriguez, *La Opinión*, 2 May 1992). *La Opinión*'s regular publication of profiles and interviews with Olmos focused less on his activities in Hollywood than on his activities in the community.

Indeed, Olmos's star image often seemed to address two different audiences. One set of texts disseminated through the mainstream media sought to explain his activities to a primarily Anglo audience and readership. Those texts typically elaborated on Olmos's roots in East Los Angeles and his decision to turn away from gang activity toward sports and eventually acting, thereby framing his subsequent success as an account of individual exceptionalism. At the same time, this biography lent his portrayals of inner-city characters like Montoya Santana in *American Me* the air of authenticity. For example, Roger Ebert praised *American Me* for its authenticity, insisting that Olmos "knows their [gangbangers'] streets" (*Chicago Sun-Times*, 13 March 1992). In the Spanish-language press and other media outlets aimed at Latina/os, Olmos more often addressed that community directly. For example, while *People*'s coverage of his Chiapas trip mobilized a doubly ethnographic gaze—directed first at Chiapas and then at Olmos himself—in describing that same trip in *La Opinión* Olmos spoke for himself, identifying his most precious treasures as "*our* Mayan and Aztec roots. We have to save them" [emphasis mine] (Francisco Linares, *La Opinión*, 6 September 1998). In this way, Olmos included himself in the imagined, transnational Latino community with historical connections to other peoples in the Americas.

Despite his address directly to Latina/os in the press and through his films, Olmos's social activism, like the use of his star image on the cover of *Time*, promoted meanings of latinidad that conformed to rather than contradicted mainstream notions of diversity and difference. This depoliticization can be seen in the exhibition *Americanos: Latino Life in the United States*, which was organized by Olmos's production company in collaboration with the Smithsonian Institution. The timing of the exhibition took advantage of a recent report that had criticized the Smithsonian Institution for neglecting Latina/os in its programming and outreach efforts (see Smithsonian Institution Task Force). Made up of photographs with accompanying wall text and multimedia installations, the project literally framed Latina/os as part of a multicultural society. Together with its accompanying corporate-sponsored book, documentary film, concert, and CD (all sponsored by TimeWarner), the exhibit celebrated the diversity of the Latino community and used an aesthetic everydayness to argue for Latina/os' inclusion in a multicultural America. Directed primarily at Anglo audiences, the exhibit offered an antidote to the relentlessly negative images of Latina/os in the media (including cinema).

The exhibit also addressed Latina/os, encouraging them to see themselves as part of the national imaginary. In regard to the volume that accompanied the exhibit, Olmos said, "This is not a book that speaks of discrimination but rather of life, pride, and humanity" (*La Opinión*, 22 April 1999). As this quote suggests, the tenor of the exhibit promoted a liberal multiculturalism predicated on the inclusion and recognition of difference in civic life. As Esteban Del Río observes, "The exhibit constructs a new and acceptable version of Latinidad for general audiences that affirms the multicultural status quo, depoliticizes Latina/o history and agency, and works within the ideology of the American dream" (148–49).

Olmos's perception that cultural representation and production could serve as the path to cultural citizenship manifested itself in other areas that drew on his star image, including his promotion of Latino book fairs and film festivals in Los Angeles as well as his appearance in a first-person essay published in *Variety* in 1998. That essay, a unique self-authored intertext conjoined with the star's average or everyman image, allowed Olmos to situate himself as a star-cum-average-American-moviegoer. He describes Sundays with his family: "We looked forward to this day because it was all of us together, off to eat as a family and to spend the afternoon in Hollywood." He goes on to construct a continuum between the films he saw in his youth, such as *Lawrence of Arabia* (1962), *Dr. Zhivago* (1965), and *The Bridge on the River Kwai* (1957), and contemporary films about diverse ethnic groups such as *The Joy Luck Club* (1993), *Soul Food* (1997), and *Schindler's List* (1993). This comparison serves as evidence that cinema provides both "entertainment and a stronger understanding of others" (Olmos, *Variety*, 17 November 1998). Olmos's liberal multiculturalism—the idea that difference should be incorporated into the fabric of American life—as a question of mutual understanding stood in tension with the ways in which his stardom was produced around his image as a social activist constantly called upon to advocate for the visibility of Latina/os in American society.

As a star whose primary labor seemed to be that of representing Latina/o interests in the mainstream media on- and offscreen, Olmos was able to leverage his stardom with a corporate America that was desperate to find ways for courting new audiences and consumers to fund projects such as the *Americanos* exhibition. His credibility as a Latino spokesperson derived in large part from the conflation of his on- and offscreen roles, an entwining that allowed the mainstream to perceive him as an individual who had himself "defied the odds" (Luaine Lee, *Pittsburgh Post-Gazette*, 15 May 1997). Despite these constraints, Olmos was able to directly address Latina/o audiences and participate in Latino/a efforts to shape their own representation in the public sphere.[2]

★★★★★ Conclusion

Latino stars of the decade were poised at the crossroads of corporate capitalism and its media imperatives that saw ethnicity as a marketable quality that could generate profit from individual and group desires for increased representation and sites of self-identification. The high profiles of Banderas, Garcia, and Olmos obscured the history of marginalization, invisibility, and negative stereotypes of Latinos in Hollywood. At once, textual constructions of both their masculinities and their stardoms inserted them into a narrative of "exceptional cultural identity" (Noriega 130) as the neo-Latin Lover, the striving immigrant, and angry social activist, respectively. They were offered up simultaneously as heirs to a tradition of Hispanic/Latino male stardom, and as visual evidence of the industry's embrace of difference. Banderas was constructed as a free-floating signifier of latinidad; as a Spaniard he could stand in for any of the subject positions created by Spain's colonial project in the Americas. Garcia, in contrast, reinforced notions of Cuban Americans as "good" immigrants who, just as Garcia had, could cross over from Latino roles to "mainstream" roles, from ethnic to assimilated subjects. Olmos, though marked as being outside stardom proper through his appearance, his decision to continue to appear in both television and film, and his adamant and public persona as a spokesperson for the Latino community, used his stardom to promote ideals of inclusive cultural citizenship, if not radical political perspectives, generated within the Latino community.

Any cursory examination of their stardom reveals the three had substantially different relationships to latinidad and to the industry and media. Even the Latina/o community within the industry gathered them under the umbrella term "Latino" in such a way that the socially real (the relative privilege afforded Spaniards vis-à-vis groups identified as minorities in the United States, just to offer one example) was replaced by "historically familiar, acceptable, and contained images of Latinos that the U.S. can integrate into its own logic" (Aparicio 92).

At the same time, each of these stars used his being typed as "Latino" to his own ends, some more progressive than others. Banderas clearly took his role as a representative of latinidad quite seriously, while also being aware of the benefits that had accrued to his own career because of his willingness to be cast almost exclusively in Latino roles. Garcia likewise used the tension between his Cuban heritage and the myths of assimilation that circulated through and in his biography to promote a specific politics of culture. Finally, Olmos leveraged his identity as the face of the "Latin Boom" in Hollywood to push beyond Hollywood's desire to cultivate a new market segment. Collectively, they were presented as part of a pan-ethnic social formation, "Latinos in Hollywood," that could be commodified and sold to target and mainstream audiences alike. Ethnic and racial difference, rendered visually on the screen but also produced in the "images, words, and sounds" that come to stand for a star, allows cinema to capitalize on our culture's fascination with the racialization of certain stars (McDonald 6; see Willis).

Further, Chon Noriega points out that the flurry of attention to Latino actors in the nineties produced a "restrictive" discourse on Latino celebrities (168). That is, discussions about Latinos and media focused on a handful of emerging stars, and on Latina/os as a market category rather than as a social group. Indeed, media attention to the Latino Boom in Hollywood might have led some to think that the social issues of discrimination, poverty, and even a lack of representation onscreen had been resolved. Statistics at the end of the decade suggested otherwise. The Screen Actors Guild study on the status of Latina/os in the entertainment industry concluded in 1999 that despite the high profile of stars such as Banderas, Garcia, and Olmos, Latinos continued to be underrepresented in all aspects of the industry, including in starring roles (Pachon et al.). Thus, despite their iconic status, on one level their celebrity obfuscated rather than reflected social reality. Given the relentless parade of negative images of Latino masculinity in the media—the illegal alien, the gang banger, the drug dealer—the discourses of immigrant striving, exotic sexuality, and liberal multiculturalism that surrounded Latino stars in the nineties offered socially acceptable Latino masculinities that would sell movie tickets. At the same time, each of these stars used the media discourse of latinidad to claim cultural citizenship and make Latino masculinity visible on and off the screen.

NOTES

1. Throughout this essay I use the term "Latino" to refer to men and the unwieldy but more specific "Latina/o" or "Latina/os" to refer to both genders. My sources use "Hispanic" and "Latino" interchangeably; I follow their lead when appropriate.

2. For a more extensive overview of Olmos's career and star image see Beltrán *Stars*. She offers a reading of Olmos's star text as reassurance that "not only were Latina/os still in marginal positions in U.S. popular culture, but they were also uplifting their race" (124), a reading that resonates with the one offered here.

7 ☆☆☆☆☆☆☆☆☆☆★

Tom Hanks and
Tom Cruise
The Box Office
and "True Masculinity"

MARY BETH HARALOVICH

Tom Hanks became the most successful male star of the 1990s, critically and in terms of box office receipts, playing sensitive and fallible men in compelling dramas and romantic comedies. Tom Cruise, on the other hand, rose to the top of Hollywood's A-list in roles that epitomized American machismo and professional cunning. The coexisting stardom of the two Toms presented two kinds of Hollywood economic power and two kinds of popular masculinity in the decade: Hanks's vulnerable bosom buddy and Cruise's exceptional hero. Both are known on the marquee as "Tom," not "Thomas." Even when playing extraordinary or loutish, they are familiar and friendly. Being a regular guy seemed to come easily for Hanks, although he protected his family life from the press ("There can be nothing more mundane or boring than my private life," he told "60 Minutes"). Cruise, dogged by rumors about homosexuality and Scientology, integrated family life into his star image.

The two Toms entered the decade in comic roles, developed breadth, and ended with strong performances in challenging roles. For Cruise's star image, *Risky Business* (1983) remained the touchstone. Critics and fans cherished the energy of that role even as they appreciated Cruise's growing maturity as an actor. When Hanks found equilibrium between the quality of his performances and the quality of his films, critics found nirvana. By the end of the decade, Hanks had become an iconic everyman associated with Spencer Tracy and Jimmy Stewart. Cruise diversified his portfolio with action, vulnerability, and an edgy sexuality that played against his star image.

Early in the nineties, Hanks and Cruise both dealt with media agitation around homosexuality. Cruise was famously cast as the homoerotic vampire Lestat in the adaptation of Anne Rice's novel *Interview with the Vampire* (1994). He responded to rumors with interviews and lawsuits that engendered discussion about what it might mean to be gay in Hollywood commercial cinema. Lauded for his performance as a gay lawyer with AIDS in *Philadelphia* (1993), Hanks challenged anxieties that playing a homosexual would trouble the career of a straight actor. The Hanks and Cruise press reveals the significance of sexual identity in the relationship of fan to star to character. Cruise's and Hanks's star images became associated with homosexuality. The issues were similar but played out differently. While Cruise defended his heterosexuality, Hanks found pleasure in gay sexuality and effused an ordinary-guy masculinity that did not carry the sexual possibilities of Cruise's.

☆☆☆★★ Intense Guy and Ordinary Guy

Against the moving background of black-and-white clips from his films, Cruise looks out directly at the viewer, standing next to the "Message from Tom" that opens Tom Cruise The Official Site (tomcruise.com). Cruise's "hello and welcome" reveals attributes of his star image that have followed him throughout his career: love of moviemaking; humility (his work is both "a privilege" and "a great pleasure"); appreciation of crew and cast; friendly engagement with fans ("to bring you in and to share with you the fun I experience every day during the filmmaking

Interview with the Vampire (Neil Jordan, Geffen Pictures, 1994). Famously cast as the homo-erotic vampire Lestat, Tom Cruise in the ruffled dandy role challenged and expanded his star image. Collection Mary Beth Haralovich.

process"); and charismatic screen presence. The filmography link leads to a page with a widescreen image from each of Cruise's films. Click on any image and find the poster, the trailer, stills, and a synopsis. Tomcruise.com plays very well. It's robust and strong. The website celebrates the twenty-fifth anniversary of *Risky Business*, whose air guitar scene has become a

Lauded for his performance as a gay lawyer with AIDS in *Philadelphia* (Jonathan Demme, Clinica Estetico/TriStar, 1993), Tom Hanks challenged anxieties that playing a homosexual would trouble the career of a straight actor. Courtesy Photofest New York.

foundation of Cruise's stardom and the hetero- and homoerotic pleasures and high-energy charisma that he generates on- and offscreen. That glorious moment lives on today, without Cruise, as grown men in underpants and dress shirts joyfully play the Wii Guitar Hero.

As Tom Hanks describes himself on his MySpace page, "I'm that actor in some movies that you liked and some that you didn't. I'm taller than some folks think, not as tall as a lot of people. Sometimes I'm in pretty good shape and sometimes I'm not because, hey, you gotta live, you know?" (myspace .com/tomhanks). Hanks's web presence is modest: "The MySpace page created and updated by, yes, Tom Hanks, and/or his crack staff of Professional Show Business Experts!" He's male, was born in 1956, lives in Los Angeles; is married, straight, and a proud parent. In a candid black-and-white photo, Hanks is driving with the top down, wearing sunglasses and a turtleneck. He points out at the camera and the viewer. Among his low-tech videos are two installments about his electric car and a self-deprecating endorsement of Barack Obama for president, titled "Beware Celebrity Endorsement." Hanks inaugurates the page with a casual twenty-three seconds of video close-up. A sliding glass door and the sound of children's voices in the background are the familiar sights and sounds of ordinary home life. Although the page is updated, the link to "new projects" is empty. Other than the MySpace page, Hanks does not have an official website or organized presence, although his MySpace friends number more than 77,200.

The Toms entered the nineties with similar statures in the film industry, for roles that delved into what it means to be a man. Cruise had a Golden Globe and an Academy Award nomination for his portrayal of disabled Vietnam vet and antiwar activist Ron Kovic in the biopic *Born on the Fourth of July* (1989). Hanks had a Golden Globe and Academy Award nomination for his portrayal of a twelve-year-old boy in a man's body in *Big* (1988).

If one considers the accolades for their film work, there is not a great difference between Cruise and Hanks. As of 2011, each had scored seven career nominations for Golden Globes. Cruise has three wins—for *Born on the Fourth of July*, *Jerry Maguire* (1996), and *Magnolia* (1999), and nominations for *Risky Business*, *A Few Good Men* (1992), *The Last Samurai* (2003), and *Tropic Thunder* (2008). Hanks has four Golden Globes—for *Big*, *Philadelphia* (1993), *Forrest Gump* (1994), and *Cast Away* (2000), and nominations for *Sleepless in Seattle* (1993), *Saving Private Ryan* (1998), and *Charlie Wilson's War* (2007). Cruise has three Academy Award nominations, for *Born on the Fourth of July*, *Jerry Maguire*, and *Magnolia*. Hanks won back-to-back Academy Awards for *Philadelphia* and *Forrest Gump* and nominations for *Big*, *Saving Private Ryan*, and *Cast Away*.

★★★★★ Tom Cruise: Playful Exhibitionism

Disappointing critics after his transformation playing Ron Kovic in *Born of the Fourth of July*, Cruise attempted to carry two epics: as a stock-car racer in *Days of Thunder* (1990) and an Irish immigrant in *Far and Away* (1992). He went on to solid performances in the thriller genre as cocky young professionals in *A Few Good Men* and *The Firm* (1993). Cruise expanded his screen repertoire as the lusty vampire Lestat in *Interview with the Vampire*, then delivered two high-energy performances as the faltering sports agent in *Jerry Maguire* and the confident action hero in *Mission: Impossible* (1996), the first output of Cruise/Wagner Productions. Cruise ended the decade with performances of oppositional masculinities: a crude misogynist in *Magnolia* (1999) and a bland society doctor in *Eyes Wide Shut* (1999).

Cruise's masculine presence has a diverse appeal. Veronika Rall offers a compelling discussion of Cruise's star image at the beginning of the 1990s, noting that he was declared "the sexiest man alive" by *People* and a "recession-proof movie star" by *Rolling Stone*. To understand the Cruise "phenomenon" and to reconcile his "success with the image of a thirty year old scientologist, married for the second time," Rall engages in a quest for Cruise's "sexual attractivity" through a survey of Cruise's presence in popular magazines (96). Rall distinguishes between photos of Cruise posing with a model's distance and Cruise engaged with the viewer. It is in the latter that she locates his hetero- and homoerotic appeal. Albert Watson's pictures for the 1992 *Rolling Stone* presented a "rather boring" image of "a young man looking sternly into the camera, mouth closed, eyes wide open . . . emptied of expression." In the *Time* cover on *Born on the Fourth of July*, Cruise is "boyish . . . an up-and-coming (male) manager." About his look outward at the spectator, Rall argues that "the gaze of the model checks the gaze of the spectator" rather than engaging it (97).

The Cruise star image is writ large in "the erotic portraits published in the 1990 issue of *Rolling Stone* taken by Herb Ritts, a gay fashion photographer, famous for Levi's market-influencing campaign displaying male semi-nudes and Hollywood star portraits" (Rall 96). The cover image drips with invitations to desire:

> The magazine's cover presents Cruise in a high angle shot dressed in jeans and a ripped tank top, walking from the sea, the water splashing around his thighs. Smiling invitingly, his gaze meets the onlookers . . . and invites the viewer's gaze. The open lips show off shiny, white, yet irregular teeth. The splashing water as well as the wetness of the muscular bronze body and the clothes, which give the shirt a body-sculpting and transparent quality, enhance the erotic subtext of the image: . . . [the body] is clearly situated with the frame of pleasure. The photograph . . . invites the female as well as the male gaze by conveying the stunning presence of a playful, exhibitionistic man in front of the camera.   (96)

This embodiment of Tom Cruise—willingly and playfully engaging the spectator, an object of desire and an object of commerce, confident in his masculinity and its display—invites fascination.

Reception of Cruise's films illustrates the centrality of his body and his charismatic intensity for the Cruise star image. Throughout the decade, critics use this intersection to present and evaluate his film performances. In her review of *Born on the Fourth of July*, Janet Maslin homed in on this key to Cruise's performance of masculinity—to become Ron Kovic, Cruise's star image had to be destroyed (*New York Times*, 31 December 1989): "The tremendous effectiveness of his performance in this film is as much a function of who he is as what he does. A perfect physical embodiment of health and strength; a reserved, polite figure with a soft voice and gentle manner;

an eager hard worker. The waste and betrayal of these shining virtues, as conveyed by Mr. Cruise's very presence, is a dreadful thing." In *Playboy* (January 1990), Cruise validates the depth of his intensity, passion, and willingness to portray what Raya Morag calls "disabled and/or impotent masculinity in the post-traumatic cinema" (201): "I remember saying, 'Ron, I promise you—I *promise* you, this film will get made. I promise you that I will give every inch of my soul and my ability to try to make this come to life and be as great as I feel that it should be'" ("Tom Cruise Gets Intense," *Playboy*, January 1990, 59). In appreciation, Kovic gave Cruise his Bronze Star (*Premiere*, February 1990, 56).

As Cruise diversified his range, his "playful exhibitionism" and intensity underscored diverse performances: signs of immaturity to be tamed (Cole Trickle in *Days of Thunder* and Joseph Donnelly in *Far and Away*) or commandeered to support a difficult mission (Mitch McDeere in *The Firm* and Lt. Daniel Kaffee in *A Few Good Men*); a foundation of manly energy (Jerry Maguire and Ethan Hunt in *Mission: Impossible*); signs to be evacuated (Dr. William Harford in *Eyes Wide Shut*); and energizing crude lust (Lestat and Frank T.J. Mackey in *Magnolia*).

In *Days of Thunder* and *Far and Away*, Cruise's "playful exhibitionism" held the screen. *Days of Thunder* was the first production of the company that would become a powerhouse of action films, Simpson/Bruckheimer Productions. "Tom Cruise" screams across the screen in the credits. *Variety* (1 January 1990) enjoyed "Cruise's likable grin and charming vulnerability" as the cocky young guy who learns from older men and matures to become a winner. Desson Howe chortled, "And it must also be [screenwriter Robert] Towne who makes [Nicole] Kidman actually call Cruise, yes, an infantile egomaniac. You gotta love him for that alone" (*Washington Post*, 29 June 1990). In *Far and Away*, Cruise's bare-chested bare-knuckled boxing was an audience lure. "Cruise's physicality is forcibly in evidence, which will not be unwelcome to his many fans. Stripped down frequently he is generally impressive in the fisticuffs action of pic's midsection" (*Variety*, 11 May 1992). Hal Hinson found the film infused with Cruise's "manly aroma" (*Washington Post*, 22 May 1992).

In the thrillers *A Few Good Men* and *The Firm*, Cruise played the smart, young, educated guy forced to become a cunning professional to combat corporate or military malevolence, a role that Howe dubbed "a testosteronal David" (*Washington Post*, 11 December 1992). With growing maturity as an actor, Cruise demonstrated his ability to command the lead of genre films where the plot twists as his character develops. Cruise stood up well against actors with considerable screen presence: Demi Moore and Jack Nicholson;

Cruise's performance as a college-educated and cunning professional in *A Few Good Men* (Rob Reiner, Columbia, 1992) helped establish him as a matinee idol. Now he evoked comparisons with Tyrone Power and Robert Redford. Courtesy Photofest New York.

Gene Hackman and Ed Harris. With *A Few Good Men* and *The Firm*, Cruise established himself as a matinee idol, evoking comparisons to good-looking old Hollywood star Tyrone Power and new Hollywood star Robert Redford (*Variety*, 28 June 1993).

Rather than continue in this strong métier, Cruise engaged his most controversial role to date in *Interview with the Vampire*. McCarthy's observation that Cruise brought a "high want-to-see and curiosity factor" to the film was an understatement (*Variety*, 7 November 1994). There was noisy and angry response to the casting (author Anne Rice complained in public; producer David Geffen defended the casting; Rice recanted after she saw the film) and concern about whether Cruise could deliver the eroticism of the vampire (see Morton). The controversy was fueled by Maslin's report in the *New York Times* that "the material's homosexual nuances have been toned down at Mr. Cruise's insistence" (11 November 1994), a rumor echoed by Mark Ebner in *Spy* (qtd. in Ehrenstein 324).

Scarlet Street: The Magazine of Mystery and Horror covered the adaptation, probing issues of casting and Hollywood pressures. The cover of this genre magazine played up homoerotism: "Tom Cruise & Brad Pitt: Vampires in Love!" (and in ruffled shirts). *Scarlet Street* explored the implications of the star-character relationship, finding justification for the casting in Cruise's previous film roles: "The Lestat of *Interview*, the first novel in the series, is shallow, gratuitously cruel, and not even especially intelligent, just clever. . . . Since Cruise has had considerable success playing selfish, manipulative young men . . . this early incarnation of Lestat may be well within his range" ("Lestat Lives!" 30). Director Neil Jordan evoked similarities between vampires and Hollywood stars: "The description of vampires in the book as young, eternally youthful, and unnaturally perfect creatures—to me, they had to be Hollywood stars, because that's what a Hollywood star is, you know?" (30).

In a parallel to her review of *Born on the Fourth of July*, Maslin delved into the transformation of "noted nonvampire" (read: heterosexual) Cruise into "the most commanding and teasingly malicious of Ms. Rice's creations": "Talk about *Risky Business*: here is the most clean-cut of American movie stars, decked out in ruffles and long blond wig, gliding insinuatingly through a tale in which he spiritually seduces another foppish, pretty young man. And here is the surprise; Mr. Cruise is flabbergasting right for this role. The vampire Lestat . . . brings out in Mr. Cruise a fiery, mature sexual magnetism he has not previously displayed on screen. Except for a few angry outbursts here, there are no signs of the actor's usual boyishness."

Lestat may be seducing Louis, but fan discourse disavowed gendered vampire eroticism. *Scarlet Street* explained: "Eroticism is neither homo nor hetero and doesn't focus on gender or genitalia. . . . It's a very erotic movie, but its eroticism is not to do with sexuality. It has nothing do with gender. It's to do with the urge to take the victim, which is an erotic urge. The taking of blood is very sexual" (31). Like rumors about homosexual encounters with Cruise, vampire eroticism is a metaphor for the sexual act.

Jordan maintained that Cruise "didn't balk at portraying Lestat's evil nature or his sexual versatility" and denied allegations that Cruise was uncomfortable with the sexual aspects of the story: "Not true, no. Very far from true. He's great, you know. He's wonderful. . . . Tom was exploring aspects of dramaturgy and characterization that he'd never explored before" (31). Carole Zucker finds Cruise's performance inflected by "Jordan's penchant for working close to the edge and for placing viewers in a position of discomfort where they must traverse a network of conflicting moods and emotions" (205). Lestat under Neil Jordan is very like Dr. Harford under Stanley Kubrick in *Eyes Wide Shut*. The masculinities of Lestat's ruffled dandy and of Hanford's tuxedoed society doctor strayed far from Cruise's star image and presented a challenge to reception.

After *Interview with the Vampire*, Cruise displayed powerful physicality, maturity as an actor, and the ability to hold a big-budget actioner as secret agent Ethan Hunt in *Mission: Impossible*. In the DVD special feature, *Mission: Remarkable, 40 Years of Creating the Impossible*, Cruise talks about how much fun it would be to make a film from the television show he loved as a kid. Producing partner Paula Wagner explains that Cruise is "physically agile and coordinated" and "actually does his own stunts." The DVD shows spread-eagled Cruise fearlessly dropping precipitously from on high to stop only inches before the camera lens waiting below. The *New York Times* crowed, "Having held the patent for more than a decade on Hollywood's notion of yuppie conqueror with a gold-plated conscience, Tom Cruise has found the prefect superhero character on which to graft his breathlessly gung-ho screen personality" ("Mission Accepted: Tom Cruise as Super-hero," 22 May 1996). *Variety* agreed: "And he looks great, too; his newly buff biceps get so much screen time they deserve separate billings" (20 May 1996).

Although grounded in Cruise's friendly masculinity, Jerry Maguire led the way to the edgier characters that Cruise would play at the end of the decade in *Magnolia* and *Eyes Wide Shut*. For *Variety*, *Jerry Maguire* reached back to the young man of *Risky Business*, but tempered him with insecurities and struggle: "Since as long ago as 'Risky Business,' Cruise has specialized in playing slick operators who get what they want. This is Jerry Maguire at the beginning, but the majority of the film has him hanging by a thread, often in embarrassing positions, and the actor conveys this with his cus-tomary enthusiasm as well as with a self-deprecatory quality and humor that are new and welcome. One can truly credit him with a fine perform-ance" (9 December 1996). Maslin appreciated how Cruise's performance deftly moderated the masculinity of his star image: "Mr. [Cameron] Crowe makes clever use of his leading man's golden-boy aspects. . . . It's a compli-cated role, one that requires [Cruise] to master the manner of a blowhard . . . while suggesting the better hidden side of Jerry is ready to be coaxed out" (*New York Times*, 13 December 1996).

In the two art films that end the 1990s, Cruise went further in playing with and against "his golden-boy carapace" (Janet Maslin, *New York Times*, 19 July 1999). Dennis Bingham finds in *Eyes Wide Shut* a parallel to the "var-ious and durable formula" of Cruise's films that "knock him off his pedestal and make him earn back his confidence in a maturer framework" (253). Bingham sees in Cruise's performance the Brechtian "heroic Everyman tradition" in which Kubrick "uses the heroic male star type and the performer who signifies that type less like an actor and more like a model" (254). Cruise's bold masculinity disappears, thus inviting audiences and fans to ponder what Cruise's star image is and can be. Bingham's analysis and Rall's description of Cruise's cover photos both conclude that the model does not engage the spectator the way the charismatic movie star does. In *Variety*, Todd McCarthy pondered how to understand a Cruise performance that turned away from engagement: "Where this leaves Cruise is the film's most debatable issue. At face value, the star gives a limited, emotionally constrained, eyebrow-crinkling and grimacing performance, nor is he entirely convincing as an established favorite doctor to Gotham's elite. On the other hand, it can be argued that the actor, who has none of the big thesping demands placed upon him that the women do, despite being onscreen nearly continuously, generously hands the picture over to his several outstanding female partners by allowing them to shine" (12 July 1999).

Meanwhile, *Playgirl* reveled in anticipation of the promise that *Eyes Wide Shut* would expose Cruise's literal sexuality onscreen. Rall finds in "*Playgirl* editor Nancy S. Martin's standing offer to feature Cruise in a nude pictorial . . . not simply the address of a fan but an offer from a business person" and offers a reminder, "One should not forget that a large group of *Playgirl*'s consumers are not women but gay men" (96). In 1999, *Playgirl* featured Cruise two months in a row. The November issue promoted "TOM CRUISE All The Right NUDES!" on the cover. Inside, photos of Cruise in his underpants in *Risky Business* accompany an alleged sighting of Cruise's penis in *All the Right Moves* (1983), "first flashing his fantastic behind then exposing The Firm little guy in a skintellating nude scene that bulged eyeballs and moistened panties around the globe." A yellow arrow emblazoned with "$20,000,0000 [*sic*] Cruise Missile" points to a blurry image. The story goes on to misrepresent, or perhaps participate in the buzz about, the sexuality in *Eyes Wide Shut*: "Lucky for us, age has only increased his appeal. . . . *Eyes Wide Shut* [has] plenty of fascinating flesh—especially in an orgasmic orgy scene."

Playgirl's December cover declares Cruise one of "the 10 sexiest men of 1999." The issue spins fantasy scenarios about Cruise in *Eyes Wide Shut*, before returning to *Risky Business*, the *ur*-source of sexual pleasure in Cruise's star image: "We wouldn't mind letting Dr. Bill Harford take a look at us— only unlike some of his patients, we'd want to be conscious for the exam. Make ours a pelvic!" (25). *Playgirl* celebrates the longevity of Cruise's sexual appeal: "The 37-year-old firecracker who has kept us *coming* back *multiple* times since *Risky Business*" (December 1999; emphasis in original). Even as Cruise presents an art-film performance that creatively depletes the masculinity of his star image, fans seek to be grounded in his sexuality.

Cruise's performance as the crude high-energy misogynist hustler in *Magnolia* was easier to grasp and appreciate. Emmanuel Levy in *Variety*: "A superlative ensemble headed by Tom Cruise" (10 December 1999). Maslin in the *New York Times*: *Magnolia*'s "biggest surprise is Tom Cruise in the role of a strutting, obscenity-spouting cult figure" (17 December 1999). As with *Eyes Wide Shut*, reception of *Magnolia* cannot resist reaching back to *Risky Business*. Rita Kempley notes that Cruise "hasn't danced in his underpants since 1983's 'Risky Business,' but he does it here with mischievous energy. He is sexy, funny, infuriating and, yes, vulnerable, in the role of Frank Mackey" (*Washington Post*, 7 January 2000). Not everyone raved. As early as 1990 Michael Pye had complained, "By now, Cruise's range and energy have been called 'surprising' much too often" (*Independent*, 18 March). Yet fans and critics continued to embrace the energetic young man of *Risky Business*, the constantly renewing template for the strength and power of Cruise's masculinity.

☆☆★★★ Tom Hanks: A Human Center

After underwhelming in *Joe Versus the Volcano* and *Bonfire of the Vanities* (both 1990), Hanks expanded his range as a dissipated women's league coach in *A League of Their Own* (1992), a grieving single father in *Sleepless in Seattle*, and a gay lawyer with AIDS in *Philadelphia*. In his last films of the 1990s, Hanks played roles set in the sweep of U.S. history: the savant with a low I.Q. in *Forrest Gump*, astronaut Jim Lovell in *Apollo 13* (1995), and Captain Miller in *Saving Private Ryan*. He brought charm to the chain bookstore executive in the romantic comedy *You've Got Mail* (1998) and the prison guard in the magical *The Green Mile* (1999). Hanks directed, wrote, acted in, and wrote songs for a movie about a 1960s pop group, *That Thing You Do!* (1996). He voiced Sheriff Woody in *Toy Story* (1995) and *Toy Story 2* (1999).

In addition to this prolific film activity, Hanks worked in television throughout the decade. He was a popular and willing television comedian, hosting "Saturday Night Live" three times in the decade: in 1990 with Aerosmith, 1992 with Bruce Springsteen, and 1996 with Tom Petty and the Heartbreakers. In the early nineties, Hanks acted in and directed episodes of cable horror-ghost series: "Tales from the Crypt" (HBO, 1992), "Fallen Angels" (Showtime, 1993), and "Vault of Horror" (HBO, 1994). At the end of the decade, Hanks executive-produced and hosted the award-winning HBO miniseries about the U.S. space program, "From the Earth to the Moon" (1998). He directed the opening part, for which he received an Emmy nomination, and made writing contributions to four others. As executive producer, he was recognized with Golden Globe, Emmy, and Producers Guild of America awards, among many others.

In the reception of Hanks's performances, attributes of his star image and expectations for his screen characters emerge. His acting is thoughtful. He is physically malleable and able to embody personality. He brings likeability and humanity to flawed and extraordinary men—through his ordinary body, poignant eyes, and beefy face. He has respect for and generosity toward his characters. He is able to open characters to the audience. He brings to the screen characters that no one else could.

With *Forrest Gump* came parallels to Spencer Tracy, the first to win back-to-back Academy Awards for Best Actor, for *Boys Town* (1936) and *Captains Courageous* (1937). In *Saving Private Ryan* and *You've Got Mail* (a remake of Ernst Lubitsch's *The Shop Around the Corner* [1940]), Hanks called to mind Jimmy Stewart, who also played vulnerable guys in romantic comedies and dramatic roles. "He shares Stewart's lovely way of speaking from the heart," observes Maslin (*New York Times*, 18 December 1998). By the end of the decade, Hanks was comfortably ensconced in the firmament of screen performers.

But the 1990s began with two films that disappointed. In *Joe versus the Volcano*, Hanks "indulges himself in some rather unfunny solo bits" (*Variety*, 1 January 1990). In an otherwise "grim" experience, Vincent Canby saw "a carefully thought-out performance" (*New York Times*, 9 March 1990). For Desson Howe, "Hanks is the only reason you'd want to see the movie" (*Washington Post*, 9 March 1990). Hanks agreed that he was miscast in *The Bonfire of the Vanities* (1990): "Me, the master of the universe!" For Canby, "He's nobody's idea of a prototypical Yale man . . . but he's a good comic actor" (*New York Times*, 21 December 1990). Rita Kempley offered sympathy: "Tom Hanks, poor dear, seems more like a lamb led to the slaughter. . . . Nobody wants to see a marshmallow like Hanks get roasted" (*Washington Post*, 21 December 1990). Hanks's likeability survived the film.

A League of Their Own and *Sleepless in Seattle* presented Hanks with roles and stories that were up to his skills. With his easy screen presence, he brought kindly humor to the loutish antics of the over-the-hill coach of a women's league baseball team during World War II. Hanks's pudgy, stubbly face, ordinary body, and revealing eyes tempered the character's eccentricities and flaws. This ability to infuse performance with human frailties would mark Hanks's career for the rest of the decade. Canby raved: "His Jimmy Dugan is a priceless, very graceful eccentric. With his work here, there can be no doubt that Mr. Hanks is now one of Hollywood's most accomplished and self-assured actors" (*New York Times*, 25 June 1993). In *Sleepless in Seattle*, a romantic comedy, Hanks plays an insecure and fragile single father. In *Variety*, Brian Lowry noted Hanks's "almost tangible grief" as a widower and concluded, "Hanks certainly figures to increase his stock as a well-rounded actor and not just a comic" (1 January 1993).

Hanks was delivering multifaceted and intricate masculinity, men whose wisdom and strength were tempered with fragility. Critics reiterated their mantra: his performances brought ordinary qualities to the screen and he connected with audiences on a human level. With *Philadelphia*, reception of Hanks's performances noted the exceptional challenges and complexity of his roles. Critics began to locate Hanks as the only screen actor who could have brought these characters to the screen.

For *Philadelphia*, Hanks not only received accolades for a performance of depth and humanity as a gay lawyer with AIDS, he was credited with making a success of the mainstream message film. Todd McCarthy in *Variety*: "Whatever else might nag about the film's treatment of a difficult subject, Hanks constantly connects on the most basic human level" (7 December 1993). Maslin in the *New York Times*: "In the end, thanks to such effects (makeup, camera, editor, production design) and to the simple grace of Mr. Hanks' performance . . . *Philadelphia* rises above its flaws to convey the full urgency of its difficult subject, and to bring that subject home" (22 December 1993). There can be no doubt that Hanks's performance as Andy Beckett fostered his offscreen legitimacy when he managed the press controversy about playing a homosexual.

Andy Beckett and Forrest Gump were both sweet and intelligent men who brought sunny dispositions to life's tragedies. Andy coped with AIDS with a quiet courage, dancing gracefully with an IV stand while listening to a recording of Maria Callas (see Fuqua). Forrest was "another career triumph for Hanks" (*Variety*, 11 July 1994). For Maslin, Hanks was "the only major American movie star who could have played Forrest without condescension. . . . [A] touching, imaginatively childlike . . . sweet, guileless performance" (*New York Times*, 6 July 1994).

As astronaut Jim Lovell in *Apollo 13*, Hanks "gives the film a human center, someone with whom the audience can easily feel at home" (*Variety*, 23 June 1995). Maslin agreed: Hanks is "the Everyone in the driver's seat" and "the empathy factor for 'Apollo 13' is through the roof. This actor's way of amplifying the ordinary side of an extraordinary character remains supremely fine-tuned" (*New York Times*, 30 June 1995). Hanks does not need to be bodily present for this achievement. When he voiced Sheriff Woody in *Toy Story* and *Toy Story 2*, the animated character became "instantly sympathetic" (*New York Times*, 22 November 1995).

Even when Hanks stepped aside from monumental screen roles to make a lightweight pop band movie, his star image saturated *That Thing You Do!* For Emmanuel Levy, "The best thing to be said about Hanks' feature debut is that it bears all the elements that have made him a movie star: boyish charm, natural ease, comic precision and, above all, generosity of spirit" (*Variety*, 16 September 1996). Maslin complimented Hanks for taking "something other than the standard movie-star route to directorial distinctions." Although the film is "lightweight and undemandingly likable . . . [i]t's to Mr. Hanks's considerable credit that this approach never turns saccharine or stiff" (*New York Times*, 4 October 1996).

For *Saving Private Ryan*, Steven Spielberg and Hanks received the U.S. Navy's highest civilian honor, the Distinguished Public Service Award ("Biography: Tom Hanks, The Luckiest Man in the World"). As a teacher thrust into heroism while reluctantly doing his duty, Hanks's ordinary man negotiated Captain Miller through the sweep of World War II. McCarthy wrote, "One comes to see clearly a decent man of the sort that America was theoretically meant to produce, and perhaps did during the generation in question" (*Variety*, 1 July 1998). In Hanks he saw "James Stewart's move into more complex, conflicted and bitter characters—in his case, after his World War II experience." Maslin raved about the way that Hanks declined heroics: "Never have Hanks' everyman qualities been more instantly effective than here. . . . There's nothing stellar about the way Hanks gives the film such substance and pride. As in 'Apollo 13,' his is a modest, taciturn brand of heroism. . . . [Miller is] a decent, strong, fallible man who sustains his courage while privately confounded by the extent that war has now shaped him" (*New York Times*, 24 July 1998). *You've Got Mail* continued the Stewart and Tracy parallels, with *Variety* seeing that he "meshes the boyish charm of Jimmy Stewart with the earthy integrity of Spencer Tracy" (14 December 1998), and the *New York Times* plumbing the depths of the comparison: "And he continues to amaze. Once again, he fully inhabits a new role without any obvious actorly behavior, to the point where comparisons to James Stewart . . . really cannot be avoided. Though he has none of Stewart's lanky grace or leading-man patina, the wonderful Hanks has all the same romantic wistfulness and the same poignant shyness. . . . He shares Stewart's lovely way of speaking from the heart" (Janet Maslin, 18 December 1998). With Hanks's last film of the decade, *The Green Mile*, Maslin brought the discussion to a close: Hanks is "so unaffectedly good that it has become redundant to say so" (*New York Times*, 10 December 1999).

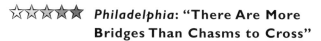 *Philadelphia*: "There Are More Bridges Than Chasms to Cross"

Anxieties about a straight male actor playing a gay character circulated openly in the press when *Philadelphia* opened. On "CBS This Morning" (23 December 1993), Harry Smith asked Hanks about the possibility that his fans would react with anger regarding his choice of role. Hanks avoided addressing homophobia directly and segued instead into an argument for human rights:

> *SMITH:* There's a whole group of people in America who are going to find the idea of this movie abhorrent, the idea of their beloved Tom Hanks playing a gay guy . . . how do you get past that? . . .
>
> *HANKS:* Well, no one is campaigning for anybody to like anybody else. The case is do we have guaranteed to us the right to pursue our own individual happiness, taking into account all of our responsibilities and all of our laws absolutely. I think I'm a better actor and a better human being after doing this movie and you can't always say that.

At the end of the interview, co-host Giselle Fernandez sighed, "Such a courageous undertaking and such a different Tom Hanks."

In the *Los Angeles Chronicle*, Edward Guthmann situated Hanks in a history of male straight-to-gay performances and the rumors that a homosexual performance could engender: "Al Pacino did it. William Hurt did it. Michael Caine's done it more than once, and so has Richard Gere. Prominent screen actors, especially in the last decade, have played gay roles without serious jeopardy to their careers. And yet, the notion persists that gay roles leave a stain of identification on an actor—a lingering question of "Is he really . . . ?" (9 January 1994).

In his response to homophobia in Hollywood, Hanks evoked his star image and personal security: "I honestly don't see how there's a risk involved. . . . One of the reasons is this cheerful, nonthreatening image that I have. . . . I mean, if the studio is looking for someone to dispel whatever fears people have about the subject . . . I'm probably the perfect guy" (Edward Guthmann, *San Francisco Chronicle*, 9 January 1994). Tom Green in *USA Today* asked, "You have kids, will your playing this role be tough on them?" Hanks: "I told my kids that there may be a circumstance where people are going to say, 'Your dad's a fag!' If you want to answer them, you could say, 'My dad's an actor!' They are very hip kids" (20 December 1993).

In *Newsweek*, Hanks offered the public a vivid picture of homosexual desire, referencing the actor who played his partner, Miguel, in the film: "People are saying that I was bold to do this, that it was a courageous choice. I don't see it. It's bold for me to what? To play a man who goes to sleep in Antonio Banderas' arms every night? Who has sexual intercourse with him somehow? Is that what's bold? As a society we should be beyond that" (14 February 1994). And to *USA Today* he mused on the diversity of Banderas's star image and possibilities of attraction: "I'm the envy of most of the women of the world—and quite a few of the men, from what I understand" (20 December 1993).

Asked by a caller to "Larry King Live" what he had learned from the role, Hanks responded: "Single-handedly, without question, how much I have in common, how much we all have in common, me specifically, with an awful lot of men out there who are supposed to be so different from us" (13 January 1994). Near the end of the King interview, a call came in from Los Angeles. It was Rita Wilson, Hanks's wife: "Honey, I just want to tell you, if I wasn't married to you, I'd have to get married to you right now after those things you said. . . . You look really cute. . . . I'm calling to say, Honey, come home." Hanks: "All right, yeah, heat up the burritos, Honey, I'm on my way." Secure in his masculinity, or at least in his heterosexual marriage, the great actor with a sunny disposition goes home to a loving and supportive wife.

The film also met with criticism from gay viewers. A frequent complaint was the absence of explicit gay sexuality and that the film depicted "normal-with-a-vengeance gay characters . . . [behaving] with such chaste, com-radely restraint that half the audience isn't sure whether they're boyfriends or just very devoted roommates" (Cunningham). In response, Hanks situated the couple's relationship within his own everyman experience: "These guys have been together for nine years. They're once-a-weekers at best. I've been with my wife now for 10 years. And the number of times we actually smooch in public is probably declining. It's just the nature of things" ("Playing the Part: Straight Tom Hanks Gives a Lesson on Being Gay," *Newsweek*, 14 February 1994, 46). To gay activist Larry Kramer's critique that the film "doesn't portray gay life realistically," Hanks argued that Andy and Miguel's sexual relationship could be intuited from other signifiers of intimacy: "There are other ways to show that these two gay men loved each other and would love each other for the rest of their lives" ("Larry King Live," 13 January 1994), as when Andy and Miguel dance at a costume party. Notably, Hanks defended the film without overt mention of Hollywood's constraints on representation.

In his Oscar speech, Hanks gave a moving and eloquent invocation. He applauded his high school drama teacher and a classmate, "two of the finest gay Americans. . . . I had the good fortune to fall under their inspiration at a very young age. I wish my babies could have the same sort of teacher, the same sort of friend." The next day, on "CBS This Morning," Hanks explained: "I just wanted to be able to point out the fact that the idea of our movie is that tolerance is practiced every day. . . . If I had been afraid of these men in 1973 and 1974, I wouldn't be where I was today."

☆☆☆☆★ Gay Rumors: "Fans' Willingness to Believe" Tom Cruise Is Straight

Rumors about Cruise being gay became an attribute of his star image in the 1990s, prompted not only by *Interview with the Vampire* but also by Cruise's physicality and energetic engagement with spectators. Cruise had a twofold response to rumors: spin and lawsuits. For spin, a 1994 *Vanity Fair* interview became a source to counter rumors as other media picked up items discussed in the story. The lawsuits were not about denial of gay pleasure in his films. Rather, they were attempts to quash published allegations of homosexual encounters and thus protect the heterosexual foundations of the relationship between Cruise's fans and the star and the characters he played. Cruise gave two responses to the gay rumors: "Tom Cruise the person" declared his openness to diverse interpretations and people of diverse sexualities; "Tom Cruise the commercial commodity" protected his status as a movie star.

Like Rall, Gaylyn Studlar argues that the performance of masculinity that made Cruise a star also made him an object of heterogeneous pleasure: "Cruise's performances of masculinity played out through the beautiful male body have allowed him to become an erotic sign that can be appropriated by more than heterosexual female audiences" (182). Studlar explains that it is because of Hollywood commercial cinema's "need to exploit a star's appeal to the broadest possible demographic (one that at the very least includes spectators of both genders)" (173) that the "transgressive quality of Cruise's screen embodiment exists extratextually as well as textually as both a homoerotic and a heteroerotic sign" (174).

Rall and Studlar demonstrate that Cruise's homoerotic appeal predates *Interview with the Vampire* by a decade. But his "mature sexual magnetism" as Lestat and promotion of the vampire film opened the door for discussion of Cruise's sexuality. The defensive positions are familiar: he is an actor, he makes films, he has a family life. Cruise does not deny or protest the possibility of homoerotic pleasure in *Interview with the Vampire*. In an interview with Ingrid Sischy, Cruise stated, "There is an eroticism. But I think if someone is a homosexual, to them it will be homoerotic. And if they're not homosexual, it will be heteroerotic" (*Interview*, November 1994). In fact, the trailer for *Interview with the Vampire*, with its man-to-man gazes through filmy curtains, is available on tomcruise.com.

The first major interview in the press coverage for *Interview with the Vampire* was in *Vanity Fair* in October 1994: "The all-American brand-name hero with a winsome smile and a winning plan. But will the public buy him as the bitchy, bisexual star?" The story brings home the key points. On the cover: "Tom Opens Up: Tom Cruise on Sex, Marriage and Romancing the Vampire." Paul Newman, his co-star in *The Color of Money* (1986), on Cruise: "It's tough when fame happens as fast as it did with Tom. So far he's kept his head on his shoulders, but he's one of the very, very few." Cruise on Kidman: "It was that special connection when you recognize your soul mate. Nicole is a person who *understands*" (emphasis in original). Kidman on Cruise: "He was just the most incredible, unusual man I'd ever met. He's *amazingly* romantic" (emphasis in original). Cruise on Scientology: "People ask me, 'So what is Scientology?' I say, 'Hey, if you want to know, read a book about it.'" Cruise on rumors: "But look at all the stuff that I've heard about myself. That I'm a misogynist. I'm a homosexual. I'm brainless. How can I be all of these things? So you've just got to go, Hey! What the fuck! Sometimes I'll turn to Nic and say 'Let's just live our lives and keep doing what we're doing.' . . . I could spend my time going around saying *that's* not true and *that's* not true and *that's* not true. But I've got so much stuff going on in my life that I'd rather spend the morning with my daughter and my wife and taking care of work."

References to the *Vanity Fair* interview appeared widely elsewhere, such as in *USA Today* (6 September 1994, 2D; 17 February 1995, 2D); *The Independent* (27 October 1994, 32); *Hollywood Reporter* (7 June 1995, 3); *New York Daily News* (6 June 1995, 14); and many more. Soundbites from the interview were circulated: Kidman's defense of Cruise's heterosexuality, Cruise's denial of the rumors but openness to homosexuality, and Cruise's response to concerns about Scientology.

Conducted by the out editor of *Interview*, Kevin Sessums (see mississippi sissy.com), "Cruise Speed" begins with the action and energy of Sessums and Cruise somersaulting in a biplane over the coast of California. Janet Maslin and Roger Ebert provide credibility for Cruise as an actor, arguing that his performances extend beyond his star image. Maslin: "The times he has been great are the times when someone uses that healthy, handsome thing of his, yet leaves him wounded and bewildered by it." Ebert: "Cruise is both a genuine star and a genuine actor, although not always at the same time." Industry power brokers validate Cruise as a filmmaking professional. Jeffrey Katzenberg (Walt Disney Studios): "Tom keeps putting himself at risk as an artist." David Geffen (producer of *Interview with the Vampire*), speaking of the casting controversy: "People are such fools when it comes to these kinds of issues. . . . I know how sensitive Tom is and I knew it would hurt his feelings."

The interview segues into the presence in the film of "the homoerotic strains that are so prevalent in the novel": " 'This is the way I feel about the homoerotic issue: I don't care either way,' confesses Cruise. 'It's nothing I worry about. I'm an actor and I play a character. I do find it a very *sensual* movie, because everything Lestat does he does out of *love* and *longing*—yet, he's *sadistic*' " (emphasis in original). Sessums asks directly about the rumors: "Part of the burden of stardom is suffering all of the rumor mongering. In Cruise's case, the rumors involve that he is a closeted homosexual. 'Why do you think people keep whispering about you being gay,' I ask him. Cruise answers, 'First of all, I don't think it's an indictment. . . . It's not true but people are going to say what they want to say.'" Sessums asks Cruise a key question about Hollywood commercial cinema: "Do you think an actor can be open about his homosexuality and still be as giant a movie star as you are?" Cruise answers: "I believe now that anything is possible. Maybe I'm being naïve. But I think that is becoming *not* a big issue."

The interview tempers the hot topics of homoeroticism and Scientology with domestic stories about Cruise's family life, his marriage to Kidman, and changes in their lifestyle with the recent adoption of their first child, a daughter. Sessums delves into the Cruise biography of growing up in a family of women, his parents' divorce, and the death of his father ("Until now he has steadfastly refused to discuss the man's absence from his life"). The *Vanity Fair* interview about *Interview with the Vampire* was an opportunity to resituate Cruise as family man, risk-taking actor, and professional, someone coping with the downside of being a huge star.

While *Interview with the Vampire* provided a canvas for Cruise to dispel rumors about homosexuality, the actor also filed lawsuits to dispel allegations of homosexual activity. For gay cultural critics, the lawsuits prompted an exploration of the effects of homosexuality rumors in Hollywood, what it means to be gay or straight as an actor, and Cruise's reflections on homosexual desire. The lawsuits and the critical reflection suggest that sexual identity undergirds the relationship of fan, star, and character.

The lawsuits certainly quashed the commercial viability of the rumors. *McCall's*, a mainstream publication, headlined its February 1995 issue with "Tom Cruise and Nicole Kidman: Can They Survive the Rumors?" ("that Mr. Cruise is sterile or homosexual . . . or that they married for any reason other than mutual love and respect"), then, two months later, printed this apology: "*McCall's* understands that some may have assumed these statements to be true, and regrets any negative effect that may have resulted from repeating the rumors."

"They Cruise Straight to Libel Win," the *New York Daily News* reported (30 October 1998, 14), announcing that Cruise and Kidman had won a libel suit against the *Express* of London for alleging "that the couple, who are Scientologists, married on the orders of their religion to cover up their homosexual inclinations." In 2001, Cruise filed two $100 million defamation lawsuits against men who claimed, in the media, to have had homosexual affairs with him (*Hollywood Reporter*, 5 June 2001; *Associated Press*, 3 May 2001).

In "That's Myth Tom to You," comedy writer Bruce Vilanch, writing with the credibility of an out celebrity—or at least self-defined celebrity ("I hear about these things")—offered an explanation about the persistence of rumors about Cruise: "The fact that we have wanted him to be gay for more than a decade has been translated in some minds into the fact that he is gay, which is, in fact, not a fact at all. That's what happens when rumors hang around long enough" (*The Advocate*, 3 July 2001). Vilanch credits the lawsuits with identifying not homophobia but "homophobiaphobia"—the fear of homophobes, the fear of coming out: "Someone has finally said that being gay can be a commercial liability, to the tune of $100 million. . . . It sets that stage for some brave star who really is gay to step out and prove that it isn't true." Or is it? Cruise's attorney stated the crux of the matter in the *Hollywood Reporter*: "The actor's career depends on his fans' 'willingness to believe that he does or could possess the qualities of the characters he plays'" (qtd. in Ehrenstein 328). The lawsuits take as their foundation an awareness of homophobia and the assumption that the commercial value of Cruise's star image would be adversely and fundamentally affected if tinged with homosexuality.

Despite lawsuits, rumors continued to have commercial viability. Cruise filed a "cease and desist" order against publisher William Morrow and Company about the 1998 publication of David Ehrenstein's *Open Secret: Gay Hollywood 1928–1998*. *The Advocate* (29 September 1998) quoted Cruise's attorneys: "We have been informed that the book repeats rumors that our client is homosexual. . . . Mr. Cruise is not homosexual, has never had a homosexual experience and is completely heterosexual." According to *Variety*, the attorneys were also protesting the book's allegation that the "Church of Scientology somehow controls all aspects of his life.' . . . While Cruise is not gay himself he 'does not disapprove of people who lead a homosexual lifestyle'" (31 August 1998).

Although Ehrenstein quipped, "I go to all this trouble to prove he's straight, and this is the thanks I get!" (*The Advocate*, 29 September 1998), the dust jacket of *Open Secret* exploits the rumors, claiming to answer "the world's most important question: 'is Tom Cruise gay?'" The answer? "Well, of course not. Sort of. And . . . well, it depends" (520). For the "of course not" answer, Ehrenstein calls upon his interviews with Chastity Bono and David Geffen, out celebrities who have personal knowledge of Cruise. For the more ambiguous answer, Ehrenstein points to the commercial value of Cruise's crossover appeal: he "has something to do with everyone. For that's why he gets the big bucks" (521).

Hanks and Cruise both took on dramatic roles that challenged them as screen artists. They were greeted with similar concerns about masculinity. Both stars stated their personal openness to sexual diversity, but they adopted somewhat different defensive positions in response to the "homo-phobiaphobia" of the Hollywood cinematic institution. For Cruise, homophobia exists and can trouble the relationship of fan-star-character. Hanks's press implies his fan-star-character nexus was secure enough to survive homophobia. Cruise and Hanks brought to light important issues for stars in Hollywood: what it means to be gay or straight as an actor; the commercial value of a star's crossover appeal; assumptions about fan and studio homophobia; assumptions about the verisimilitude that a star's sexuality brings to roles; and the sexual identity that appears to be the basis of the relationship of fan, star, and character.

8 ☆☆☆☆☆☆☆☆☆☆☆☆

Angela Bassett and Halle Berry
African American Leading Ladies

MIA MASK

      The complex and contradictory discourse of African American women's celebrity throughout the 1990s is clearly exemplified by the artistic accomplishments and professional endeavors of two towering talents and the institutional barriers they surmounted. Angela Bassett and Halle Berry stand out as iconic figures in American popular culture. Both

The portrait of Angela Bassett is reprinted here courtesy Photofest New York.

have become mainstream crossover film stars with national accolades and international name recognition. Their celebrity itself is remarkable given the paucity of quality scripts with substantive roles for women in general, women of color specifically, and black women in particular.

Actor-writer-director Kasi Lemmons—who performed small roles in *School Daze* (1988), *The Silence of the Lambs* (1991), and *Candyman* (1992)—has spoken openly about the paucity of quality roles for women of color. After the release of *Eve's Bayou* in 1997, for example, Lemmons told *Ms.* magazine's Erika Muhammad, "As an actress I couldn't empty my soul because the parts I was playing (Black Girl Best Friend, Black Girl Next Door, Black Girl Cop) would not allow that sort of artistic relief. . . . I was frustrated" (March/April 1998, 74–75). This frustration ultimately led Lemmons into a career as a writer-director, during which she has created substantive roles for Lynn Whitfield, Debbie Morgan, and Diahann Carroll in *Eve's Bayou* (1997); for Aunjanue Ellis and Tamara Tunie in *Caveman's Valentine* (2001); and, more recently, for Taraji Henson in *Talk to Me* (2007).

Not only women directors have addressed the issue publicly; the academic community has responded with rigorous scholarship on stardom, exemplified by Mary Beltrán's provocative work. In her discussion of Hollywood's history of exoticizing Latinas, Beltrán acknowledges the relatively privileged position of Latinas and Latinos vis-à-vis other people of color within the American racial hierarchy (80). The academic literature parallels the journalistic community's response, which has repeatedly questioned Hollywood's exclusionary practices. Take Allison Samuels's "Why Can't a Black Actress Play the Girlfriend?" (*Newsweek*, 14 March 2005), which makes the same argument with inquisitive bravado, or Pamela Lambert's cover story "Hollywood Blackout" (*People*, 18 March 1996), as cases in point.

Angela Bassett and Halle Berry have confronted and surmounted these career frustrations with aplomb. Their extraordinary and—in some ways—parallel careers invite comparative analysis as a way of understanding their negotiation of the exclusionary practices of Hollywood and the American film industry more generally. Evaluating the similarities and differences between their career trajectories reveals the various ways these women have participated in the marketing and consumption of their star personas. Understanding their star personas requires knowledge of their background, identity politics, and personal positions on sensitive topics like nudity, sexuality, religion, and racial politics, since these inform their career goals and decisions to accept certain film projects and roles.

☆☆☆☆☆ Bassett and Berry Chart Their Hollywood Careers

Both Bassett and Berry proudly self-identify as African American. Their black pride clearly distinguishes them from some actors of color who have insisted their ethnicity or racial background is coincidental, irrelevant, or even an unacknowledged detail they would like audiences to kindly forget. For Berry and Bassett know well the difficulties of otherness, of being considered gender and racial minorities in predominantly white patriarchal Hollywood. Although Halle Berry's mother, Judith Berry, is Caucasian and her father, Jerome Berry, is African American, she has not identified as "biracial" or "multiracial," unlike countless other actresses, musicians, and entertainers who foreground or celebrate their multiraciality in interviews—Lisa Bonet, Alicia Keys, Mariah Carey, Dwayne "The Rock" Johnson, Tracee Ellis Ross, Vin Diesel, Veronica Webb, Thandie Newton, Nicole Ari Parker, Rosario Dawson, Jessica Alba, and Lenny Kravitz, among others. Berry, however, stands out as having precluded her biraciality from overdetermining her public persona. She credits her mother with having empowered her with a sense of racial pride in her African American heritage. While many young celebrities rightly feel proud of their mixed-race heritage, this newfound celebration of multiracial identity marks significant generational, demographic, and cultural shifts. It distinguishes those raised by parents influenced by the 1960s era of Black Pride from those raised by parents influenced by the 1980s millennial multiculturalism.

Berry's career was set in motion by a significant occurrence when she was seventeen years old. Without informing her, her boyfriend sent her high school yearbook photograph to the Miss Teen Ohio beauty pageant. Three weeks later she received a letter saying she had been selected as a finalist. Wearing her prom dress, she won the title of Miss Teen Ohio. She went on to compete in—and win—the 1985 Miss Teen All-American Pageant. According to biographer Frank Sanello, Berry has reflected on her "time with the tiara" with contradictory and sometimes critical remarks. In 2001, she remarked, "It was very shallow in many ways, because it perpetuated my physical self more than I ever wanted to, but it was very significant in a way because I gained confidence in myself" (Sanello 16–30). Bored with the modeling work that followed her beauty pageant experiences, she began taking acting classes and eventually moved to New York in 1989, where talent manager Vincent Cirrincione began managing her career. Only two months after relocating, Berry landed a role on a sitcom about something with which she was already familiar: modeling. The show was

ABC's "Living Dolls," a spin-off of the successful "Who's the Boss?" but it was a critical and commercial disaster and was canceled after only thirteen episodes, last appearing on 30 December 1989 (Sanello 26). Soon after, however, Berry's 1990 audition for Spike Lee's *Jungle Fever* helped relaunch her career, resulting in an unglamorous but highly visible role that enabled her to demonstrate the range of her talent.

Angela Bassett is also committed to her African American identity, family, and heritage. She has expressed and emphasized the importance of maintaining family roots, and she has appreciated the virtues of her modest southern upbringing. Growing up in St. Petersburg, Florida, Basset and her older sister, D'nette, were raised by their single mother in a housing project where everyone helped watch the girls while Mrs. Bassett was working at the state's juvenile welfare board. The actress told one interviewer that her mother didn't want her daughters duplicating any aspect of her own single-mother experience. Instead, she expected excellence from her girls, and excel is exactly what the Bassett girls did.

Angela's academic excellence took her to Yale, where she completed a bachelor's degree and, in 1983, an MFA in theater. After graduation she toured with the prestigious NEC (Negro Ensemble Company), one of the oldest theater companies in the United States dedicated to performing and promoting black theater; the group was also the subject of Bassett's undergraduate thesis (Hollinger 167). In addition to maintaining her commitment to family, community, and her religious faith over the years, Bassett has also shown a deep personal and academic interest in African American cultural idioms, displaying a down-to-earth mode of self-expression steeped in black vernacular culture. According to African American essayist Hilton Als, who in 1996 interviewed Bassett for the *New Yorker*, Basset smoothly transitions in and out of vernaculars. "In conversation," writes Als, "she indulges in many forms of black American colloquial speech, in the accents of her native St. Petersburg, Florida—'Mm-hmm,' 'Girlfriend,' 'You know what I'm sayin"—and with a jocularity that her control doesn't allow her to show onscreen, where she often portrays characters who never refer to their ethnicity in the company of white people (and hence the camera)" ("A Crossover Star," 29 April and 6 May 1996). Als was also one of the first to identify Bassett's "aura of dignity and pride," which is detectable by most spectators but stands out for African Americans who value her ability to represent the kind of dignified womanhood we know from our mothers, aunts, sisters, and cousins but that has historically been underrepresented in Hollywood films, mainstream television, print journalism, and interactive technologies.

While their upbringings (under the guidance of a watchful maternal eye) may have been similar and their professional pursuits as leading ladies likewise, the career trajectories of Berry and Bassett have diverged considerably. In fact, existing scholarship compares their career paths, recognizing Bassett as the classically trained dramatic artist and Berry as the commercially viable, eye-catching ingénue. Author Karen Hollinger, for example, has argued that "although Halle Berry won the distinction of being the first black star to win the Academy Award for Best Actress . . . Bassett's career has more longevity and is much more distinguished and accomplished overall" (165). Hollinger maintains that Bassett's "career trajectory, image configuration, and views on acting offer an interesting study of the difficult position of the black actress in the overwhelmingly white milieu of Hollywood filmmaking" (165). Hollinger's views typify the critical consensus and popular view. Even spectators and magazine readers have come to view Berry as celebrity sex symbol and commercial crossover star but envision Bassett as the formally educated, respectable, and reputable artist. Nowhere is this more evident than in the journalistic coverage of their careers, which corroborates the distinction between artist and sex symbol. For example, Berry has regularly appeared on magazine covers and has frequently been listed among the coveted A-lists of "the most inspiring Americans," "the sexiest people," and "the hottest stars." These lists are usually reserved for the rich, famous, and preternaturally beautiful (see *Essence*). Such rosters are merely an indication of popular sentiment and public perception rather than anything concrete or tangible.

Bassett's career is revealing because she has often chosen the politically minded, socially progressive problem pictures and television shows. For example, even after having established her box office mojo with many respectable roles, Bassett joined NBC's primetime hospital drama "ER" for the fifteenth and final season as a "tough-as-nails" attending physician (Marti Parham, *Jet*, 8 September 2008, 18). Playing resilient, ethical, and professional women is a niche Bassett has carved out for herself in film and television.

It stands to reason, given her background and formal certification, that Bassett would gravitate toward and cultivate a more sophisticated screen persona predicated on the careful selection of conservative, dignified female characters and family-based roles. In addition to her star discourse garnering enthusiastic popular press coverage, her powerful roles readily lend themselves to academic, discursive analysis. By contrast, Berry's pathway to celebrity may have harvested more coverage in fanzines, advertisements, and tabloids, but it also evokes suspicion, disapproval, and backlash since critics, scholars, and even audiences are wary of models-turned-movie-stars. As a society, we tend to look askance at such individuals, suspecting that otherwise talentless people have been cast for their good looks (or cheeky personality) alone. This sentiment is particularly acute in the era of reality TV and game-show programming, when charismatic contestants and winners alike seek to convert their telegenic personalities into celebrity franchises. Over the course of her career, Berry has been perceived as a similar kind of opportunist. In fact, some scholars have gone so far as to call for a boycott of her films on the basis of ideological criticism alone, without recognition of the ways she has pushed the envelope and broken barriers with strong performances in *Jungle Fever* (1991) and *Losing Isaiah* (1995) and her Academy Award for *Monster's Ball* (2001).

Berry's evolving career deserves consideration. She may have started out as a model with little experience, but like many before her she developed as an actor and leading lady. More important, she shares this career path with other Hollywood stars (black, white, Asian, and Latina). Long before the era of supermodels, some of the most celebrated American and European starlets began, or spent part of their careers, as models, cabaret singers, and nightclub entertainers (for example, Anna May Wong, Lauren Bacall, Rita Hayworth, Audrey Hepburn, Greta Garbo, Dorothy Dandridge, Cybill Shepard, Diana Ross, Rene Russo, Julia Roberts, and Angelina Jolie).

Like Bassett, Berry also offers an interesting study of the choices black actresses must make to succeed in an otherwise exclusionary, white, heterosexist, and predominantly male industry. Their respective career trajectories reveal something about the configuration of stardom and the varying brands of star charisma. Each represents a distinct brand of charisma: Bassett embodies black bourgeois respectability, unconditional maternal love, and sociopolitical responsibility. Berry aligned herself with hip-hop culture, urban sassiness, and coquettish sexuality in a multicultural era.

The divide between Berry's sensuality and Bassett's morality is even evident in box office returns. According to online industry databases, the average opening gross for a motion picture in which Bassett starred or was featured was roughly $10 million. By comparison, the same figure for Berry is estimated at $22 million. The fact that Berry's films have grossed twice as much is an indication of the different demographics to which the women's celebrity personas appeal. Berry has been more marketable in mainstream crossover pictures like *Bulworth* (1998) and franchise films such as *X-Men* (2000) because her celebrity charisma reached the youth market and a larger cross-section of the moviegoing population. Bassett, by contrast, always appealed to a more mature crowd with biography pictures like *Malcolm X* (1992) or *What's Love Got to Do with It* (1993), women's movies such as *Passion Fish* (1992), and maternal roles as in *The Jacksons: An American Dream* (1992), which was made for TV. Today, the fastest growing segment of the U.S. population is the over-fifty crowd, but in the 1990s studios were primarily catering to the eighteen-to-twenty-four-year-old demographic (Brian Lowry, *Variety*, 6 November 2005).

To demonstrate versatility, both women diversified their repertoire of characters. Each accepted roles against her earlier image to avoid typecasting. Bassett softened and sensualized her steely, professional, sometimes puritanical persona (as the incorruptible Betty Shabazz in *Malcolm X* [1992]; the innocent Anna Mae Bullock turned into chiseled Tina Turner in *What's Love Got to Do with It*; Detective Rita Veder in *Vampire in Brooklyn* [1995]; limousine driver Lornette "'Mace'" Mason in *Strange Days* [1995]; and Dr. Betty Shabazz in *Panther* [1995]). She expanded her opportunities by taking on more romantic roles like Bernadine Harris in *Waiting to Exhale* (1995), Stella Payne in *How Stella Got Her Groove Back* (1998), and Dr. Kaela Evers in *Supernova* (2000). *Vampire in Brooklyn* is a particularly interesting case in point because Bassett demonstrated a combination of tough professionalism softened by damsel-in-distress vulnerability. I discuss this film in greater detail below.

In Berry's case, she attempted to add gravitas to her ingénue screen persona and portfolio with biopics and prestigious literary adaptations. She portrayed Shelby Coles in *The Wedding* (1998) and the eponymous starlet of *Introducing Dorothy Dandridge* (1999). *The Wedding*, a two-part television miniseries directed by Charles Burnett, was based on Dorothy West's acclaimed novel published when the author was already in her eighties.

Because celebrity is not only an ideological construct but also always relational, we gain a more comprehensive understanding of it when we view film stars in relationship to one another. The ensuing comparative reading of Bassett's and Berry's film roles, and my examination of their individual brands of charisma and their different negotiations of the media, offers a broader window on the American star system and a study of their relative positions therein.

★★★★★ A New Era for Black Women Stars

Spike Lee's *Jungle Fever* put interracial relationships in mainstream moviegoers' consciousness. In the film, Halle Berry plays the bit part of Vivian, the drug-addicted girlfriend of Gator (Samuel L. Jackson),

Flipper Purify's wayward brother. Berry's performance is evidence of her early dramatic potential. Stripped of her glamour, she is so convincing as a homeless crack addict as to be unrecognizable as her otherwise strikingly attractive kewpie-doll self. And with a steady stream of larger parts capitalizing on her youth and beauty—including *The Last Boy Scout* (1991), *Boomerang* (1992), *The Rich Man's Wife* (1996), and Burnett's TV movie *The Wedding*—it is likely that spectators forgot Berry's impressive early portrayal of such an uncharacteristic and unglamorous character.

Lee's motivation for *Jungle Fever* derived—in part—from the highly publicized slaying of Yusef Hawkins, to whom the film was dedicated. Hawkins was a sixteen-year-old African American youth who was shot to death on 23 August 1989 in Bensonhurst, a white, working-class neighborhood in Brooklyn. Hawkins and three friends had gone to Bensonhurst that night to inquire about a used 1982 Pontiac that was for sale. The four were attacked by a crowd of ten to twenty youths, with at least seven wielding baseball bats. One, armed with a handgun, shot Hawkins twice in the chest, killing him. It was the third murder of a black man by mobs in New York City during the 1980s.

This climate of both racial hostility and black-on-black crime involving young males was the focus of John Singleton's *Boyz N the Hood* (1991), the very film that proved a major vehicle for Angela Bassett. Up to that point, Bassett had been cast in scores of television programs and small movie roles, including the soap opera "Ryan's Hope" (1975), the scifi show "F/X" (1986), the yuppie drama "thirtysomething" (1989), the alien invasion mini-series "Alien Nation" (1990), and the movies *Kindergarten Cop* (1990) and *Critters 4* (1991). But none were as socially significant or emotionally weighty as her role as Reva Styles, ex-wife of Furious Styles (Laurence Fishburne) and mother of young Tre Styles (Desi Arnez Hines II). Nearly two decades after its release, *Boyz* still stands as a classic example of the new, gritty, realist 'hood cinema and the prototype of what S. Craig Watkins called the "ghettocentric imagination."

Like Berry's character in *Jungle Fever*, Bassett's character in *Boyz* was a supporting role but an important part. Bassett dignified the image of the single black mother by making her character strong yet supportive, even if somewhat reluctant to give her estranged partner a second chance at fatherhood. Although Reva was a respectable character, *Boyz* is not remembered for its uplifting portrayals of black women. African American critics, feminists, and reviewers felt the film reaffirmed the stereotype proffered by the 1965 Moynihan Report.[1] For example, Michelle Wallace asserted as much in her insightful essay on the film:

But then, a black single mother brought the demonization of black single mothers in the film to my attention. In a second viewing of *Boyz N the Hood*, what made me most uneasy about the portrayal of these single black mothers was how little we're told about them, how we, as viewers, are encouraged, on the basis of crucial visual cues, to come to stereotypical conclusions about these women. We never find out what Tre's mother does for a living, whether or not Doughboy's mother works, is on welfare, or has ever been married, or anything whatsoever about the single black mother whose babies run in the street.   (123)

On the other hand, the role enabled some mainstream and black audiences to connect with Bassett's clean single-mother personification, in the Lifetime Television mode. The role required no nudity, no sexuality, and no foul language. Like most of Bassett's performances, it was a respectable and dignified role with political valence that resonated with the era's zeitgeist. Single motherhood was under assault by conservative Republicans at the time of the picture's release.

In May 1992, Vice President Dan Quayle took up the family values mantle when he argued in a San Francisco speech that the Los Angeles riots earlier that year had been caused, in part, by a "poverty of values" that included the acceptance of unwed motherhood, as celebrated in popular culture by the CBS comedy series "Murphy Brown." The program, which aired from 1988 to 1998, starred Candice Bergen in the title role as an investigative journalist and news anchor for a fictional CBS television newsmagazine. A white, upper-middle-class, thirtysomething Washington, D.C., resident, Brown was a long way from John Singleton's South Central L.A. and Angela Bassett's single-mother character. But there was widespread concern among right-wing conservatives that middle-class white women were beginning to take lifestyle cues from single mothers of color. Family values were paraded on the campaign trail, and single African American and Latino mothers were objects of national disdain.

In short, both Halle Berry's and Angela Bassett's 1991 roles raised critical, contemporary social issues. Both gave amazingly focused performances lauded by critics and audiences. The difference, however, was that as their careers progressed Berry allowed herself to be exposed, to be sexual, and to be sexualized in ways that Bassett did not. Whether or not this distinction would redound to Berry's credit depended on individual and personal attitudes about black women's sexuality in the cinema.

All genres and cross-sections of cinema in the nineties—African American, Asian American, Hispanic American, European American—became increasingly graphic, especially where sex was concerned. For example, in

Basic Instinct (1992), Sharon Stone played the beautiful, seductive, and wealthy writer Catherine Tramell, giving the film its NC-17 rating for graphic content with a revealing shot of her nude crotch. The film also emphasized lesbianism and bisexual relationships. In a similar vein, Quentin Tarantino's *Pulp Fiction* (1994) included an unexpected image of male sodomy. Choosing the higher ground, Bassett sought to circumvent sexual roles and sexual stereotypes that have shaped beliefs about black women's bodies (in Western visual economies for hundreds of years) by circumventing sexuality altogether. Since the days of the Venus Hottentot (Sara Baartman) through to the silent cinema of *The Birth of a Nation* (1915), the tragic mulatto of Douglas Sirk's *Imitation of Life* (1959), and the oversexed video vixens of the rap music industry's iconography (see Steffans), black women's sexuality has been promoted, policed, patrolled, pathologized, and paraded in popular culture in denigrating and dehumanizing ways. Bassett has responded to this history of representation in the Western visual lexicon with a form of cinematic abstinence, a kind of celebrity-celibacy wherein she always represents reputable black womanhood that keeps its clothes on. Her celebrity persona is defined by the discourse of respectability, decency, and propriety. In some ways, she is the cinematic equivalent of a linguistic eradicationist who would prefer that the racial epithets of bygone days completely disappear from spoken language (see Kennedy).

Alternately, Berry has been less concerned with African Americans' iconographic or cinematic past and more interested in making her own history. Her star or celebrity persona was defined by the discourse of desirability, the allure of nubile femininity, and sexual attraction. Her professional disposition was analogous to the New Age linguist, poet, or performance artist who believes that signs, signifiers, and images can easily undergo resignification and reassignment. Bassett's and Berry's different choices of roles reflect diverging cultural philosophies and inform the differences between their career paths and celebrity trajectories. Romance, sexuality, and interracial relationships have figured prominently in Berry's early screen persona and throughout her career. Bassett veered away from risqué and taboo roles.

For instance, Berry's character Angela makes eyes at Eddie Murphy's Marcus in *Boomerang*. The following year she was falling in love and getting laid as an eager college coed in *The Program* (1993). She turned to tragic motherhood briefly in *Losing Isaiah*, but moved on to make various kinds of films featuring racy interracial relationships, as in *The Rich Man's Wife*, *The Wedding*, and *Bulworth*.

Halle Berry stars as Angela in *Boomerang* (Reginald Hudlin, Paramount, 1992) opposite Eddie Murphy. She plays the innocent ingénue who helps Marcus (Murphy) reform his womanizing, playboy lifestyle. Collection Mia Mask.

Meanwhile, Bassett made movies about distinguished celebrities and innocent girls turned into rock stars throughout the 1990s. She played matriarch Katherine Jackson in *The Jacksons: An American Dream*; embodied righteous Muslim Betty Shabazz in *Malcolm X*; fought her way to the top as Anna Mae Bullock (later Tina Turner) in *What's Love Got to Do with It*; and tried to pick up the pieces of her broken heart in *Waiting to Exhale*, playing aggrieved wife Bernadine Harris. Given their respective career choices, it is not surprising that Berry's riskier, sexier, miscegenation-taboo-breaking movies caused more controversy (and made more money) than Bassett's more moralistic family films. By the time Bassett made *Supernova* (2000), the first film in which she had an interracial relationship (with James Spader), her star persona was already well established. She was more generally known for portraying uptight, religiously conservative women who had been to the school of hard knocks.

However inequitable it might have been, Berry's edgier roles—and the concomitant sexuality she displayed onscreen—helped facilitate the transition to leading parts in franchise blockbuster movies like *X-Men*, making the difference between their star signs a matter of Bassett's reputability and respectability versus Berry's sexuality and desirability. Since interracial romances were trendy box office, Berry was willing, and able, to take the risk of moving into this taboo territory early in her career with a range of films, however uneven and problematic. In so doing, she chose to climb the entertainment celebrity ladder in a more conventional way, sometimes playing the sensual, scantily clad ingénue. By taking on some of these roles, Berry inserted herself into a collective reworking and rehashing of national myths and fundamental ideals about race, ethnic difference, and romance. As problematic as some of her films were, they enabled Berry to diversify her performance portfolio—mixing it with social problem pictures like *Jungle Fever* or dignified roles like Khaila Richards in *Losing Isaiah*—and hedge her proverbial bets against typecasting in character parts. By contrast, Bassett appears to have chosen the cinematic high road, a road less traveled.

What's Love Got to Do with It reignited the onscreen chemistry between Bassett and Laurence Fishburne. The film was based on Tina Turner's autobiography, *I, Tina*, co-authored with MTV's Kurt Loder. Given the tumultuous life and times of Anna Mae Bullock—watching her parents' turbulent marriage, being inexplicably abandoned by her mother, being discovered by Ike Turner, rising to international stardom, suffering physical abuse from her husband, having a whirlwind career and children to raise—this film was the first textured, complex life story to challenge Bassett to deliver the best that was in her at that point.[2]

Much of *What's Love Got to Do with It* deals with the relationship between Ike and Tina Turner and how their marriage went from romantic and idyllic to one characterized by physical and emotional abuse. Ike descends deeper and deeper into cocaine-fueled paranoia as Tina increasingly becomes the sole focus of the public's attention. Out of spite, envy, and drug addiction, he beats her regularly, which she stoically accepts for seventeen years. Then, inspired by Buddhism, she decides to leave him.

In his study of cinematic representations of domestic violence, Duncan Wheeler praises the movie for strong performances and a compelling narrative. As critic Aldore Collier noted, "The film portrays Ike as a musical visionary plagued by deep-seated feelings of insecurity that exploded in acts of violence. . . . It followed Tina's life from the time she was an undisciplined, musically gifted grade school girl, to her triumphant solo career and the release of her mega-hit record 'What's Love Got to Do with It'" ("'What's Love Got to Do with It': Larry Fishburne and Angela Bassett Portray Ike and Tina Turner in a New Movie," *Ebony*, July 1993, 110; see also Collier's articles in *Ebony*, September 1998, 68; and May 2006, 182–84). As comprehensive as the filmic text was, director Brian Gibson and screenwriter Kate Lanier deleted much of the brutality Turner says she endured for years. This omission is interesting given the fact that some of the film's critics praised *What's Love Got to Do with It* for its nuanced depiction of domestic violence.

Diane Shoos, for example, argued that *What's Love* sets itself apart from other recent film representations of abuse by offering audiences a powerful, nuanced portrait of a battered woman *and* the complex psychology and tactics of a male batterer. Most important, the film's focus on a black man and woman whose musical success became their ticket out of poor, working-class families provides the opportunity for an analysis of the ways in which larger societal ambivalences about race and class become caught up with and support those who circulate within abusive situations. Shoos reminds us that there was tacit acceptance of Ike's behavior by her family and most of her friends and colleagues. The film not only avoids the trap of blaming the victim; it reveals the powerful societal pressures and deterrents that keep women imprisoned in abusive relationships.

One of the most powerful scenes in *What's Love Got to Do with It* occurs when Tina finally fights back and defends herself from Ike. After arriving in Dallas, where she was scheduled to open at The Academy, Tina refuses to be Ike's punching bag. In the limousine en route to the hotel, he begins to beat her. For the first time, she returns the blows and a fistfight erupts. When they arrive at the hotel, both are beaten and bloodied. They check into their room, where Ike shouts at Tina to clean herself up. Upon seeing her swollen face in the mirror, she falls apart. She comes out of the bathroom to find Ike asleep on the couch. She tiptoes out of the room and to the lobby, then bolts from the hotel, running across the highway and into a Ramada Inn where—without a penny—she begs to check in to find refuge from Ike. In this sequence, Bassett takes the audience through a range of emotions: anger, fury, fear, desperation, and relief.

Many found her rendition compelling. *Variety* noted, "Nothing in Bassett's earlier repertoire suggested the consummate skill she brings to the part. It is a full-bodied, nuanced portrayal" (1 January 1993, 116). But not all critics celebrated her performance. Writing for *Entertainment Weekly*, Ty Burr epitomized critics who found the film unconvincing and Bassett's lip-synched acting somewhat disappointing:

> Based on Turner's autobiography *I, Tina*, and filmed with her cooperation, *What's Love* is saddled with a stilted, as-told-to caution. It's a glorified TV movie—even more so on video—that happens to have great musical numbers and two astounding, Oscar-nominated lead performances. One of which is troublesome in the extreme. Angela Bassett is a gifted, hardworking actress

who, with any justice, has a major career ahead of her. . . . Bassett's Tina is a thought-out creation, and that's a problem. . . . In her defense, she has to lip-synch the songs to the real Tina's voice, a jarring technique that severs any link between character and actress the moment Bassett opens her mouth to sing. Someone also convinced the actress to buff her body up with anachronistic muscle tone; you're distracted by sinew. Given these stumbling blocks, it's a marvel that she does in fact create a Tina Turner for whom you root, especially in the private battle against the husband who beats her up, body and soul.   (18 March 1994)

Apparently, Bassett was intimidated about the prospect of meeting the legendary Tina Turner. Bassett told Collier, "When I met her at the studio, she looked at me and said, 'She's gorgeous.' We embraced and she started showing me pictures of her and the Ikettes [the background singers]. . . . When I left, I was energized. I was inspired to do my best." A bond obviously developed between them. "I wanted to convey that she is a bright woman, a survivor and a fighter," said Bassett. "When she came to the set, she just came and did things she didn't have to do. She could have sat back, but she helped me with my make-up. She took the wigs, cut them for me, went to the store and bought shoes for me. She's so generous and loyal. She showed me choreography and dance movements" (Collier, "'What's Love Got to Do with It,'" 111). To watch the film is to witness the connection that developed between Turner and Bassett.

It is no wonder, then, that Bassett was disappointed when she did not win an Oscar after being nominated for Best Actress (Fishburne was likewise nominated for Best Actor). It also contextualizes her response to Halle Berry's subsequent Oscar win for *Monster's Ball*. Controversy ensued in the months following the 2002 Oscars. Bassett's caustic comments in *Newsweek* (in which she criticized the explicitly sexual aspect of Berry's Oscar-winning role in *Monster's Ball* and subtly questioned Berry's choice to accept the role in the first place) reignited a fierce debate inside and outside the African American entertainment community about Berry and the bittersweet significance of her victory. Reporting on the debate, Allison Samuels wrote:

Bassett is clear she isn't criticizing Berry—just the way Hollywood views women in general and black women in particular. Several actresses, including Vanessa Williams, passed on *Monster's Ball*. "Film is forever," says Bassett. "It's about putting something out there that you can be proud of ten years later. I mean, Meryl Streep won Oscars without all that." . . . Bassett is the first to admit her career hasn't gone the way she'd dreamed it would when the spotlight swung her way after *What's Love Got to Do with It*. "I remember

sitting at the Oscars and thinking this is great! This is the beginning of something big for me. . . . But I didn't work again for another year and a half. I
guess I was pretty naïve to think it would be different—that it was just about
the talent—particularly for someone who looks like me."

("Angela's Fire," *Newsweek*, 1 July 2002, 55; see also Mask)

Although she did not win an Oscar for *What's Love*, Bassett did go on to star
in other powerful films. Meanwhile, the early 1990s proved to be a dry spell
for Berry as well. After the success of *Boomerang* (1992), with an amazing
African American cast that included Robin Givens, Eartha Kitt, Martin
Lawrence, Grace Jones, Chris Rock, Lela Rochon, Geoffrey Holder, and
Tisha Campbell-Martin, Berry thought she was on her way to the top. But
in fact she had a few duds ahead of her.

In 1993 she appeared in the TV miniseries adaptation of Alex Haley's
"The Queen," a noble but unremarkable project that did not live up to its
prologue, "Roots." She starred in the little-known *Father Hood* (1993) before
making the popular and financially successful family comedy *The Flintstones*
(1994), and then made the serious film *Losing Isaiah*, which reunited her
with *Jungle Fever* co-star Samuel L. Jackson. Also co-starring Jessica Lange,
Losing Isaiah tells the story of a baby boy born addicted to crack cocaine and
thereafter accidentally abandoned by his homeless, drug addict mother,
Khaila Richards (Berry). Shortly after being admitted to the hospital, Isaiah
is adopted by white social worker Margaret Lewin (Lange) and her husband
Charles (David Strathairn). As a family with other children, the Lewins
experience some growing pains but ultimately adjust to Isaiah and his special needs. A few years later, Khaila is released from prison and living in an
overcrowded apartment in the projects with another single mother, Marie
(Joie Lee). When she discovers that the baby she never agreed to put up for
adoption is still alive, she fights to regain custody.

Director Stephen Gyllenhaal took Berry seriously enough as an actor to
cast her in a role that put her career on a more serious dramatic track. With
the exception of the powerful films *Jungle Fever* and *The Program*, Berry had
not made many serious dramas. She certainly had not yet carried one as a
leading actress. The pairing of Berry and Lange proved beneficial since
Lange's beginnings as a fashion model enabled the two former beauty
queens to bond. From the more experienced Lange, Berry received some
valuable mentoring. Although not a major commercial success (earning
only $7.6 million on an investment of $17 million) or a critical sensation
(opening to mixed reviews), *Losing Isaiah* stands out in Berry's career trajectory because it allowed her to prove herself as a dramatic actress. Afterward she was poised to accept the role of Josie Potenza in Amy Holden

Jones's thriller *The Rich's Man's Wife* and meaningful parts such as Shelby Coles in *The Wedding*.

The Wedding was not uniformly applauded by critics. Writing for *Variety*, Ray Richmond disparaged the effort, as well as the role of Oprah Winfrey as executive producer:

> The mega-powerful talk show queen rolls out a Black History Month project that's more bluster than bite, more soap than substance. It's a two-night miniseries that's gorgeous to look at and mostly tedious to endure, content as it is to play like *Dynasty* in brown-face. . . . The issues raised in scribe Lisa Jones' adaptation are generally compelling ones about class struggle, biracial interaction and familial commitment. But Jones' execution never quite clicks, due in part to some weak casting. Halle Berry is asked to carry "The Wedding" in the role of Shelby Coles, a gorgeous debutante who has bummed out her snobby Martha's Vineyard relations in 1953 by getting engaged to a penniless, very white musician named Meade Howell (Eric Thal).   (20 February 1998)

But it hardly seems fair to dismiss *The Wedding* as *"Dynasty* in brown-face" given director Burnett's progressive background and screenwriter Jones's track record. The miniseries would have benefited from more context and screen time to allow the complexity of its characters (and race relations in the fifties) to come through.

One of Berry's strongest roles was in the political farce *Bulworth* opposite Warren Beatty, who also wrote and directed the film. Set in 1996, the film stars Beatty as Senator Jay Billington Bulworth, a liberal California senator forced to resort to the right-wing politics of the day to retain his Senate seat. Bulworth's true political leanings are disclosed during the film's opening sequence, which rolls over photographs of Martin Luther King Jr., Bobby Kennedy, Rosa Parks, and Thurgood Marshall hanging in his office. Depressed by the state of the union and his career, Bulworth puts out a $10 million contract on his own life. In the meantime, he publicizes the ugly backdoor deals struck by fellow politicians. But his fatal plan is complicated when he meets and falls for Nina (Berry), a stunning biracial beauty and lollypop-sucking fly girl from South Central L.A. She ignites his long dormant libido and desire to realize his liberal democratic political goals—however confused they might be.

Clearly, Beatty's script left something to be desired. The film's political commentary and the charades the plot sets in motion fail to offer the kind of biting progressive satire Beatty was seeking. Perhaps a different writer might have provided more perspective and shaped the script into the sort of biting, political satire Beatty claims he sought. Nevertheless, Berry stood out in the film, although many viewers were disturbed by her line at the end when she casually (and rather lovingly) refers to Beatty with the "N" word: "You know you my nigga." The interracial May-December relationship between Beatty's burned-out Bulworth and Berry's mischievous Nina was already too implausible for most audiences to swallow. Adding the frequently enunciated "N" word to the mix just made an already curious and unfunny satire more bizarre and troubling.

However ideologically problematic *Bulworth* and *Losing Isaiah* were, the films gave her the opportunity to work with A-list stars (Lange, Jackson, and Beatty) and benefit as well from studio financing, large advertising budgets, and easily reachable target audiences. As a result, these pictures left her poised to connect with other Hollywood insiders.

Around this time, Bassett was working on one of her more politically charged star vehicles. *Strange Days* (1995) opens in an incendiary Los Angeles close to the brink of destruction from prostitution, larceny, fire-bombing, police corruption, and urban decay. It's (virtually) the eve of the new millennium: 30 December 1999. The film's protagonist is Lenny Nero (Ralph Fiennes), a sleazy peddler who runs a black-market video recording operation. Using government-initiated technology, he records and sells X-rated, underground sensory experiences for virtual-visceral-vicarious experiential playback. His recording mechanism is known as SQUID: a Superconducting, Quantum Interference Device, which can be worn undetected. With it, he promises customers and returning clients: "I can get you what you want. I'm your priest; I'm your shrink. I'm your main connection to the switchboard of the soul. I'm the magic man . . . the Santa Claus of the subconscious."

But Lenny is not only a provider. He's also the ultimate user. He gets off on his own black-market escape technology. His private collection preserves vivid fragments of his past love affair with former girlfriend Faith (Juliette Lewis), a rising pop star now attached to ruthless promoter Philo Grant (Michael Wincott) (Strick 53–55). In the beginning of the film, Lenny pleasures himself watching reruns of their lovemaking. The only grounded person in his world is Lornette "Mace" Mason (Bassett), who tells him, "Come on . . . You sell porno to wire heads!" But despite Mace's friendship, stewardship, and unrequited love, Lenny can't see the forest for the trees.

On the brink of the new millennium, L.A. is a war zone. Every establishing shot of the city streets is of burning cars, baton-wielding police, store looting, drug trafficking, and prostitution. Amidst all this, Lenny can think only of Faith. Adding fuel to the city's burning fires is the news that black revolutionary rap star Jeriko One has been murdered. When Lenny discovers that Faith's friend Iris (Brigitte Bako) witnessed and recorded Jeriko's murder, he sets out to discover how the pieces—including Iris's rape and murder—fit together.

Strange Days proved a box office failure (earning only $8 million on an investment of $42 million) and a critical curiosity among progressive audiences and critics. As Karen Hollinger has noted, Bassett played the female leads in three major films in 1995 (*Waiting to Exhale, A Vampire in Brooklyn,* and *Strange Days*), a year that also marked "the beginning of the end of Bassett's rise to stardom" (171). While Bassett's performances were not held responsible for these failures—critics saw her portrayals as among the best aspects in the films—her role in *Strange Days* stands out as particularly problematic.

Andrea Hairston's incisive reading of the film spells out why Bassett's Mace is amiss:

> In *Strange Days* Angela loves Ralph for no good reason. Her black ex is in jail and she knows better than to love his triflin' ass anymore. A working single mom, Sister Angela is taking care of business and not as a slut for hire like all the white women in the film. She offers state of the art chauffeur and security service. Like Sigourney Weaver and Linda Hamilton in other James Cameron scripts, Bassett is the kick-butt heroic one in *Strange Days.* She's got the principles, the balls, nerves of steel, and charismatic muscles. She risks her life over and over to save Ralph and champion truth and beauty, but despite her elegant super-heroism (she's almost lynched at the end for doing the right thing), it ain't Angela's story. It's Ralph's and this angsty lover boy anti-hero doesn't do one thing to deserve her love or loyalty—except be the white male star of the movie. Emotional maid and chauffeur, Angela drives him everywhere, all the way to his best self.

Indeed, watching *Strange Days* it is difficult to suspend disbelief and become sutured into the film's spectacle. Manthia Diawara has dubbed this experience "resisting spectatorship." Spectators watch Bassett's Mace pine for Fiennes's pathetic Lenny the loser. Oddly, Lenny never notices Mace's chiseled figure or remarkable beauty. Instead, he longs to have Faith. What's more, the film's mise-en-scène flaunts the scantily clad bodies of the two white female characters (Lewis and Bako) as seen through the eyes of white male spectator/beholders via SQUID. When seeing what SQUID users are watching, the movie's spectators are positioned as white heterosexual viewing subjects. Even if they find Lewis attractive, most African American spectators cannot help but notice and resist the racial and gendered hierarchy of *Strange Days* and the way this film positions Bassett's Mace as the abject object, while privileging Lewis as the desired object of the male gaze.

Take the lovemaking scenes or the scene of Iris's rape as examples. The scene of Lenny making love to Faith is shot from a high angle. Iris's rape is shot in exactly the same way. These scenes, like many in the film, recall Laura Mulvey's seminal essay on visual pleasure in narrative cinema (see Mulvey). The essay has not fallen into obsolescence. The director of *Strange Days*, Kathryn Bigelow, privileges its white, heterosexual male protagonist and his point of view as the narrative agent of action. Concomitantly, it spectacularizes white womanhood, making it the object of the film's—and by extension the audience's—sexualized gaze. In fact, all the film's sex scenes (replete with lingering topless shots) are shown from the male perspective and filmed from high angles looking downward at the female form. In addition to objectifying womanhood, this technique has a secondary (narrative) effect. Precisely because Mace is in love with Lenny, the continual fixation on white womanhood and negation of black womanhood underscores the desirability of white femininity and implies the unrecognizability of black womanhood as desirable. It is not only a question of seeing Bassett objectified. It is a matter of not seeing her beauty acknowledged within the narrative. What is truly problematic about this is that most spectators are unaware of the film's careful narrative sutures. So the technique of stitching spectators into these scenes goes unnoticed as a natural element of film form.

In *Vampire in Brooklyn*, Bassett stars as Brooklyn-dwelling, churchgoing, tough-as-nails police detective Rita Veder. Comedian Eddie Murphy produced, co-wrote, and starred in this romantic-horror-comedy film, working with veteran horror director Wes Craven. The result was a hodgepodge of generic flourishes and cinematic styles, one part vampire movie and one part black romantic comedy. Blaxploitation aficionados might describe it as *Blacula* (1972) meets *Tales from the Hood* (1995). The movie tells the story of Maximillian (Murphy), the last surviving vampire of African ancestry, who arrives in Brooklyn on a ship full of people who have been brutally murdered. One of the corpses resembles Rita, a detective assigned to the case. Recognizing her as his long-lost love, Maximillian targets Rita, hoping to get a dance with her that will bring her under his spell, making her his eternal soul mate. Though he uses supernatural powers to interfere with the budding romance between Rita and her partner Justice (Allen Payne), Max is unable to turn her into a vampire because her morals are too deeply entrenched.

It is not surprising that the film, which earned only $19 million on a budget of $14 million, flopped with audiences and critics. As reviewer James Berardinelli noted, "*Vampire in Brooklyn* doesn't live up to its promise or

Angela Bassett in *Vampire in Brooklyn* (Wes Craven, Paramount, 1995) opposite Eddie
Murphy (again). As the working detective, Rita Veder (Bassett) is the object of Maximillian's (Murphy's) diabolical affections. Collection Mia Mask.

premise. The humor is hit-and-miss and the horror just isn't all that frightening. Eddie Murphy proves that he still has screen presence, but he needs a better showcase. The problem here isn't as much the talent in front of the camera as it is the weak and hackneyed script" (www.reelviews.net/movies/v/vampire_brook.html).

Worse still, *Vampire in Brooklyn* may even have offended some of its target Afro-Caribbean-American audience with the way it positioned the Caribbean as the site of sinister, supernatural secrets, mysticism, and hidden vampirism. Murphy's on-again, off-again Jamaican accent is also bewildering. Then there is the inexplicable use of reggae music on the soundtrack, making the Caribbean references undeniable. As it turns out, Rita is the half-human, half-vampire offspring of an interspecies Caribbean romance. But the movie never clarifies why the film relies on the Caribbean to create the image of an unexplored, exotic Other.

As for Bassett, her satisfactory performance in an otherwise silly horror film cannot be taken seriously. *Vampire in Brooklyn* leaves one wondering what kind of onscreen chemistry the talented Bassett and the popular Murphy could have created with a decent script and adult characters. Three years after the release of *Vampire*, Bassett appeared in *How Stella Got Her Groove Back,* then followed with the drama *Music of the Heart* (1999) and the star-trekking escapade *Supernova* (2000). Among these, *Waiting to Exhale* and *How Stella Got Her Groove Back* stand out as two of Bassett's more notable 1990s vehicles. But in *Waiting to Exhale* she was part of an ensemble cast. And in *Stella* she and actor Taye Diggs lacked the onscreen chemistry to make their May-December romance credible.

Supernova is one of the first major crossover pictures to present her as an intelligent professional who is also a sexually desirable woman. Here she is both the agent of narrative action and the desired object of the heterosexual male gaze. She is the woman over whom the two male leads will fight in hand-to-hand combat. It is an indication of her crossover star power that she was able to carry a major film role that could have been given to any actress regardless of race. It is also significant that her character and her love interest both survive at the end of the picture. Nevertheless, *Supernova* was a lackluster performer with audiences and a whopping disappointment for MGM (earning only $14 million on a $90 million budget). The movie's poor reception was a consequence of the film's reliance on a mélange of clichéd ideas leftover from the *Aliens* and *Terminator* franchises, however, and not due to Bassett's performance.

Bassett and Berry would go on to more successes. Bassett starred in *Boesman and Lena* (2000) with Danny Glover, followed by *The Score* (2001)

In *How Stella Got Her Groove Back* (Kevin Rodney Sullivan, Twentieth Century–Fox, 1998), Bassett performs to sensuous perfection as the eponymous leading lady opposite Taye Diggs as a much younger love interest. Collection Mia Mask.

with Robert De Niro and the progressive real estate development drama *Sunshine State* (2002). Berry completed the musical *Why Do Fools Fall in Love* (1998) and the made-for-TV movie *Introducing Dorothy Dandridge*, then appeared as Storm in the very popular *X-Men* and became a Bond girl in *Die Another Day* (2002). Not only did Berry become the first African American actress to win an Oscar for Best Actress, she also was the first to be contracted for a second James Bond film. While her roles may not have been as distinguished or reputable as Bassett's, she has managed to break various barriers. Both Bassett and Berry have represented different brands of womanhood and different forms of star charisma—no easy feat for black women actors in Hollywood at the time of their remarkable star turns.

It may not be necessary to demonize or valorize one celebrity over the other. Rather, it may be more fruitful to consider these stars in relationship to one another so that we have a better understanding of their individuality, the paths they have taken, and the kinds of branded celebrity charisma they have come to embody.

NOTES

1. "The Negro Family: The Case for National Action," now commonly referred to as the Moynihan Report, was a document in which Assistant Secretary of Labor Daniel Patrick Moynihan urged the federal government to adopt a national policy for the reconstruction of

the Negro family. He argued that the real cause of the American Negro's troubles was not so much segregation or a lack of voting power, but the structure of the Negro family, which he called "unstable and in many urban centers . . . approaching complete breakdown." Moynihan attributed this to the increasingly matriarchal character of American Negro society, in which a husband was absent from nearly two million of the nation's five million Negro families and in which some 25 percent of all births were illegitimate (Moynihan).

2. In *The Devil Finds Work*, James Baldwin writes that in his day the sorry roles black actors were given did not challenge them to deliver performances to the best of their abilities.

9 ☆☆☆☆☆☆☆☆☆☆☆

Michael Douglas
An Ordinary Man

DONNA PEBERDY

Michael Douglas quickly became synonymous with the popular figure of the man-in-crisis in the 1990s. Linda Ruth Williams calls Douglas "*the* representation of flawed, crisis-ridden masculinity and the concomitant decline of male cultural and social authority" (*Erotic* 177). Michael Kimmel argues that Douglas "offers an allegory of the besieged middle-class white male in today's society" (309). Celestino Deleyto adamantly asserts that Douglas is "the paradigm of the male in crisis . . . of course" (20). Whether portraying masculinity threatened by a duplicitous female, as in *Basic Instinct* (1992), *Disclosure* (1994), and *A Perfect Murder* (1998); or threatened by social forces beyond his character's control, as in *Falling Down* (1993) and *The Game* (1997), Douglas's screen persona has consistently been read as the epitome of contemporary renderings of masculinity in crisis.

Often described as "talkies" or "social-problem movies," Douglas's films have sparked debate concerning their often-controversial content and messages. A number of critics have made parallels between Douglas and suspect notions of the era's zeitgeist, a problematic alignment instigated by his 1987 performances as Gordon "greed is good" Gekko in *Wall Street* and as family man Dan Gallagher, sexually harassed by a "bunny boiler" in *Fatal Attraction*. For *Daily Variety*, *Basic Instinct* "marked Douglas as a consistently savvy reader of the zeitgeist" (Strawberry Saroyan, "Douglas on Douglas," 9 January 2004). In its review of *Falling Down*, the *Washington Post* claimed Douglas "again takes on the symbolic mantle of the zeitgeist" (26 February 1993). Similarly, Philip Green asserts that Douglas did not "invent" his crisis-ridden character "out of thin air," but instead "clearly tapped into the zeitgeist, or part of the zeitgeist, as well" (195). In each case, Douglas is seen to represent a specific cultural and historical moment, iconic of prevailing issues and concerns around capitalism (*Wall Street*, *The Game*, *Disclosure*), feminism (*Fatal Attraction*, *Basic Instinct*, and *Disclosure*), homosexuality (*Basic Instinct*), and ethnic minorities and racial discrimination (*Falling Down*). Not only are Douglas and his films perceived as paralleling trends in American society, but his characterizations themselves are discussed as a recognizable social type: the "persecuted figure" (Tasker 132).

The typing of Douglas is particularly apparent in discussions that position him as the Everyman: "an example of a specific type, the Average White Male, facing a crisis of power at a particular moment in US history" (Davies, "Gender" 216) and who is "acutely symptomatic of the masculinities of his moment" (Williams, *Erotic* 194). The statements aligning Douglas with zeitgeist notions of masculinity are significant for the credit they allow Douglas in constructing his contemporary characters; it is Douglas who has "tapped into," "takes on," and "reads" the zeitgeist. Rather than the writers or filmmakers, it is Douglas himself who is afforded a sense of authorship concerning the roles he plays.

Academic accounts of Douglas's films of the decade have been primarily concerned with what the star represents rather than what he does to represent it. In particular, studies have focused on the star's "whiteness" and how dominant female characters continually threaten his masculinity (see Davies, "Gender"; Davies, "Bad Guy"; Savran; Gabriel). While these ideological readings highlight the sociocultural implications of Douglas's films and how such representations react to or fuel particular moments in the nineties, they do little to explore Douglas himself in relation to these controversial gender, race, and class moments. In each case, the ideological message of the film determines and, indeed, overwhelms, the star image. As Jude

Davies and Carol Smith argue, Douglas's "star persona is built on making explicit some of the contradictions and multivalencies in constructions of white masculinity" (25). It is my intention to complicate the idea of Douglas as an icon of contemporary masculinity by locating the role of the actor in the construction of his characters. How did Douglas "tap" into the zeitgeist? Why is Douglas so symptomatic, so "consistently savvy" in his presentation of nineties masculinity? In other words, what did Douglas *do* to become paradigmatic of the decade's male in crisis?

Linda Ruth Williams has suggested that Michael Douglas "has chosen roles which overlap, presenting a continuation of contemporary issues which develop certain character types" (*Erotic* 178). In exploring Douglas's role in constructing character, we can problematize the social typing of the actor as "Average White Male" by exploring the nuances and departures in his screen persona, considering his persona as comprising several themes that are "differentially activated" from role to role (King 47). Ultimately, we must examine the significance of contradictions and differences in the construction of Douglas's star and screen personas.

☆☆☆★★ Consistencies and Deviations: Variations on a Type

Fatal Attraction, *Basic Instinct*, *Disclosure*, and *Falling Down* are the four most widely discussed of Douglas's films. *Fatal Attraction*, *Basic Instinct*, and *Disclosure* have generally been explored together as exhibiting a similar Douglas image alongside recurring themes and characteristics and, according to Linda Ruth Williams, "male failure/retribution essays such as *Falling Down* and *Wonder Boys* only seem to underpin what has been etched out in the erotic thriller" (*Erotic* 177–78). However, rather than demonstrating an extension of the themes displayed in his three "erotic thrillers," Douglas's role in *Falling Down* significantly departs from such representations, a portrayal of male angst that, I suggest, Douglas returns to and revises later in *The Game* and *Wonder Boys* (2000) at the end of the decade.

Falling Down and *Wonder Boys* differ from the majority of Douglas's 1990s films in their emphasis on Douglas's characters "as" crisis-ridden, while his other roles foreground the male protagonist's gradual downfall. In this respect, *Fatal Attraction*, *Basic Instinct*, *Disclosure*, and to a large extent *Wall Street* can be considered "fall from grace" narratives. Dan Gallagher in *Fatal Attraction*, Nick Curran in *Basic Instinct*, Tom Sanders in *Disclosure* are, at the start of each film, self-confident and dominant men. It is during the course of each narrative that their self-confidence is pulled apart by a

Douglas as a somewhat confident Detective Nick Curran in *Basic Instinct* (Paul Verhoeven, Carolco, 1992), charged with investigating "the monstrous/muderous feminine." Digital frame enlargement.

duplicitous female (Alex Forrest [Glenn Close], Catherine Tramell [Sharon Stone], and Meredith Johnson [Demi Moore]), to be replaced by paranoia, apprehension, and insecurity. The initial security of the male protagonist's identity is increasingly threatened to the point where he is forced to retaliate or be destroyed fully. This is the case in *A Perfect Murder*: Douglas's Steven Taylor is being cheated on by his young wife (Gwyneth Paltrow), but his failed attempt to have her murdered backfires and results in his own death at the hands of his unfaithful spouse. In this way, *A Perfect Murder* can be seen as a reversal of *Fatal Attraction* in its presentation of the unfaithful *wife* in a sympathetic light while Douglas adopts the domineering and dominating *homme fatal* position.

In *Falling Down*, however, the Douglas character's fall from grace occurs prior to the film's narrative; he is a fallen man from the outset. D-Fens (alluding to his car's license plate) has recently been made unemployed; a restraining order prevents him from seeing his young daughter and ex-wife Beth (Barbara Hershey); and he lives with his mother, factors suggesting that a more apt title for the film would have been "Fallen Down" or "Fell Down Further." Rather than focusing on the process of destabilizing and re-stabilizing male identity, *Falling Down* is fundamentally concerned with Douglas "as" crisis-ridden; the presentation of pathetic, unstable masculinity is the prevailing image.

The Game initially appears to have more in common with *Basic Instinct* and *Disclosure*, with Nicholas Van Orton (Douglas) as a "bloated millionaire fatcat" who is stripped of his power and money and left for dead in Mexico. Instead of a dominant woman threatening his power, the source of manip-

Douglas as *homme fatal* Stephen Taylor in *A Perfect Murder* (Andrew Davis, Warner Bros., 1998), with Gwyneth Paltrow. Courtesy Photofest New York.

ulation is Consumer Recreation Services, a company that creates real-life games for wealthy patrons. However, Nicholas's initial position of stability is called into question and revealed as a mask hiding the truth: he is a loner, haunted by his father's death, divorced, estranged from his brother, and a ruthless businessman who favors profit over morals. *The Game*, then, is closer to *Falling Down* in its narrative trajectory of fallen masculinity than in the case of falling men in the erotic thrillers.

Departures in Douglas's roles can be further considered in relation to the agency of his leading men. The male characters of *Basic Instinct* and *Disclosure* are more characterized by reaction than action; protagonists Dan Gallagher, Nick Curran, and Tom Sanders have a limited control over their environment. They respond to, rather than instigate, events. Specifically, it is the dominant female who determines the narrative trajectory, dragging the male character along, often against his will. In both films, order is seemingly restored at the end, yet this is not a result of the male's doings: *Basic Instinct*'s ambiguous conclusion suggests that Curran continues to be deceived by his bisexual lover, Catherine Tramell; in *Disclosure*, Sanders only manages to outwit Meredith Johnson with the help of "A Friend," a female colleague who has been sending him anonymous tips in order to expose Johnson's corrupt actions. The female colleague is ultimately promoted over Sanders at the film's close, once again denying Sanders the opportunity to dominate the workplace.

Conversely, Douglas's character in *Falling Down* is motivated by action rather than reaction, beginning with D-Fens abandoning his car in the middle of a traffic jam to "go home." His violent rampage across Los Angeles is presented as conscious and calculated rather than as a rash decision reinforced by Douglas's poker face throughout the film. Nonetheless, *Falling Down* also emphasizes the futility of action since D-Fens's actions do not move him any closer to mollifying his anger and frustrations. By the film's close, he is even further away from the possibility of being reunited with his family. *The Game* is similarly complex in its presentation of male agency. Like Nick Curran and Tom Sanders, Nicholas Van Orton is mostly reactive, helplessly dragged along by the game in which he is playing, forced to respond to events beyond his control. However, Nicholas breaks away from reacting by attempting to "pull back the curtain and meet the wizard," and while the extent to which he achieves this goal remains ambiguous, Nicholas's redemption by the end of the film is attributed more to his own actions than is the case for Curran and Sanders.

While distinctive depictions of falling and reactive men, and fallen but active men, highlight important narrative differences between Douglas's films and his leading male characters, notable differences can also be observed by considering Douglas's visual appearance from role to role. Drawing from James Naremore, Philip Drake has argued that the recurring elements of the star's performance, carried over from one role to another, "operate, for those who recognize them, as ostensive intertextual signifiers, offering the return of familiar pleasures" (74). In Douglas's case, a recurring theme in his "Average White Male" roles is the presentation of ordinariness. In the first instance, his characters are professional men: he is police detective Nick "Shooter" Curran in *Basic Instinct*, computer company executive Tom Sanders in *Disclosure*, defense worker (albeit unemployed) Bill Foster/ D-Fens in *Falling Down*, investment banker Nicholas Van Orton in *The Game*, and college professor Grady Tripp in *Wonder Boys*.

Work for each character is much more than a plot point; the male status of each is not only defined in relation to his work but success in the workplace is presented as inseparable from male identity. Bill Foster/D-Fens experiences a crisis of identity when he is fired from his job as a defense worker, instigating his Los Angeles rampage. Tom Sanders is twice passed over for a promotion in favor of a woman, causing him to question his masculine privilege. Grady Tripp has writer's block and his blackouts and incompetence are attributed to his inability to finish his second novel. The inseparability of maleness and a professional work ethic present Douglas's characters as Middle Americans, in search of the American Dream that rewards hard work and ambition.

In the erotic thrillers, the gradual unraveling of the male characters' "ordinary" appearance assists in the construction of Douglas as experiencing a crisis of male identity. Each film starts by establishing Douglas's ordinariness via a mask of masculine heteronormativity, or what Jude Davies terms "hypernormality" ("Gender" 216); he is clean-shaven, suit-wearing, a middle-class, well-educated professional, and married with children (in the case of *Fatal Attraction* and *Disclosure*).With work and occupation as key framing devices, it is not surprising that the business suit functions as a marker of Douglas's white male professionalism, building on the iconic image established in *Wall Street*. Whether a sharp suit and designer shirt (*The Game*, *A Perfect Murder*) or informal suit, shirt, and tie (*Basic Instinct*, *Disclosure*), the manner of dress serves as an immediate indicator of Douglas's status; his masculinity is coded through his characters' business attire (Roper; Edwards). The absence of the suit jacket in *Falling Down* underscores Bill Foster's loss of identity, indicating that the status of worker has been stripped from him. Later, his loss of status is amplified by the replacement of business wear with combat gear. However, if Douglas's appearance in the films highlights the similarities between his roles, it also brings attention to the differences.

Falling Down hints at Douglas's departure from earlier film roles through the visual contrast of D-Fens and Bill Foster: his earlier identity. The narrative begins before his divorce and while he is still employed. There is a home video showing a relaxed, caring, friendly, and happy man. His soft and "natural" brown hair, his blue-and-white checkered shirt, unbuttoned slightly, work together to give Bill a reassuring homely look comparable with Douglas's fatherly image in *Fatal Attraction* and *Disclosure*. The home video flashback scenes in *Falling Down* are intercut with present-tense cinematic images of a now radical-looking D-Fens/Douglas watching the video, wearing a dark buttoned-up shirt and a severe militaristic buzz-cut. His face is stiffer, older, unhappy. He wears the same glasses in both scenes and yet, on D-Fens, the glasses look larger, overwhelming his face and creating a more sinister feel as the light from the television reflects on the lenses.

Not only does this conspicuous transformation highlight D-Fens's increasing anxiety and paranoia regarding his separation from his family, it also foregrounds Douglas's changing screen image. Indeed, critics singled out Douglas's atypical hairstyle in the film (Caryn James, "Using One's Head: The Bad Haircut as Starturn," *New York Times*, 21 March 1993; Marshall

D-Fens/Bill Foster (Michael Douglas) has lost his marriage, his family, and his job in *Falling Down* (Joel Schumacher, Alcor/Canal+, 1993). Digital frame enlargement.

Fine, "Buzzcut Sends Michael Douglas 'Falling Down,'" *Chicago Sun-Times*, 7 March 1993). However, while this visual difference—what Paul Gormley refers to as Douglas's "strangeness" (22)—foregrounds difference over similarity, it is not really a clear departure from his erotic thriller roles. Rather, the images of Bill Foster deliberately play on Douglas's other versions of the crisis-ridden male, visually aligning Bill with Dan Gallagher, Nick Curran, and Tom Sanders. D-Fens suggests a conscious awareness of this screen type, a reflexive comment on the "familiar pleasures" of the actor's idiolect while, at the same time, foregrounding his "strangeness." A similar tactic is also evident in *The Game*, whose protagonist is a visual and performative amalgamation of Gordon Gekko's ruthless confidence, polished attire, and slick-backed hair and Nick Curran's self-assured obnoxiousness.

Douglas's differences and departures are apparent in terms of narrative and visual appearance, yet the most significant departure is evident in how male instability is exhibited in his films. As was the case with *Fatal Attraction*, *Basic Instinct*, *Disclosure*, and *A Perfect Murder*, external factors are blamed for usurping male power—specifically the threat of a castrating *femme* who must be contained. *Falling Down* also seemingly blames external factors: the emasculating effects of the consumer-driven modern world and resentment of immigrant communities gaining a foothold in the United States. D-Fens deems himself "not economically viable" and strikes out against what he perceives to be the "problems" in contemporary American society: he demolishes a shop owned by a Korean American because the prices are too high and holds up a fast-food restaurant for not serving breakfast after 11:30 A.M.

Yet the film differs from Douglas's earlier roles in exhibiting an *interiority* of crisis. D-Fens's masculinity is ultimately threatened from within; it is his own paranoia that constructs society as threatening. This is not an "ordinary man at war with the everyday world" (DVD sleeve, *Falling Down*), but a broken man masquerading as ordinary, living on the border between sanity and insanity, at war with his inner demons. In *The Game*, while the CRS company is initially presented as the cause of Nicholas Van Orton's paranoia and instability, his insecurities are later revealed as stemming from his detachment from his family and his fears of repeating his dead father's mistakes. It is the emphasis on interiority that constitutes the most significant departure for Douglas from the erotic thrillers. What, then, does Douglas actually do to project inner emotion?

☆☆☆★★ Wiping Himself Off: Performing Ordinariness

Rather than presenting male instability through something he does, that is, something he exhibits or displays, the key to Douglas's performances is in what he apparently does not do. The portrayal of ordinariness so central to Douglas's image of Everyman seemingly hinges on the actor's ability to restrain his actions and "do" very little. However, as John Ellis rightly notes, "Under performance is not a question of restraint or lack of histrionics. It is a question of *producing the effect of behaving* rather than performing" (104). Douglas's minimal acting in *Falling Down* and *Wonder Boys* is still acting, even if the technique is not immediately apparent.

The projection of interiority, or what Andrew Higson terms "externalizing emotion" (153), is central to Douglas's performance of ordinariness. In *Falling Down*, scenes of activity are interspersed with moments of introspection with his angst projected outward. The opening scene is indicative in this regard. A four-minute sequence juxtaposes images of D-Fens/Douglas trapped in unmoving traffic with the triggers of his escalating agitation: road signs flashing incessantly, schoolchildren shouting, car radios blaring, broken air-conditioning, lines of unmoving traffic with exhaust fumes and beeping car horns, garish bumper stickers, and a fly buzzing round his hot car.

Each time the camera returns to Douglas, it offers the actor in fragments: extreme close-ups of his mouth, nose, and eyes; a medium close-up of the back of his neck; a medium shot of his hands. A number of critics have singled out this sequence in their discussion of the film, focusing on the framing of D-Fens/Douglas in relation to these external irritations. Fred Pfeil, for example, sees the combination of close-ups of Douglas's face and body, with the swiveling and panning camera and build-up of diegetic and nondiegetic sounds, as creating an unsettling position for the viewer that problematizes the actor's hero status (239–40). Similarly, Paul Gormley singles out the long takes, fast edits, and close-ups, along with the "over-bearing soundtrack," as contributing to Douglas's "strangeness" in the film: "The discomfort caused by the fast editing and the rising soundtrack," he notes, "places the audience in a mimetic relationship with the figure trapped in the car, and it comes as a huge relief when D-Fens ends both his, and the audience's discomfort, by getting out of the car, and telling other drivers he is 'going home'" (45; see also Davies, "Gender" 217; Clover "White Noise"). Douglas's part in creating this discomfort is barely acknowl-edged in either reading, implying that it is technology, not actor, that cre-ates meaning.

While the camera and soundtrack certainly feature heavily in the con-struction of agitation in the opening sequence, Douglas's actions frame the scene and contribute to the overall meaning in significant ways. His mouth trembles slightly, with droplets of perspiration visible across his upper lip. He slowly closes his eyes with heavy, weary eyelids. His breath-ing is shallow and labored. He forces a swallow, a weak gulp, in an attempt to moisten his mouth. The trembling, sweating, closed eyes, stilted breath-ing, and gulping all take place before the first pan away to the blaring radio, a demonic-looking Garfield toy, screaming children. As we pan back to Douglas, the actor swats the back of his neck, followed by a medium shot of him as his hands tightly grip the steering wheel. His pupils dart frantically from side to side. He slowly closes his eyes again. He clenches his jaw and purses his lips. His brow creases slightly. He vigorously rattles the car window handle. He furiously swats the fly with a rolled-up news-paper. It is perhaps not surprising that Pfeil, Gormley, and others focused their reading of the traffic-jam scene on the movement of the camera, yet in doing so they bypass the instigator of the discomfort and "strangeness": Douglas's D-Fens himself.

Douglas's shift in this scene from subtle, slight gestures and expressions to excessive, hysterical outbursts is repeated throughout the film. Moments of interiority are punctuated by violent outbursts. D-Fens uses violence (verbal and physical) as a cathartic release for his anger and frustration; his "flooding out," as Erving Goffman terms those moments of extreme emo-tion that burst from containment (91), is projected onto a rocket launcher (when he obliterates some roadworks with a weapon acquired earlier from the homophobic white-supremacist owner of a military surplus store) or baseball bat (in destroying the Korean American shopkeeper's overpriced goods), while his face and gestures remain calm and relatively motionless. In *The Game*, Nicholas Van Orton struggles to keep a straight face when his briefcase fails to open, causing him to delay firing an employee. Moments later, we see Nicholas thrashing the briefcase against a bench, unable to contain his anger and frustration any longer. In both cases, anxiety and the performance of emotions are restrained and internalized to the point of becoming damaging to the male characters: D-Fens and Nicholas bottle it up until they explode into verbal or physical aggression. Both characters are characterized by a conflict between action and inaction, while the protagonists of *Basic Instinct* and *Disclosure* can only react to the forces out of their control.

Douglas's presentation of ordinariness as D-Fens is particularly evident in the home video sequence. Watching himself as Bill Foster, D-Fens self-reflexively reads his own performance of fatherhood. At first, Bill Foster is presented as an "ordinary" father. D-Fens wistfully watches the scene. His fingers gently rub the knuckles on his left hand in anticipation of what the video will show. He smiles openly, mouthing along to Bill singing "Happy Birthday" to his daughter. The smile quickly fades as his daughter begins to cry and refuses to sit on the toy horse birthday gift. As Bill's voice gets angrier and more frustrated, swearing and demanding that his wife put their daughter on the horse, D-Fens realizes the ordinary father is a false act and his nostalgic anticipation quickly gives way to melancholy and regret; he looks away from the screen and lowers his head in shame.

Significantly, Bill Foster is seen only briefly in the home video at this point, trying to feed his daughter cake. He is present in voice rather than image, underscoring his disembodied and estranged fatherhood. At first, Bill/Douglas's voice is soft, encouraging, nurturing. With his daughter's refusal to eat the cake and sit on the horse, his voice becomes harsher and demanding. At the end of the film, after D-Fens has been killed, a police officer returns to Beth's home and the camera focuses on the home video for a final time. Bill Foster holds his smiling daughter on one arm and a Labrador puppy on the other. Talking softly and lovingly, he kisses his daughter's head and hugs her tightly. Beth is heard laughing in the background and then joins father and daughter in front of the camera. The final scene underscores the performance D-Fens has struggled to maintain throughout; his status as "ordinary man" is a complete fabrication.

Ordinariness, then, is revealed as a façade and masquerade, evident only as far as the surface: the stiff white shirt with pens clipped in the top pocket, the smart tie, the leather briefcase. However, in his response to everyday irritations the construction of Foster's ordinariness is immediately evident. D-Fens's ordinary image breaks down in bursts of irrational violence and hostile action. D-Fens is also unable to meet the norms of his male social roles. At the start of the film, D-Fens is presented as a white-collar worker, a husband, and a father. His inability to maintain the "ordinary" male roles is gradually revealed as the source of his angst: the divorce, the restraining order, the loss of the job, and the forced residence with mother. In each case, D-Fens fails to perform the ordinary or to fit male social norms. It is only in coaxing police detective Prendergast (Robert Duvall) to shoot him at the film's finale that D-Fens is able to regain some sense of ordinary fatherhood; it is only in dying that he is able to fulfill what he deems to be his obligation as a man and father, and that is leaving his life insurance benefits that provide for his daughter in a way he was unable to when alive.

Reflecting on his performance in *Fatal Attraction*, Douglas has talked about the act of "wiping yourself off" in order to become an everyday character:

> I think what was a big breakthrough for me as an actor was when you start preparing for a part, you start thinking about your character: what are you going to do, what mannerisms, who's the character? And I remember having a moment where I said: wait a minute, what character? This is not about putting on the makeup, or putting *on* the character, this is about wiping yourself clean; wiping yourself *off*. Because I *could* be a lawyer in New York City, I *could* possibly have had an affair, this nightmare *could* have happened to me.
>
> ("Remembering *Fatal Attraction*," *Fatal Attraction* DVD)

Rather than putting *on* a performance, Douglas considers his performance as taking *off*, removing a mask in order to present that which is underneath. The mask in this case is the Douglas star persona that must be wiped off or contained in order to portray an Everyman, highlighting a disparity between star and screen persona. Douglas's performance of ordinary Everyman is problematized by his star status. The portrayal of ordinariness so central to Douglas's image of the "Average White Male" thus hinges on the actor's ability to restrain his actions, that is, by emphasizing "being," not "doing." However, the foregrounding of Douglas's ordinariness, while central to his screen characterizations, both opposes and complements the extraordinariness of his star persona. As John Ellis notes, "The star is at once ordinary and extraordinary," offering a paradox that is "repeated and intensified in cinema by the regime of presence-yet-absence that is the filmic image" (91). His extraordinary identity clashes with his ordinary characterization so that the very act of taking off the mask—"wiping yourself off"—is also revealed as a performance since it involves an identity that must be hidden or suppressed (see Holmes; Bennett).

Douglas's extraordinariness is revealed by his star status—as an Academy Award–winning actor and producer and son of classical Hollywood star Kirk Douglas—and amplified by his celebrity status via frequent appearances on chat shows and in gossip magazines. In these respects, his star identity starkly opposes his "Average White Male" screen persona and yet also supplements it. In 1992, rumors circulated that Douglas had admitted himself into a rehabilitation clinic after then-wife Diandra Luker accused him of having a sex addiction. Ordinarily, such an accusation would have a damaging effect on a star's image, yet the news followed the release of *Basic Instinct*, blurring the boundary between person and persona with a "confirmation" of the actor's hypersexuality. Despite categorically denying his ex-wife's claims, stating that he was being treated for an alcohol dependency problem, Douglas is still widely referred to as a "self-confessed sex addict," reinforcing the power of celebrity gossip in determining star identity. In this case, Douglas's performance in *Basic Instinct* was less about "wiping off" his star identity than extending his star persona onto the screen. The blurring of person and persona was evident once again at the end of the decade when Douglas appeared as an aging college professor in *Wonder Boys*. Not only does his performance as Grady Tripp significantly depart from the endangered males of his earlier films, but it also reworks Douglas's "contemporary" masculinity, offering a contradictory mix of conflict and consistency that is evident throughout his nineties output.

★★★★★ Aging and Departure: *Wonder Boys*

While only a spattering of critics drew attention to Douglas's visual difference in *Falling Down*, reviewers readily highlighted his change of image in *Wonder Boys*. Reviews stressed the visually different Douglas: "In a calculated reversal of his standard lethal-lothario persona," one critic noted, "Grady is overweight and unshaven, with a bad haircut, glasses, and a stocking cap" (Peter Keough, *Boston Phoenix*, 24 February 2000). Grady Tripp is a patently visual man in crisis. The publicity poster that accompanied the film's initial release featured a close-up head shot of Douglas. Peering over his large-frame tortoiseshell glasses, his face unshaven and hair unkempt, the image was a clear departure from the slick-backed coiffure and professional clean-shavenness that were signature trademarks of Douglas's earlier characters. A red scarf and tweed jacket replaced the sharp suit and designer shirt he so often wore in his other roles. If the visual transformation was not immediately apparent, the poster's tagline— "Undependable. Unpredictable. Unforgettable."—underscored the intention to foreground Douglas's uncharacteristic image (a move later blamed for the film's box office failure: Douglas himself even commented that the poster made him "look like Elmer Fudd"). As Tripp's problems increase during the course of the film, his appearance deteriorates: his clothes get shabbier, his hair is messier, and his beard becomes increasingly unkempt; the limp that he gains after being attacked by a dog accentuates his vulnerability and incompetence.

It is intriguing that *Wonder Boys* received more attention from critics than *Falling Down* regarding the different Douglas; while the latter film presents a direct contrast in D-Fens, particularly in the severe buzzcut and military uniform, Grady Tripp is much closer to Nick Curran and Tom Sanders in visual terms. Tripp could be considered to be a grayer, older, messier, and overweight version of his earlier dominant persona. As one critic noted, "Unshaven, unkempt and frequently clad in a fuzzy pink woman's bathrobe, Douglas actually resembles a middle-aged human being for the first time" (Andrew O'Hehir, *Salon*, 25 February 2000). Yet it is the new emphasis on age that marks Douglas as different. His graying hair suggests an aging Douglas, not the timeless and unchanging Douglas from *Fatal Attraction*, *Basic Instinct*, and *Disclosure*. Whereas all his characters prior to his role in *Wonder Boys* were in their forties, as Grady Tripp Douglas played a fifty-year-old for the first time (although age fifty-five at the time of filming, Douglas was still not "acting his age").

Further, the actor's weight gain for the role reinforced his departure from earlier roles and blurred the line between persona and performance. His twenty-five-pound gain can be considered as what James Naremore terms "pure biological performance" (20). Aging, he notes, is an "involuntary biological process" to the extent that we cannot stop the process of growing old (although apparently it can, as Sylvester Stallone demonstrates, be delayed or reversed via health care regimes and surgery). Douglas's weight gain for *Wonder Boys* can be considered as a voluntary biological process of sorts, with the actor speeding up the aging process. His performance of ordinariness therefore requires Douglas to adapt his extraordinary star body (made extraordinary via Hollywood fitness regimes and plastic surgery). Yet in the case of *Wonder Boys*, his body became hyper-ordinary when Douglas "put on" rather than "wiped off" for the role. Putting on weight in order to maximize authenticity in the role of an aging college professor necessitates a departure from the extraordinary star persona of "Michael Douglas."

As with *Falling Down*, *Wonder Boys* did not just offer a visual departure. Reviewers also acknowledged the narratively different Douglas: "*Wonder Boys* found [Douglas] acting against himself," commented one reviewer (Alistair McKay, *Scotsman*, 10 July 2003), while another noted: "He has put his seething away; his paradigmatic, oppressed white male has found a character in which to lose himself" (Wesley Morris, *San Francisco Examiner*, 25 February 2000). Douglas himself remarked that he saw in the film "an opportunity to do a different type of role than some of the 'Prince of Darkness' roles I've done in the last couple of years" ("Wonder Boys: A Look between the Pages," *Wonder Boys* DVD).

While D-Fens and Nicholas Van Orton move between action and inaction, Grady Tripp is more firmly associated with inaction, waiting for events to take place around him in moments of what Andrew Higson has termed "doing nothing": "Whether in a stylized acting practice, or in a naturalist acting practice . . . there are moments when one or more actors are required to '*do nothing*,' thus calling for a minimalist style of acting (although still calling for work and concentration): shots involving characters waiting or watching, or thinking, or day-dreaming, where the key to the success of the scene is the absence of movement or expression (which is expressive in itself, of course)" (116). Rather than the absence of movement being the key to the success of the scene, however, doing nothing still requires the actor to do or not do something as part of the process of "externalizing emotion" (Higson 121–22). "Doing nothing" in film performance is an oxymoron that involves a level of skill and engagement on the part of the actor in order to convey the effect of not-acting or being rather than doing. Waiting, watching, thinking, and day-dreaming all involve some movement, action, gesture, and expression, even if that movement is slight and apparently insignificant. In *Wonder Boys*, for example, numerous scenes depict Douglas seated in front of his typewriter or on his doorstep "doing nothing." With a voiceover narrating Tripp's motivations (or lack thereof), his thoughts and feelings are projected more through his low and gravelly monotone than as gestures, expressions, or corporeal movements.

Props continue to be significant in determining emotion, but instead of his projecting anger and frustration onto a briefcase or baseball bat, the business of smoking marijuana during moments of introspection provides Douglas with an "expressive object" (Naremore 83–88) onto which he can project Tripp's melancholy via deep inhalations and extended exhalations. Commenting on his role in *Wonder Boys*, Douglas has drawn comparisons between the film and his character in *Falling Down*, noting a difference from earlier roles: "Compared with the characters in *A Perfect Murder* or *Wall Street*, this guy was much more uncertain about himself, more like the guy in *Falling Down*. . . . *Wonder Boys* allowed me to play a man of inaction as opposed to a man of action" (qtd. in *Movieline*, December 2000/January 2001; see also Carrie Rickey, "Wonderful Mr Douglas," *Advertiser*, 20 July 2000, where Douglas makes a distinction between his "Prince of Darkness" roles and his "quirk" films). Indeed, the audience is denied the opportunity to witness Tripp's most excessive moments of emotion: Grady experiences anxiety attacks that cause him, and the screen, to black out. Whereas D-Fens erupts into physical aggression, Tripp passes out from his restraint, imploding rather than exploding with emotion.

It is in those moments of "doing nothing" and relative inaction that Douglas's performance of angst and his presentation of ordinariness come together. As with *Falling Down*, ordinariness in *Wonder Boys* is revealed as a masquerade, an image that is put on and enacted. The scenes of Tripp privately "doing nothing" demonstrate the artificiality of his public actions. For example, when Tripp stands outside at a party to escape the networking and small talk, his pronounced intake and deep exhalations of cigarette smoke suggest his relief at exiting the room, as well as his boredom, an acknowledgment that his jovial attempts to converse with guests a few moments earlier were forced and superficial. Grady may present an image of ordinariness—a successful writer and college professor—but it is in performance, especially in his social performance, that he fails. His presentation of angst is particularly evident in moments of private introspection, the quiet moments of thinking, typing, smoking, and passing out that are confirmed by his voiceover narration.

Despite these adjustments and departures, the ending of *Wonder Boys* suggests that the film is more in line with the images of stability presented in the closing scenes of *Fatal Attraction*, *Basic Instinct*, and *Disclosure* than the ambiguity and uncertainty of *Falling Down* and *The Game*. Tripp's physical appearance at the end of the film reinforces his emotional journey: dressed in a smart polo-neck shirt, clean-shaven with his hair combed (and, importantly, less gray), his crisis seemingly resolved. Yet this idealistic ending offers a paltry conclusion to a film that has, until that point, been dominated by the image of pathetic masculinity.

While offering a departure from the Average White Male persona presented in his erotic thrillers, *Wonder Boys* reworks the notion of contemporary masculinity that was so central in the alignment of the actor with the zeitgeist during the eighties and nineties. While his alleged sex addiction in the early nineties complemented his characterizations in *Basic Instinct* and *Disclosure*, his performance in *Wonder Boys* sparked comparisons with his offscreen relationship with Catherine Zeta-Jones, twenty-five years his junior and then expecting their first child. "In this case, it's life imitating art," Douglas quipped (Marshall Fine, *Seattle Times*, 25 February 2000). The comparison once again highlights the inseparability of star and screen image, person and persona.

If typing suggests that "change or 'development' is kept to a minimum" (Dyer, "Stereotyping" 28), the adjustments and departures foregrounded in *Falling Down*, *The Game*, and *Wonder Boys* problematize readings of Douglas as a "type," suggesting that even an actor so firmly aligned with masculine instability can perform it in different ways. Visually, this is achieved by putting something on or taking something off: graying hair or weight gain, for example. Narratively, the character's trajectory is more concerned with emphasizing instability over resolution; even in a film such as *Wonder Boys*, Douglas's angst takes precedence over his restabilization.

In terms of performance, the differences are evident in the movement from reaction to futile action and inaction, which are, in Barry King's words, "differentially activated" from role to role (47). While *Falling Down* and *The Game* can be considered more nuanced in their movements away from Douglas's established persona, *Wonder Boys* offers a more conscious break by the end of the decade that is continued in the 2000s with "quirky" films foregrounding a visually different Douglas, such as *One Night at McCools* (2001), *King of California* (2007), and *Solitary Man* (2009), which sees Douglas once again blurring the line between person and persona in the role of a sex addict and womanizer. Despite these departures, critics continue to draw comparisons with the earlier Douglas, the Average White Male presented in *Fatal Attraction, Basic Instinct,* and *Disclosure* (see, for example, Laura Emerick, *Chicago Sun-Times*, 22 September 2007), indicating the power of a few roles to dominate conceptions of persona despite an actor's attempts to change and adapt.

10 ☆☆☆☆☆☆☆☆☆★

Pierce Brosnan
Licensed to Sell

TRACEY HOOVER AND TOBY MILLER

In 2005, *Entertainment Weekly* wrote that Pierce Brosnan's "illustrious stint as James Bond is in the past . . . having ended a year ago with a single surprising phone call in which producers informed him that, for reasons he can't explain, his secret services would no longer be required. 'After that,' [Brosnan said], 'I thought, F— it! I can do anything I want to do now. I'm not beholden to them or anyone. I'm not shackled by some contracted image. So there was a sense of liberation'" (Joshua Rich, "Gentlemen Don't Prefer Bonds," August 2005). Brosnan's words are also reproduced on his website, piercebrosnan.com. The sentiment is typical among superannuated Bonds, an ex-post facto rationalization of rebirth following putative industrial imprisonment—the chance to make art rather than chase mammon. And no doubt it really was a transcendent experience to enter, inhabit, and depart the Bond identity. Brosnan has talked of how he was running through a Papua New Guinea village two days after the London press conference that announced his selection as 007 and happened upon some children who already knew to address him as Bond.

But there is another side to this global recognition. The magazine *ENcontrARTE* explained its reasons for creating a special dossier on Marilyn Monroe like this: it was to illustrate how "the great Powers . . . draw the maps of the World, create icons, mold them, imprint them, commodify them . . . and when they cease to be of use, withdraw them from circulation" ("Marilyn Monroe: Construcción y comercialización de un mito," n.d.). In a way, that describes the trajectory of many actors who take on the Bond role and then are tossed aside, losing their capital currency. You get to join what Brosnan calls "that coterie of men, that small club" (Paul Fischer, "Sundance Interview: Pierce Brosnan for 'The Greatest,'" *Dark Horizons*, 20 January 2009). Then you are summarily cashiered.

When asked by *GQ*—in an interview also included on Brosnan's website—about advice he would give to future Bond actors, he replied, "Get a good attorney," and lamented how quickly each subtlety in the character was quickly subsumed and controlled by "the fucking straitjacket" of "the Remington product-placement razor" (John Naughton, "Editor's Special Award: Pierce Brosnan," *GQ*, October 2005). Then again, consider an earlier remark Brosnan made in an open dialogue with a British audience at the height of his career as Bond, rather than after it, when he heralded product placement in the series as in the spirit of Ian Fleming's own branded journalism and fiction—as well as furthering his own haul of commodities ("Questions from the Floor," *Guardian*, March 2003). Fleming was a populist snob, that rare breed of writer who lords his knowledge of fine commodities over readers while letting them in on the secret of his own cultural capital, thereby debasing its exclusivity as knowledge even as he markets its status. In both his travel writing and his novels, nothing but the finest tobacco, coffee, and cars sufficed. Brosnan was a model vocalist for Fleming's latter-day incarnations. For he is an international cinema-to-cinema salesman, marketing products in his films by using them in the most glamorous ways.

Cars have been subject to product placement in Bond films since *The Man with the Golden Gun* (1974). And BMW paid a premium (some estimates put it at $30 million) to displace the Aston Martin for *GoldenEye* (1995) with its yet-to-exist Z3 Roadster (Edward Jay Epstein, "Pushing the Pseudo-Reality Envelope," *Slate*, 27 March 2006). A month after *GoldenEye* opened, the company had received 9,000 orders. Most of the first year's production was presold, and when it actually arrived in showrooms, demand was massive; the arrangement continued for two more Bond pictures, showcasing successive models of the automobile ("Band Aid," *Hollywood Reporter*, 25 April 2005).

When not getting in and out of his BMW in *Tomorrow Never Dies* (1997), Brosnan was knocking on theater doors to sell viewers Swedish cell phones, Swiss timepieces, and German vehicles—for all the world he was a European-Union Revlon gentleman. The use of a BMW motorcycle in the film set a record for a product placement—it lasted ten minutes (Galician and Bourdeau 22). The results were spectacular; the promotion coincided with a 100 percent increase in sales for Omega and ten thousand advance orders for BMW's forthcoming roadster (Stock 37–38). After BMW's successful launch of the Z8 sports car featured in *The World Is Not Enough* (1999), the company explained the decision to engage in product placement via Brosnan's Bond in these terms: "Global publicity, communicated in part by subliminal means and partly by overt ones, is positive and important, because it reaches a wide section of the public quite often on a world-wide scale" (www.bmw education.co.uk/coFacts/linkDocs/marketingProd-Placement.asp).

In return for such product placement, the studio had half its massive advertising budget dedicated to billboards and commercials. These were funded through merchandising carrying Bond's moniker and picture, thereby promoting the film through advertisers' words and images just as the film itself was to promote their wares (Phyllis Furman, "Bonding with Advertisers," *Daily News*, 9 December 1997, 54). This was too much for some. The *Philadelphia Inquirer* thundered that Brosnan had "become a top sales agent—a human Sharper Image catalog, shilling pricey products in suave Britspeak. The name is Brand, James Brand" (Steven Rea, "James Bond, Suavely Spying and Selling," 19 December 1997, 3), and the *St. Petersburg Times* archly referred to an "era of junk Bonds" (Steve Persall, "The Era of Junk Bonds," 19 December 1997, 8).

Ford paid $63 million to displace BMW as the carbon-emitter of choice for *Die Another Day* (2002), whose release was heralded by eleven firms expending $200 million on TV commercials to buttress their unofficial advertising within the text. The film was spoofed by the British advertising industry as *Buy Another Day*, in (dis)honorable recognition that it set a record for money paid to promote goods in a movie ("New Bond Film 'A Giant Advert,'" *BBC News*, 18 November 2002). The *Times* of London worried that "Millennial Bond may offer more product placement than plot" ("Vulture Classic Choice," 2 November 2002), and almost a decade later it was still renowned "as the most product placement-heavy film ever made," even given that the Bond production house, Eon, has an entire division dedicated to amortizing production costs in advance through clandestine advertising (Hugo Rifkind, "The Secret Plot to Change Bond's Suits," *Australian*, 10 March 2008).

☆☆☆☆★ Stardom and Identity

Brosnan represents one segment of a huge but critically underexplored commodity phenomenon of covert marketing. U.S. magazine and newspaper stories include well over $200 million in product placements each year. The cinema has been rife with it since Hollywood began, with agreements between studios and corporations covering long-term onscreen use of cigarettes, cigars, diamonds, cosmetics, and telephones. In 2005, the U.S. product-placement market was $1.5 billion, an increase of 50 percent over 2004 (see Beckerman; Berry; Stuart Elliott, "Greatest Hits of Product Placement," *New York Times*, 28 February 2005; Michal Lev-Ram, "James Bond's New Temptress," 17 November 2006, CNNMoney.com).

The theme of corporate identity and stardom as intermingled suffuses our chapter. We do not accept the tortured artist's complaints about the distortions of studio production on face value, preferring to see such remarks as paradoxical components of an image, rather than alienated signs from beyond it. For Brosnan is very careful about his star signage as a commodity fetish, having brought a celebrated case before the World Intellectual Property Organization (WIPO) over the domain name piercebrosnan.com to get a Canadian website shut down for using it without permission. WIPO established in its decision that the sign "Pierce Brosnan" has "secondary meaning"; that is, everything done under it is associated in the public mind with the person, Pierce Brosnan. As a consequence, the actor has trademark-protection rights over his name (WIPO Arbitration and Mediation Center, Administrative Panel Decision: *Pierce Brosnan v. Network Operations Center,* Case No. D2–003–0519, 27 August 2003).

This directs us to a methodological remark: that stars are not just signs to be read; they are not just coefficients of political and economic power; and they are not just industrial objects. Rather, they are all these things. Hybrid monsters, stars are coevally subject to rhetoric, status, and technology—to text, power, and science—all at once, but in contingent ways (see Latour). We therefore propose a tripartite approach to analyzing texts: first, reconstruction of "the diversity of older readings from their sparse and multiple traces"; second, a focus on "the text itself, the object that conveys it, and the act that grasps it"; and finally, an identification of "the strategies by which authors and publishers tried to impose an orthodoxy or a prescribed reading on the text" (Chartier 157, 161–63, 166). We draw on the work of both Roger Chartier (1989) and Pierre Macherey (1977), who argue that texts, including star texts, accrete and attenuate meanings on their travels as they rub up against, trope, and are troped by other fictional and social texts, and as they are interpreted by viewers. Such approaches fruitfully connect text to performance, what Ian Hunter calls an "occasion," or "the practical circumstances governing the composition and reception of a piece" (215). Those circumstances may reflect, refract, or ignore social tendencies.

Screen texts are part of a multi-form network of entertainment, via commercial-free and commercial-driven television stations, video, CD-ROMs, the Web, DVDs, theater, electronic games, telephones, newspapers, magazines, radio, and multiplexes. Engagements with audiences and texts must be supplemented by an account of the conditions under which materials are made, circulated, received, interpreted, and criticized. The life of any screen text is a passage across space and time, a life remade again and again by institutions, discourses, and practices of distribution and reception—in short, all the shifts and shocks of a commodity. To take the "game" example, although the first Bond electronic games were released in the 1980s, *GoldenEye 007*, released in 1997, was a sea change. Developed for the Nintendo 64 system as a first-person shooter immersion, it situated players as Bond himself and added more storylines to those of the original film while diminishing its pro-feminist aspects. *Tomorrow Never Dies* followed in 1999, and here Bond was not merely occupied by players, but could also be seen by them as a third person resembling Brosnan (see Elvis Mitchell, "Pity Pierce Brosnan's Poor Commercialized 007," *Fort Worth Star-Telegram*, 22 December 1997; Mera).

Our analysis is a materialist one, not in the sense that we seek a reflection of social relations in cinema, but that we track the way screen texts travel, attenuating and developing links and discourses across their careers. We are following several examples here, such as Toby Miller's 1997 research on the television series and characters "The Avengers" (1961–1969) (Miller, *Avengers*) and the way that Tony Bennett and Janet Woollacott, through close intertextual study of Bondian books, comic strips, films, and merchandising, determined how these different commodities contributed to a reading formation that slipped and slithered between reality and fiction, in accordance both with their material nature and history and prevailing geopolitics, notably the Cold War and the era of détente, and such social movements as national liberation and feminism (Bennett and Woollacott). Stars, too, are themselves texts that accrete and attenuate meanings as they rub up against, trope, and are troped by other texts and by the social. We must therefore consider all the shifts and shocks that characterize their existence as cultural commodities and proprietors.

To understand stars, we need to see how the private and public sectors meet across the body, in the form of a fetish. This is very important to comprehending Brosnan's appeal, for he is one of those people whom millions of us believe we actually know. Brosnan is a stranger who is also part of daily life, one of the key myths and symbols of masculinity and happiness, reified by capitalistic, sexual, and cinematographic processes in the space where personal qualities and social impacts fabricate something that then functions as a resource of commerce, art, and fantasy—and who is loaded with the prior signification of his predecessors in the role. We would like to reach out to the capacious world of cultural and social theory on the one hand, and on the other to consider the work of "Yanqui" (U.S.) social science and its positivistic, experimental fetishes that utilize regression analysis and artifice to examine the complex commodity careers of stars. We do not analyze Brosnan's films in depth to explain his stardom; rather, we look for the meaning of "Pierce Brosnan" in commercials, websites, political causes, and women's magazines. We are most concerned with his *persona* as Bond, since this has marked him, for complex reasons, before, during, and after the period in question.

It is necessary to stretch time in order to make sense of Brosnan. First of all, his career was transformed through becoming "James Bond," which only occurred in 1995, and he continued playing the role through 2002—but his career was also transformed by *not* becoming "James Bond" in the 1980s, when the producers wanted to cast him in the role but were unable to do so for contractual reasons. He became a "Bond in waiting," so to speak. Today, Brosnan's celebrity is clearly articulated to his popular run as Bond, which is associated with the 1990s. The after-effect of those years can be most clearly discerned by examining his star signage today as well as yesterday; such is the cultural encrustation of Bond (consider the latter-day careers of other actors who have played the role). So our account of Brosnan in a particular decade has to deal with his prehistory and afterlife. "The 1990s" must be addressed—at least in his case—both before and after their numerical ordering.

We also take inspiration from social theory and its collaboration with cinema studies, particularly Marcel Mauss's plans in the 1930s for a renewed discipline of sociology, which relied on historical and comparative perspectives that drew on the cinema as a record of how societies thought about and represented themselves (Mauss, "Fragment"). Mauss built his famous 1936 paper "Les Techniques du corps" (Techniques of the Body) around the way that different peoples learn to move and gesture. Movies provided his crucial modern examples. Film's international mobility and mimetic impact saw people start to walk and talk as if they were members of cultures they had never experienced personally. Drawing on these ideas, Norbert Elias (1994) constructed his figurational sociology of the civilizing process around mobility, with film an index of change (Elias). Zygmunt Bauman's theory of consumption (2001)—that individuals buy things to give meaning to their world because societies no longer provide them with a sense of continuity—takes the desire that audiences exhibit for movies as an epitome of the never-ending treadmill they are on in search of meaning (Bauman). Below, we trace our way through Brosnan's career as a pitchman for commercial products and environmental concerns, from cigarettes to coasts, and his metrosexual persona inside the career of James Bond.

☆☆☆☆★ Stardom and Products

What does Pierce Brosnan's celebrity "mean"? The idea of celebrity has been around since the first portraits of writers and painters in twelfth-century Europe, which marketed their subjects to potential sponsors. In the seventeenth century, portraits had been transformed into methods of instruction; depictions of the daily life of royalty became model rituals for courtiers. Democracy and capitalism invented the idea of publicity as a means of transferring this kind of legitimacy from the court and religion to their incarnation in upwardly mobile businessmen, whose esteem did not derive from their family background. Hence today's debates over icons and authenticity: their trans-historical as opposed to ephemeral value, their realism versus their manufacture, and their public and private lives—in other words, the full catastrophe (and pleasure) of forming a *nouveau riche* (see Briggs and Burke; Marshall; Gamson).

Yet we may know less about stars than we imagine—for instance, some film theorists probably agree with Hollywood that the key to its financial success is stardom, despite the evidence of regression analysis, which highlights such factors in addition to stars as genre, corporation, director, and so on (see Simonet; S. Rosen; Adler; Chung and Cox; Wallace, Seigerman, and Holbrook; Albert; De Vany and Walls, "The Market"; De Vany and Walls, "Uncertainty"). More than that, we negate the centrality of institutions in the creation and the life of the star. The industry paper *Variety* avows that a star is a mixture of a person and a work of art at a specific moment in time. And, as is well known, stars have at least three faces: their characters in films, their private selves, and their public personas.

In the Hollywood framework, stars are favorites of advertisers and marketers. The public supposedly shows immense trust in them, because they are regarded as likeable and trustworthy. This is known by marketers as the "referent effect." It was the key to Brosnan's endorsement of cologne and watches, for example, though it backfired when a cover of *Redbook* depicted him embracing his girlfriend while she breastfeeds their son, a pose considered offensive and potentially alienating to many U.S. consumers (Silvera and Austad; Johnstone and Dodd; Sørum, Grape, and Silvera; Cox et al.). A similar picture of Deborah Norville in a 1991 *People* spread reportedly caused a public furor (*USA Today*, 4 November 1997).

By 2005, celebrity endorsements were said to amount to over a billion dollars in expenditure, based on the assumption that audiences infer qualities from stars that can be transferred to commodities (Till, Stanley, and Priluck 180). This may be the clearest case we have of commodity aesthetics: commodities elicit desire by wooing consumers, smelling, sounding, tasting, or looking nice in ways that are borrowed from romantic love, but then reverse that relationship: people learn about correct forms of romantic love *from* the commodities themselves. The term "commodity aesthetics" covers the division between what commodities promise (pleasure) and what animates them (profit) (Haug). Stars represent the apparent human element to this process that rescues it from reification. The polite, Yanqui term for this in marketing is "associative learning," whereby there is a "match-up" between objects and the stars endorsing them that seems natural and can be transferred to consumers. University tests have shown that Brosnan is deemed "trustworthy" by viewers when he is associated with practices and products (Till, Stanley, and Priluck 188).

Consider smoking. Although U.S. tobacco corporations claimed to cease paying for product placement in Hollywood films twenty years ago, the incidence of actors smoking onscreen has magically increased eleven-fold, while use in youth-oriented films has doubled since the 1998 Master Settlement Agreement between the tobacco companies and forty-six U.S. states. These companies also offer cigarettes free "for life" to stars, with the quid pro quo that they smoke incessantly during magazine interviews (World Health Organization).

Pierce Brosnan is deeply implicated. When the United States forced Japan to open its cancer market to imported cigarettes in the late 1980s, Brosnan was on hand as a key spokesperson for Philip Morris via TV commercials; industry research showed that his image in particular and that of Bond in general were of mass appeal to young people (Lambert et al.). Although he had appeared on the cover of *Cigar Aficionado* magazine, Brosnan had previously drawn approbation from activists and scholars for not smoking as Bond. But he lit up a cigar for *Die Another Day* (2002), supposedly in homage to the Cuban setting (Paul Chuktow, "Brosnan. Pierce Brosnan," *Cigar Aficionado*, November–December 1997). The American Lung Association protested the movie for glamorizing this deadly practice (Julie Keller, "Critics Fume over Smoking Bond," eonline.com; Distefan et al.). Studies have disclosed that young people subsequently associated Brosnan's smoking with excitement and sophistication (Jones and Rossiter), yet he proudly displays pictures of himself engaging in this deadly practice on his website.

More overtly corporate (and a crucial part of audience surveillance) is the Hollywood Stock Exchange (HSX), founded in 1996 and sold to Cantor Fitzgerald, a Wall Street firm, in 2001. Brosnan has been tradeable on it since 1997 (via an icon of him holding a cigar). "HSX was conceived as a game to take advantage of the public's obsession with box-office numbers," said one of the founders, but the real plan was to sell forecasts based on "information it has collected on the folks who frequent the site" (James Bates, "Site Hopes to Put Profitable Spin on Hollywood Fame Game," *Los Angeles Times*, 19 May 2000, C1). By 2009, HSX had 1.7 million registered users, mostly affluent young men, who trade stocks of movies and bonds of stars ("Traders Hit 88% of Oscar Winners," 23 February 2009, HSX.com). HSX makes up starting prices based on past performances and sales, then lets trading determine price fluctuations, which it tracks as per a Wall Street exchange. Cantor sells HSX research to film studios as "a real-time update of consumer opinion . . . using the predictive market versus going out on the street with a clipboard and asking people questions" (Norm Alster, "It's Just a Game, but Hollywood Is Paying Attention," *New York Times*, 23 November 2003, C4). The company refers to its capacity to syndicate "the data collected from the Exchange as market research to entertainment, consumer product and financial institutions and as original content to radio, television and print media" ("Traders Hit"). Players are played, as they turn into samples for predicting cultural taste. Thus surveillance became "the interactivity that matters," by "cracking human personality in real time" and turning it into global data (David Burke, "Your TV Is Watching You," openDemocracy.net, 6 March 2003). Cantor also announced plans in 2010 to make its virtual dollars real. Stars are evaluated through TAGs, which represent their average total box-office performance over their last five credited films by release date. As of 30 March 2010, Brosnan's TAG was $48,860,402 (whatsontv.co.uk/blogs/movietalk/tag/pierce-brosnan/). The page's biography of him is articulated entirely around his time as Bond, even though he has played many roles before and since. This is typical of how his work is promoted.

Pierce Brosnan, happy to be the Bond of the 1990s.

From *Tomorrow Never Dies* (Roger Spottiswoode, Danjaq/Eon/MGM/United Artists, 1997). Even in hot pursuit, Brosnan's Bond is perfectly groomed.

Then there is the altruistic side to Brosnan's image. A part of his philan-
thropic portfolio is the work he has done for cancer charities and testifying
before Congress, so ironic given his endorsement of carcinogens, yet so
tightly linked with his first wife's death in 1991 and the sad events of his
early career. He chairs Concentric Circles, a theater group that connects
youthful and experienced actors; the Prince of Wales' Trust; Irish UNICEF;
and other children's and environmental causes (Barbara Ellen, "'I Am the
Sexiest Man in the World! I Know I Am. I Read It,'" *Observer*, 13 January
2002). It has been a theme ever since his time as Bond. Causes, corporations,
and characters cross-fertilize on his website, where Brosnan promotes practices, products, and parts, illustrating the seamless link between public personas from star sign to third-sector maven. His celebration of Earth Day has
included a link on his website enabling visitors to petition the California
government to prevent offshore gas production—in Brosnan's luxurious
gated community of Malibu. This consumerist message was confirmed by
tips on purchasing products in a way that furthered his family's "quest to be
environmentally conscience [*sic*]." He favors an "eco-friendly gardening or
car service" and proudly notes that the Brosnan Trust has donated over $1
million to schools, activists, charities, and third-sector environmental bodies
(piercebrosnan.com). This has become a key part of his public image; just as
Cigar Aficionado celebrates his stylishness, the Sustainable Style Foundation
names him, along with Angela Lindvall, as the "most stylish environmentalists on the planet," and he's a member of the "Celebrity Cabinet" of the
American Red Cross (redcross.org). Brosnan appeared in the documentary
Whaledreamers (2006), and in 2009 he lobbied Congress and the Obama
administration on behalf of the International Fund for Animal Welfare (Ted
Johnson, "Hollywood: Causes and Effects," *Variety*, 12 June 2009). Brosnan
and his second wife, Keely, also blogged about the AcademyAward–winning
2009 documentary *The Cove* to great effect. Their post on the TakePart.org
blog deserves consideration and bears quoting at length:

> There is a cove in Taiji, Japan that is completely off limits to the public.
> Activists have long suspected that dolphins and porpoises were entering the
> cove and not coming out, but there was little evidence of what took place in
> those closely guarded waters. Film director Louie Psihoyos and prominent
> dolphin advocate Ric O'Barry assembled a team of activists, divers and spe-
> cial effects experts to embark on a covert mission to infiltrate the cove in the
> dead of night. It sounds like the plot of a Hollywood spy thriller; but in this
> film the danger is real. . . . We have long been passionate about marine
> mammal protection. After watching *The Cove*, we were astonished to discover
> that more than 20,000 dolphins and porpoises are slaughtered in Japan each
> year, and that their meat—which contains toxic levels of mercury—is sold to

consumers and in grocery stores across Japan. Without this kind of investigative journalism, the plight of dolphins and the safety of some of Japan's
seafood may not have been adequately reported. This powerful and moving
film is an urgent cry for help—and now that the public finally knows the
truth, we *must demand change*.   (takepart.org)

That roster of commitments fits Brosnan's fourfold "definition of citizenship": "get informed," "take a stand," "get involved," "give your support"
("Peace and Nuclear Disarmament," piercebrosnan.com). In following this
type of activism, Brosnan fits into a popular Hollywood ethos. The ecorazzi
(paparazzi on the eco-celebrity beat) oblige with nonstop, if sometimes
rather arch, coverage of star environmental activists, especially since the
advent of the Environmental Media Association's awards and a 2007 "Hollywood Goes Green" summit meeting (see Alessandra Stanley, "Sounding the
Global-Warming Alarm without Upsetting the Fans," *New York Times*, 9 July
2007, E1; Bryan Walsh, "Living with Ed—in a Green Hollywood," Time.com;
Brockington; Corbett and Turco; Boykoff and Goodman; Wells and Heming).
Hollywood Today boasted in 2009 that actors give green gifts of "vintage-
inspired" camisoles and recycled jewels, but in 2008 MSNBC.com admon-
ished that, although "the Prius reigns supreme as the current status symbol"
in Hollywood, "trucks that carry equipment from studios to locations and
back continue to emit exhaust from diesel engines," as do generators on-
set (Michael Ventre, "It's Not Easy Being Green, Hollywood Discovers,"
MSNBC.com, 23 April 2008; Gabrielle Pantera, "Hollywood Goes Green,"
Hollywoodtoday.net). A study of Hollywood's environmental impact has disclosed massive use of electricity and petroleum and the release of hundreds
of thousands of tons of deadly emissions each year. In fact, the motion-
picture industry is the biggest producer of conventional pollutants in Los
Angeles. Municipal and statewide levels of film-related energy consumption
and greenhouse-gas emissions (carbon dioxide, methane, and nitrous oxide)
are about the same as the aerospace and semi-conductor industries (Corbett
and Turco 11–14). Film consumers are also major producers of pollutants,
from auto emissions, chemical run-off from parked cars, and the energy to
power home-entertainment devices (Roth and McKenney; Mitchell).

The key need for environmental movements has long been to combat
hostile media and co-opt them. Stars are considered correctives to the neglect
and derision of the mainstream, because they supposedly guarantee coverage of activism. But they have been accused of having a NIMBY (Not in My
Back Yard) attitude that is distant from the subsistence conservation of
environmentalists from the Global South, and a trivializing rejection of the
political-economic analyses required to understand corporate-state rela-

tions (Brockington 556–57). And empirical studies bring into serious doubt the assumption that celebrities—specifically Brosnan—really bring concerted attention to environmental causes. At the same time, it should be noted that Brosnan can transcend this consumerist model of activism, as per his advocacy for Greenpeace, the Natural Resources Defense Council, the Sea Shepherds, and the Global Security Institute in opposition to nuclear arms. He also spoke out against the 2003 invasion of Iraq. In 2009, he addressed the Environmental Protection Agency and went to the White House to lobby officials and politicians against whaling (James Osnard, "Pierce Brosnan," *Metro*, 17 May 2004; Alex Pasternack, "Pierce Brosnan Bonds with Lawmakers over Whales," *Treehugger*, 20 May 2009; Brockington; Thrall et al.).

☆☆☆☆★ James Bond—World's First Metrosexual?

> If you happen to be looking for a product spokesman, how about a skirt-chasing spy in his 80s who drinks too much, has an unfortunate taste for cashmere turtlenecks and glib one-liners and who clung to his fear of the communist menace long after the Berlin Wall came tumbling down?
>
> —"Buy Like Bond," *New York Times*, 27 October 2002

At a political level, of course, the sign "James Bond," so closely associated with Brosnan, is routinely held up as a contributor to, and a symptom of, imperialism, sexism, Orientalism, class hierarchy, and jingoism. The character's stylishness and understated but ever-ready violence have led to Brosnan's celebration within hegemonic masculinity, for example the *Jamez Bond* animutations, where to be other than Bond is to be queer—and "lame" (Kendall). Yet the Bond signage is more cluttered and contradictory than this model might allow. The cold-warrior pop philosopher Ayn Rand adored the 007 books for what she saw as their unabashed Romanticism and heroic transcendence. But she was appalled by the early films because they were laced with "the sort of humor intended to undercut Bond's stature, to make him ridiculous" (Rand 138). This suggests that Brosnan inherited a far more contradictory role than is usually supposed. Sean Connery's Bondian sex, fairly progressive for its day, was too much for U.S. critics. He was frequently criticized as a wuss, in keeping with the notion that his s/m style embodied the weak-kneed and decadent cosseting that was losing an empire. *Time* labeled Bond a "used-up gigolo" (14 August 1961, 61) after the very first film in the franchise, *Dr. No* (1962), and *Newsweek* condemned him as of interest solely to "cultivated sado-masochists" (19 April 1965, 95), while many other U.S. magazines objectified him mercilessly by listing his bodily measurements. As far as the *New Republic* was concerned, Bond was "stupid. . . . His only genius lies in an infinite capacity for taking pain" (30 May 1964, 150). Britain's *Daily Worker* noted the hero's "appeal to the filmgoer's basest instincts" and "perversion," while on the other side of politics, the *Spectator* deemed *Dr. No* "pernicious." *Films and Filming* called the character's "sex and sadism" a "brutally potent intoxicant" and identified Bond as a "monstrously overblown sex fantasy of nightmarish proportions . . . morally . . . indefensible" and liable to produce "kinky families." But for proto-feminist Susan Douglas growing up, *Dr. No* was a sign that "sex for single women [could be] glamorous and satisfying" (all quoted in Miller, *Spyscreen* 141).

In short, Bond was a sign of the end of British confidence *and* a newly pleasurable display of masculinity. If *You Only Live Twice* (1967) is a high point of Orientalism, with Bond's body wiped clean by Japanese women, it is also the moment of the withdrawal from the East, a recognition of a dream (and a tyranny) that had faded and failed, and a male who is on display. The period was marked by a begrudging acceptance of middle-power status, in keeping with the disasters of Suez, Kenya, Malaya, and Cyprus. And for all that, we might now construct a lineage of Bond as the first muscle-bound Hollywood action adventure hero of a kind that proliferated in the 1990s. He was seen as quite another kind of figure in his own time.

Brosnan had visited the set of *For Your Eyes Only* (1981), which featured his then-wife, the late Cassandra Harris. Cubby Broccoli, one of the producers, noticed Brosnan and decided he would make a fitting Bond one day. He was not alone; Brosnan became so popular in the successful television series "Remington Steele" (1982–1987) that he was selected by readers polled by a national magazine as the favored actor to replace Roger Moore as 007. In 1986, "Remington Steele" was due to be canceled, and Broccoli signed Brosnan to play Bond in *The Living Daylights* (1987). The publicity created by this announcement increased the ratings of "Remington Steele," and as a result Brosnan was optioned for additional episodes, making it contractually impossible for him to play Bond. After two films featuring Timothy Dalton, the franchise lay dormant for six years in the face of legal entanglements over rights—which had dogged the movies from the first— and uncertainty over the form a post–Cold War Bond might take. Then Brosnan finally took the part in 1995.

Brosnan as Bond was up for grabs as both sexual icon and commodity consumer, in ways that borrowed from but also exceeded earlier commodification of the male form. His appearances as Bond coincided with the emergence of the "metrosexual," a term coined in the mid-1990s by queer critic Mark Simpson after he encountered "the real future" and found "it had moisturised" (www.marksimpson.com/pages/journalism/metrosexual_beckham.html). Historically, male desire for women has been *over*-legitimized, while female and male desire for men has been *under*-legitimized. The metrosexual represents a major shift in relations of power, with men subjected to new forms of governance and commodification. Simpson calls his discourse of metrosexuality "snarky sociology, which is no good to anyone." But it has been taken up and deployed—as a *pre*scription as much as a *de*scription—because it promises "highly profitable demography" guaranteed to stimulate any "advertiser's wet dream" (Miller, *Makeover*).

The metrosexual has been joyfully embraced by Western European, Australian, South Asian, Latin American, East Asian, and U.S. marketers, who regard it as "about having the strength to be true to oneself" (Salzman, O'Reilly, and Matathia 55) rather than being the sign of a vain cad. Based on its rapid diffusion, acceptance, and national usage, "metrosexual" was declared word of the year for 2003 by the American Dialect Society, ahead of "weapons of," "embed," and "pre-emptive self-defense" (www.american dialect.org/index.php/amerdial/2003_ words_of_the_year/). Euromonitor's 2006 report on the phenomenon was entitled *The Male Shopping Giant Awakes* (www.euromonitor.com/Metrosexuality_the_male_shopping_giant _awakes). Simpson even gave his term to a prominent 2006 Thai film. The metrosexual endorses equal-opportunity vanity, through cosmetics, softness, women, hair-care products, wine bars, gyms, designer fashion, wealth, the culture industries, finance, cities, cosmetic surgery, and deodorants. Happy to be the object of queer erotics, and committed to exfoliation and web-surfing, this newly feminized male blurs the visual styles of straight and gay. He is supposed to be every fifth man in major U.S. cities. Single, straight men now embark on what the *New York Times* calls "man dates," nights out together without the alibis of work and sport or the props of televisions and bar stools—although people in the U.S. shy away from ordering bottles of wine together (10 April 2005).

From the moment of "Remington Steele," Brosnan represented a new kind of man leading us into a new millennium: he was unflappable as he challenged evildoers while still maintaining his well-manicured hands. Brosnan became the classic metrosexual *avant la lettre*, a contradictory, desirable amalgam of "italicized good looks" and a "restrained air of machismo" (Ellen, "'I Am the Sexiest Man'"). He was often taken to represent the politically correct masculinity of the 1990s—polished, witty, well dressed, and well groomed, and the first avowedly green Bond, at least off-set. Publicity shots as 007 generally had him looking boldly into the

From *GoldenEye* (Martin Campbell, Eon/United Artists, 1995): the iconic Bond image, complete with tuxedo and revolver.

camera wearing a tuxedo, and not a hair out of place; his emotional range was narrow, which could be interpreted as coolness; and his style was flawless. Janet Maslin in a *New York Times* review welcomed Brosnan to the role as the "coffee-bar James Bond: mild, fashionable and nice in a very 90's way." She found him "the best-moussed Bond" and "a fabulous clothing model" (17 November 1995, C17).

It comes as no surprise that Brosnan has often been invoked as a classic metrosexual, given the softness of his looks, the elegance of his approach, and the style of his habiliments. But he has also been hailed as the oppo-site of the metrosexual, in his cigar-smoking, devil-may-care attitude. We've found debates about Brosnan as metrosexual versus non-metrosexual from Britain to Malaysia to Ecuador to the United States to Spain to Ireland to Mexico to India: was he the first Bondian metrosexual, or the last hold-out before Daniel Craig (see Richard Torregrossa, "The New Gentleman," *San Francisco Chronicle*, 25 February 2007; Rubin Khoo, "Mirl of the Moment," *Star*, 8 August 2006; Paul Harris, "Metrosexual Man Bows to Red-Blooded Übersexuals," *Observer*, 23 October 2005; Dan Majors, "Trend Watchers Have a New Label for a Refined Man's Man: Ubersexual," *Pittsburgh Post-Gazette*, 26 November 2005; Alfonso Ruiz Alfonso and S. E. Santander, "¿Y tú de quiéneres?" *El Diario Montañés*, 7 May 2006; Deidre Reynolds, "It's the Last Stop for Metro Man," *Independent Ireland*, 21 June 2007; Beatriz Gue-vara, "2006, El Ano del Hombré Ubersexual," *El Universal*, 20 December 2005; Namrata Sharma Zakaria, "The Female Gaze," *Express India*, 4 July 2004; "Los ubersexuales jubilan a los metrosexuales en el mundo," *El Com-ercio*, 29 July 2007)? For example, in the United Kingdom, the *Daily Mirror*, a working-class leftist paper, plumps for Brosnan as anti-metrosexual (Clemmie Moodie and Danielle Lawler, "James Bond in Metrosexual Make-over Shock," 17 April 2008). But the *Daily Mail*, its working-class conser-vative rival, sees him as the acme of metrosexuality (Martin Newland, "'Bond' Heralds the Return of Pure 'Pecs' Appeal," 23 November 2006). And the *Daily Telegraph*, a ruling-class conservative paper, plumps for him as post-metrosexual (Nina Goswami, "Ken Counts on a Make-Over to Win Back Barbie," 23 October 2005). In the true traditions of bourgeois U.S. journalism, the *New York Times* places an each-way bet (Suzy Menkess, "Past Present; Secret Agent Man," 12 March 2006).

Brosnan's confused and confusing personas—secret agent/citizen, smoker/cancer activist, NIMBY/environmentalist—represent neatly the split subjectivity and increased alienation of contemporary stardom and contemporary life. Produced by consumer capitalism, stars were raised to a high level with the general development of bourgeois society: mounting mechanization, greater diversification of commodity production, hyper-consumerism, further alienation of the individual (and new, unforeseen dimensions of that alienation). Ernest Mandel argues that this search for identity is a necessary process for fictions that are produced in bourgeois societies, where individuals are divided amongst a variety of selves (Man-del). The worker, the buyer, and the capitalist are utilitarian figures who calculate all their actions to the maximum benefits for themselves. As prop-erty owners, they uphold and even materialize laws of ownership of both objects and people. As citizens, they are concerned with the general good rather than their own. And as sexual subjects, they are driven by needs that take them beyond reason, the family, and property. A weird mix of hyper-bourgeois individualist, technocrat, and empty signifier, the star can never relax, never truly know who he/she is.

The James Bond series enacts the dilemmas posed by this contradictory, split subjectivity. It also brings up all the mystique of law and order, the where and why of sovereignty, in a physical, material way, via the daily actions of secret agents. In the films Bond acts as a delegate of the people, the monarchy, or the army in foreign camps. The arbitrariness of this dele-gation, and its reliance on instant decision and action, is paradoxically cyn-ical. Loading up one person with such power and responsibility, and hence signing away the right to democracy, makes the myth of bourgeois soci-ety—popular endorsement of overt governmental processes under the pub-licly ratified rule of law—unsustainable. Binary divisions between good and evil, police and felon, spy and counter-spy, West and East, become unstable (Mandel 65, 122).

This chapter has endeavored to look at the corporate underpinnings, the property relations, that color Pierce Brosnan on television, on the Web, and in his Bond movies. Brosnan is not unusual in doing celebrity endorse-ments—about a quarter of U.S. commercials use people in this way (Silvera and Austad). It would be churlish to single him out for his part in corporate signification. Our wish is rather to see him as very, very ordinary. The same applies to his environmental activism—a norm for U.S. celebrities (Thrall et al.).

Our point, then, is not to typify Brosnan as venal or unusual, either as a spy or a fetish. Arguably, he is venal and banal by U.S. standards of pro-bity. Instead, we wish to argue for a method of interpreting stardom that goes beyond interpreting film characters, transcending that form of critique in favor of engaging the full set of texts that circulate under the commod-ity signage of the star, and doing so by drawing on a more complete inter-disciplinarity than film studies generally allows, especially in its desire for periodization. For to understand Brosnan as a figure of the 1990s, one must go back to the 1960s and the origins of Bond on film, and also shuttle for-ward to the 2000s and the afterglow of Brosnan as a social sign banking on his years in the part.

11

Johnny Depp and Keanu Reeves
Hollywood and the Iconoclasts

ANNA EVERETT

Hollywood's visual imagery and other cultural tropes of American masculinity underwent an enormous recalibration in the nineties with the cinematic star breakouts of Keanu Reeves and Johnny Depp. As the decade's quintessential celluloid bad boys, Depp and Reeves crafted both personal and professional personas that fans loved to love, and sometimes hate. Among Reeves's and Depp's lovable attributes that helped propel their individuated and similar star turns are their smoldering pretty-boy looks, lean and sexy physiques, youthful agility and sometimes extreme physicality, sensitive and often gentle masculinity, feminist leanings and anti-misogynist propensities, queer-friendly coding, and quirky character tendencies (tendencies writ large in both their reel and real lives). What is important to note here about Depp's and Reeves's effective resets of celluloid masculinity in 1990s America is each actor's participation in the decade's changing gender norms, including calls for men to reject hegemonic machismo and instead embrace their so-called "feminine side." Arguably, then, it was through some of their earliest films that Reeves and Depp lent form, acceptance, and desirability to such an epochal attitudinal shift. For Reeves's part, films such as *Tune in Tomorrow* (1990), *I Love You to Death* (1990), *My Own Private Idaho* (1991), and *A Walk in the Clouds* (1995) construed new masculine character types. And for Depp *Edward Scissorhands* (1990), *Benny &Joon* (1993), *What's Eating Gilbert Grape* (1993), and *Ed Wood* (1994) showcased iconoclastic characters that challenged masculine orthodoxy without alienating either young male or young female film audiences.

☆☆☆☆☆ Masculinity Reset

When we contrast Richard Dyer's typology of classic masculine character and star types to the later development of Depp's and Reeves's postmodern enactments of American masculinity, several transformations occur that warrant closer analysis. Consider that Dyer (following Orrin Klapp) singled out and problematized James Cagney's quintessential 1930s "tough guy" character (*Stars* 49), which ossified a brand of hyper-masculinity and gender differentiation that persisted well into the 1990s. In varying degrees, male stars aligned with the nineties-era action film genre, such as Arnold Schwarzenegger, Mel Gibson, Bruce Willis, Pierce Brosnan, and even Denzel Washington, achieved industry successes portraying hyper-masculine archetypes cut from the indelible Depression-era tough-guy pattern that Cagney and others instantiated.

Moreover, long-established cinematic gender norms often necessitated that male and female star images register clearly as binary oppositions, although subversive characterizations occurred in classical Hollywood and new Hollywood cinemas from time to time (Dyer, *Stars* 52). For example, women stars Joan Crawford, Marlene Dietrich, and Greta Garbo in the 1930s and Sigourney Weaver, Linda Hamilton, and Sandra Bullock in the 1990s performed historically situated powerful female roles that, in Judith Butler's words, troubled the "cultural matrix through which gender identity has become intelligible" (*Gender Trouble* 23). Further, Dyer underscores the point that enormously popular male stars Montgomery Clift and James

Dean "did something to launch a non-macho image of a man," which Dyer attributes to their being gay (*Stars* 61). These popular stars and their iconic films illustrate well Butler's incisive deconstructions of hegemonic social constructions of gender and their requisite performances, whether on-screen or off. Accordingly, then, it is perfectly understandable to see Reeves and Depp as legatees of Clift's and Dean's influential postwar and mid-century non-macho man-star texts. More important, however, it is crucial to acknowledge that Depp's and Reeves's extracinematic exploits and daring career moves many decades later were not as vulnerable to persistent and potentially ruinous rumors of closeted homosexuality that even in the 1990s could be career-limiting, if not career-ending. At the same time, both Reeves and Depp deliberately chose film roles with high degrees of sexual ambiguity and gender subversion, particularly Reeves's *My Own Private Idaho* and Depp's *Ed Wood*, among others.

Indeed, their ascendancies to A-list Hollywood stardom represent, within limits, a scaling back, a celluloid do-over, if you will, of film's hyper-masculine performance standards recoded for the changed nature and in-creasingly flexible gender and sexuality dynamics operating at century's end. Melvin Donalson helps us grasp this significance. His book *Masculinity in the Interracial Buddy Film* explores "the contemporary reading of masculinity," how "the norms articulated have been maintained even while enduring efforts at transformation." He notes that "certain trendy concepts such as 'metrosexual' have entered the public discourse on masculinity, suggesting revision of the prevailing attributes" (4). Still, he argues, there is a funda-mental truth that underpins popular debates about doctrinaire gender roles and their support of the dominant political-economic system: "Amer-ican cinema, whether viewed as an art form or a commercial endeavor, becomes an expressive form that emanates from . . . socialized gender [roles] within a patriarchal power structure. Therefore, the stories, images and icons of masculinity will extend themselves from that source, whether camouflaged with labels of 'entertainment' or coded in terms such as 'film genre' or 'film cycles'" (5). While Donalson rightly cautions against over-emphasizing certain transformative powers associated with such trendy masculine concepts as "metrosexual," I want to stress that it is also impor-tant to appreciate the pivotal function of stars and the culture of stardom in promoting counter-hegemonic ideals of maleness and their expressive pos-sibilities at particular historical junctures. In this light, Reeves and Depp offer fascinating near-mirror images of *fin-de-siècle* young male cinematic stardom rooted largely in their parallel career trajectories and similar off-beat personal backgrounds, which generate a form of data mining that production studio publicists and celebrity stylists cannot get enough of (Harris, "Building"; Herzog and Gaines).

Let us consider briefly some tropes of nineties-era masculine character-istics in a representative sample of Depp's and Reeves's films. For Depp, who learned the craft of acting and honed his natural performance talents during four years as a star on Fox's popular TV series "21 Jump Street" and in the quirky films *Edward Scissorhands*, *Benny & Joon*, and *Don Juan DeMarco* (1994), an uncanny fit with enigmatic, enchanting, and sexually atypical characters rescued his star image from the shackles of the highly manufac-tured and endlessly circulated teen-idol personality that he loathed. He was thrilled to exchange his straitlaced, teen- and 'tween-girl-dreamy Officer Tom Hanson character in "Jump Street" for the excitingly bizarre and delib-erately anti-glamorous characters of Edward, Sam in *Benny & Joon*, and even Don Juan, characters that he fashioned so adroitly and compellingly. In April 1990, *Los Angeles Times* film critic Chris Willman conveys a key fac-tor motivating Depp's curious film choices in the wake of his phenomenal television success. Quoting Depp himself on the occasion of the actor's selection of John Waters's *Cry-Baby* (more about this later) as his first star-ring film role while at the height of his TV stardom on "Jump Street," Will-man notes:

> "Maybe" it's a risk to take such a comic turn this early in his career, he con-ceded, "but for me it's the only thing to do. I hate that in order to sell a TV show and sell a product, it involves exploiting one person or another, and I have no control over those commercials that were DEPP DEPP DEPP," he says mocking the . . . ad campaign Fox developed for the show after Depp's star-dom among the under-18 set exploded. "It was such a shock to me to see it. If I had control over that and the posters and the amount of merchandising, I would have put the kibosh on it a long time ago. But unfortunately when you're starting out and they have products to sell, they shove you down America's throat, basically. It's pretty ugly. . . . I felt fortunate not having to pose with a revolver in my hand and kiss a girl wearing Lycra and do *the same old expected leading man stuff* [my emphasis].
>
> (*Los Angeles Times*, 4 April 1990, 1)

Apparently lost on Depp in this instance is the fact that the enormous visual appeal and charisma of young male stars endowed with matinee-idol good looks and personal magnetism hardly necessitate tactics of the hard sell or an unwanted shoving down the audience's throat. Still, Depp's genuine protestations during this period make sense when we consider that he was desperate to reinvent himself from the fleeting teen-idol, heartthrob sensa-tion of TV fame to the more enduring serious and versatile film actor. However, for film critics, for growing hordes of Depp fans, and for directors and studios eager to exploit his movie star mettle, those star build-up years on "Jump Street" and the specific cultivation of a passionate female consumer/ fan base signified potential box office gold and increased newspaper and magazine sales. For our purposes, though, we are concerned with Depp's specific transmedia appeal across print, TV, film, and the growing digital media in his expanding star appeal, as well as how his early film choices contributed to a diversification in popular films' repertoire of masculine star types in the nineties.

As the outlandish yet sympathetic title character in *Edward Scissorhands*; the simple-minded yet mesmerizing Sam in *Benny & Joon*; and the psychologically unstable yet romantic Don Juan in *Don Juan DeMarco*, Depp certainly succeeds in disrupting, if not altogether murdering, the teen-idol star text of his "21 Jump Street" years. In "Johnny Depp Contemplates Life As, and After, 'Scissorhands,'" Glenn Collins's interview with the star confirms Depp's satisfaction "that his teen-king image has been superceded [*sic*]" by his "stunning creation" of social outsider Edward Scissorhands, with whom the twenty-seven-year-old actor confessed a powerful and surprising identification (*New York Times*, 10 January 1991, C17). *New York Times* film critic Janet Maslin elaborates on the theme in "Johnny Depp as a Soulful Outsider." Her effusive 1993 review of Depp's performance in *What's Eating Gilbert Grape* helps us recognize how cinematic codes of masculinity and, by extension, gender significations at large were shifting and becoming much more fluid than in past eras.

In her review, Maslin singled out "Johnny Depp's tender, disarming performance as the long-suffering Gilbert Grape." She continues, "In films like 'Edward Scissorhands' and 'Benny and Joon,' Mr. Depp has made a specialty of playing gentle outsiders, and doing so with enormous charm. He brings much the same soulfulness and strength to this role [Grape], even though for once he is cast as a pillar of the community" (17 December 1993, C3). Here, Maslin's enfolding of Depp's star image within Swedish director Lasse Hallström's enchanting auteurist perspective of middle American quirkiness and whimsy works well to situate Depp's own actorly auteurism after a series of notable outsider character performances. However, it does not address Depp's penchant for selecting and performing unconventional masculine types, nor his dedicated fans' willingness to embrace them, to which *Edward Scissorhands*' surprising box office returns (reported on box-officemojo.com) in excess of $56 million attest. Simon J. Bronner's investigation into the emergence of nineties-era metrosexual masculine types is revealing and can perhaps shed some light on alternative masculinities at play during this period, when Depp's nontraditional male characters none-theless connect with audiences. Regarding this particularly resonant new masculine type, Bronner notes:

> Usually, the label of "metrosexual" is for a straight man who satisfies his male ego by being up-to-date, setting trends for the twenty-first century, and flat-tering himself. Besides examining its links to the culture of "cool," metro-sexual identity also invites query of its folk roots in the mainstreaming of gay and feminine culture in urban life. . . . Wearing of earrings by men and hair dyeing, for example, once considered too gay or feminine by many men, have been incorporated into various masculinities, including supposedly *macho* men's groups such as bikers, professional athletes and tradesmen.   (38)

Bronner's observations shed light on Depp's "soulful outsider" charac-ters as resonating specifically within the spirit of the times, especially the changes in straight men's embrace and resignification of the once-abhorred markers of what I am calling "sissy-boy culture." By sissy-boy culture, I mean that aspect of changing masculine norms in nineties America that, unlike hegemonic bad-boy and bad-man cultures, rejects hostility toward and oppositional politics against feminism and homosexuality far beyond those urban safe havens for metrosexuals that Bronner articulates. Thus, it is Depp's anti-macho, subtly subversive, and obviously endearing screen hero types performed in *Edward Scissorhands*, *Benny & Joon*, *What's Eating Gilbert Grape*, and *Don Juan DeMarco* that suggest this pro-feminist and pro-gay sissy-boy cultural referent. Also, it is inspired largely by Dyer's lament that "it clearly is acceptable for a girl to be a tomboy (whereas it is not acceptable for a boy to be a sissy), presumably because . . . she does not prove a threat to a grown man" (*Stars* 83). And certainly Depp's very gen-tle man-boy characterizations in these films seem hardly capable of pur-posefully threatening grown men, except perhaps as a romantic rival, as in the case of Gilbert Grape's adulterous affair with the lusty, married Betty Carver (Mary Steenburgen). Bronner's insights about real men in the nineties and their acceptance of earrings, hair dye, and other outward visual expressions of female-beauty culture among other changing gender identity politics illuminate the crucial signifying function of Depp's gender-bending physical appearances early in his film career. As Sam, Gilbert, and Don Juan, especially, Depp's strikingly chiseled facial features are framed with long, wavy, and dyed hairstyles and occasional earrings, all evoking a soft, girl-like countenance that the camera emphasizes perfectly. In *Benny & Joon*, Depp's Sam occupies the traditional female role of housekeeper and caregiver for brother and sister Benny and Joon, at one point wearing a frilly apron while preparing the family breakfast. At the same time, Sam's

Sam (Johnny Depp), with Ruthie (Julianne Moore), anxiously awaits medical news about Joon (Mary Stuart Masterson) in *Benny & Joon* (Jeremiah Chechik, MGM, 1993). As Sam, Depp's genteel masculine look registers as prettier than either of his female co-stars. Courtesy Photofest New York.

eccentric impersonations of silent film stars Buster Keaton and Charlie Chaplin function to destabilize this otherwise unisex or sissy-boy discourse through an enchanting heterosexual romance that ensues between the misfits Sam and Joon. Still, when framed in medium and close-up shots with Joon (Mary Stuart Masterson) and Ruthie (Julianne Moore), Sam's "soulful outsider" (in Maslin's terms) certainly looks prettier, more feminine, and unquestionably more photogenic.

This genteel look obtains even as Depp portrays the mustachioed, earring-wearing, hairless-chest-baring Don Juan. Adding further to his characters' blurred gender signage are his costumes, and particularly emblematic are his dress and character positioning alongside supporting actors in the film. In pivotal scenes, we see Don Juan dressed in a blousy white shirt with a waist-accentuating cummerbund, red fitted vest, gold hoop earring, black fitted trousers, black hat, Zorro-inspired cape, and black knee-high boots that, absent the cape, strike altogether a quite feminized hourglass pose.

Depp's feminized Don Juan is foregrounded even more when he is shown charming not only the entire female staff at the mental hospital but also his very large, imposing, no-nonsense male nurse Rocco (played to menacing and then cuddly perfection by Tommy "Tiny" Lister). Lister's Rocco, with a hulking body-builder physique, gleaming bald head, tall stature, and black skin, strikes a fantastic image of opposition and alterity with Depp's Don Juan, as the two unlikely characters dance around the hospital grounds to an extradiegetic music track that animates them. Murray Pomerance puts it best when he takes account of how fascinating Depp is onscreen and more importantly "the way Depp fascinates" (*Johnny* 16). In this scene of playful embrace between the two men, Pomerance gets it right when he observes that, in fact, "there is a sense of homoeroticism in Depp's performances" (26). This quality is always simmering below the surface in Depp's other sensitive nineties-era male characters.

Character speech and dialogue also reinforce the gender ambiguity theme in *Don Juan DeMarco*. At one point in the film, Don Juan utters the phrase, "I apologize for this unmanly display," in a self-conscious reflexivity that betrays the character's subversive gender performance that, according to Simon Bronner, certainly gestures toward a nineties-era ethos characterized by a "suppression of brutish manly 'instincts'" (7). Situating the anti-manly man discourse of the period in the cult of the metrosexual, if you will, Bronner's study of manly traditions in folk cultures describes a crisis of masculinity that toggles between two poles of manliness, the "men" or the "guys." For him, "'Guys,' it appears, stand for traditional stereotypes, conflated with working-class images, deemed inappropriate in a modern age of 'sensitivity.' This folklore of 'guys' has precedents in humor of 'real men' differentiated from the modern or 'gentle' men who have supposedly abandoned their manly traditions" (2). And it is precisely the ways in which these early films of Johnny Depp and Keanu Reeves arbitrate and negotiate this so-called crisis of masculinity that concerns us now. Whereas we have considered some aspects of Depp's sensitive male character types, we turn now to Reeves's performances of new masculinities.

Reeves had a previous star image that desperately needed updating for the times. In his earliest films of the decade, including *Tune in Tomorrow* (1990), *Point Break* (1991), *My Own Private Idaho* (1991), and *A Walk in the Clouds* (1995), he effectively puts considerable distance between himself and his slacker, stoner-dude character Ted Logan of the hugely popular *Bill & Ted* comedies. First of all, Reeves's stunning success in films has been a topic of much debate and bewilderment. However, Karen S. Schneider's comments on the young star's meteoric rise up the Hollywood A-list are revealing of stardom's ineffability, particularly after the collapse of Hollywood's classic studio system and its dream factory of manufactured and organic stars from an earlier period. In her article "Much Ado about Keanu" for *People*, Schneider articulates what most fans and observers of Reeves's unlikely celebrity and star quality already understand. Despite reams of newsprint, endless online chatter, and entertainment TV shows all decrying Reeves's acting inabilities, he nonetheless broke through and blew up. Discussing what "transformed him overnight from the quirky kid in *Bill & Ted's Excellent Adventure* [1989] into the full-grown, full-blown $7 million-per-picture superstar every agent dreams of," Schneider points implicitly to the role of audiences and fans in assisting the conferral of stardom: "Reeves's acting style—a detached deadpan somewhere between artful and awful—has never been the primary reason for his success. . . . Three reasons why Reeves may be the biggest thing to happen to Brooding Boys since James Dean: beautiful dark, brown eyes, perfect white teeth—and a soul that whispers the blues" (*People*, 5 June 1995). Schneider's mention of "Brooding Boys" returns us to our discussion of Reeves's varied representations of sensitive males, 2.0 (or nineties) style. For unlike the anxiety-producing fear of a domesticated masculinity run rampant among postwar American males in the 1950s as described by writer Louis Lyndon (qtd. in Cohan 34), nineties-era men were becoming habituated to the changed sociopolitical nature of gender politics obtaining in the wake of sixties- and seventies-era second-wave feminist activism. As Steven Cohan points out, "The hegemonic masculinity of a historical era does not define a proper male sex role for all men to follow so much as it articulates various social relations of power as an issue of gender normality. At any given time . . . one form of masculinity rather than others can be defined as the culturally exalted. Hegemonic masculinity can be defined as the configuration of gender practice" (35). And it is precisely to the practices of gender in specific Reeves and Depp films in this period that this section is addressed.

Whereas Depp's gentle, man-boy physique (height estimated between 5'7" and 5'10") and beautifully chiseled facial features (especially reminiscent of Montgomery Clift and James Dean) may conjure up effete masculine types (the pretty boy, the "sissy boy"), Reeves's gentle-giant body image (6'1") fits within yet contrasts well with the hypermasculine or übermanly-man tall stars of the era such as Arnold Schwarzenegger (6'2"), Pierce Brosnan (6'1"), and Denzel Washington (6'0"), with perhaps the exception of Tom Cruise (5'7"). But unlike these high-octane action-film-genre stars, for the most part Reeves began the nineties in films that represented counterhegemonic masculine character types and ego ideals whose gendered practices were neither threatened by nor fearful of strong and subversive female, homosexual, and racially and ethnically diverse character types and co-stars.

Most illustrative in this regard are Reeves's Martin Loader in *Tune in Tomorrow*, John "Johnny" Utah in *Point Break*, Scott Favor in *My Own Private Idaho*, and Paul Sutton in *A Walk in the Clouds*. In these characterizations Reeves makes his own unique contributions to the period's changing gender and sexual norms. On the one hand, what Reeves brings to these new-age, sensitive male portrayals are youthful, screen-idol good looks, an aura of innocence and trustworthiness, and a lean, lithe, and fit bodily specimen that the camera seems to enhance. On the other hand, Reeves's tall, hulking, and strong bodily presence resists childlike or feminine-genteel associations or equivalences. Rather, Reeves's body signifies traditional manliness, a staple of action cinema where hard bodies and the physical perfection of the genre's hero are requisite (see Paul McDonald's supplementary chapter in Dyer, *Stars* 182). At the same time, Reeves's traditional masculine body is enlisted in generic regimes of gender and sexuality (action and romance) that trouble these orthodoxies in remarkable ways.

As Martin Loader, Paul Sutton, and Scott Favor, Reeves portrays a range of diverse characters who are near-perfect representations of the problematic politics surrounding gender, sexuality, class, and race and ethnicity identity issues during this decade. Acting the parts of Martin and Paul, Reeves performs the traditional masculine good-guy character types, inflected with a bit of the rebel, whose nontraditional romantic choices are more in keeping with those of a 1990s era of increasing social permissiveness than what is allowed in the historical settings of *Tune in Tomorrow*'s and *A Walk in the Clouds*' respective narratives. In the former, a taboo relationship in 1950s New Orleans revolves around Martin's unacceptable passionate love for his older Aunt Julia (Barbara Hershey). Importantly, she is his relative not through blood ties but through marriage. And while May/December romances between older men and younger women are staples of novelistic and romantic comedies and other genres, the inverse is rarely the case. The fundamental gender bias of this dichotomy is challenged in Reeves's and Hershey's campy performances. In *A Walk in the Clouds*, Paul breaks other romantic taboos, one class-based and the other involving miscegenation between Paul and Victoria (Aitana Sanchez-Gijon), a young Mexican American woman. Paul's failed marriage leads him to a chivalrous encounter with Victoria that blossoms into love, prompting Paul's heroic rescue of the family's burned-out Napa Valley vineyard. The class friction or taboo, reviewer Godfrey Chesire notes, revolves around Victoria's father's "sneering at [Paul's] undesirable orphanage upbringing and lowly occupation" in relationship to the Aragon's Napa Valley wine-producing estate that's been in "[Victoria's upper-middle class] Hispanic family for generations" (*Variety*, 31 July 1995, 35). Both Martin and Paul are nontraditional characters situated at crucial historical removes from the evolving contemporary gender politics and practices of the nineties. Through these distinctive characters, Reeves strikes an effective balance of alternative masculine portrayals. At once he conveys a sensitive, nineties-era cool manliness possessed of independent thought and actions that reflect new expectations for masculine behaviors, and he refracts and challenges established masculine codes of domination and superiority at the center of normative heterosexual male identity.

As Paul and Martin, Reeves's own understated and tentative persona functions to imbue these leading-man characters with a gentle yet virile sensuality readily picked up by the camera through many facial close-ups and some bare-chested wide shots that satisfy his ardent female fan base. Among his most unusual characters is Scott Favor, a sexually complex figure whose bi-sexual exploits enact a significant boundary-pushing challenge to, or reset of, traditional Hollywood-style masculinity. Not only does *My Own Private Idaho* participate in a corpus of long overdue (Hollywood and independent) film narratives featuring complex lesbian, gay, bisexual, and transgender (LGBT) characters, communities, and issues, including such titles as *Philadelphia* (1993), *Interview with the Vampire* (1994), *Threesome* (1994), *Bound* (1995), *All Over Me* (1996), *The Birdcage* (1996), *Chasing Amy* (1997), *Before Night Falls* (1999), *The Talented Mr. Ripley* (1999), and *Boys Don't Cry* (1999), among others; but it is reviewers' remarks on Reeves's riveting portrayal in *Idaho* that are a revelation. Vincent Canby describes the film as "essentially a road movie that, in its subversive way, almost qualifies as a romantic comedy except that its characters are so forlorn." In his assessment of the powerful acting of River Phoenix as Mike Waters and Reeves as Scott Favor, Canby notes the latter's differential characterization: "Favor . . . has the manners, self-assurance and handsomeness associated with an idealized preppie. He is an untroubled bisexual . . . [who] stands to inherit a fortune. He hustles not because he has to but to satisfy his ego, to infuriate his father" ("A Road Movie About Male Hustlers," *New York Times*, 27 September 1991, C5).

Speaking specifically to the performative aspect, Canby writes, "The performances, especially by the two young stars, are as surprising as they are sure. Mr. Phoenix ('Dogfight') and Mr. Reeves (of the two 'Bill and Ted' comedies) are very fine in what may be the two best roles they'll find in years. Roles of this density, for young actors, do not come by that often." Harvey Greenberg's review of the film and Reeves's acting is less enthusiastic but nonetheless affirmative. In his contemporaneous review for *Film*

Keanu Reeves as sexual hustler Scott Favor in *My Own Private Idaho* (Gus Van Sant, New Line Cinema, 1991) evokes what Elia Kazan called "the 'bisexual' effect of Brando's image" (qtd. in Naremore 194). Reeves, here with River Phoenix, displays a nonthreatening homosociality. Digital frame enlargement.

Quarterly, Greenberg notes, "Reeves' rather narrow range and shallow handsomeness are actually helpful on this score." Of director Van Sant's creation of Reeves's "lowlife" character, Greenberg asserts, "Scott's assumption of heterosexuality is also too pat by half. It's presented as a betrayal of gay bonding as stereotypical as any straight stereotype about gay love" (25). On the whole, Greenberg finds more to commend than condemn in *Idaho*. And, given Reeves's inauspicious career launch in the *Bill and Ted* comedies, these considered opinions do seem prescient of his imminent stardom. On the other hand, Scott and Mike in *Idaho* suggest rearticulations of Bill and Ted who have taken a turn from irreverent juvenile slackers to twenty-something gay/bi-sexual "lowlife" sexual hustlers. As a star vehicle for River Phoenix, *Idaho* also engenders a specular "look"ism that promotes an erotic consumption of both Reeves's and Phoenix's highly sexualized performances. Notably, in Scott's kissing scene with fat Bob (William Richert) and in Reeves's ingénu sexual allure, here and elsewhere in the diegesis stress is placed on the fact that Scott only makes love/has sex with men for money. This is hardly surprising, and it creates a productive tension between Reeves's scintillating homosexual performance and the economics of preserving his hunky heterosexual star brand in the making, a tension that Miriam Hansen's star study of Rudolph Valentino and his female fan base enables us to appreciate. "As Hollywood manufactured the Valentino legend, promoting the fusion of real life and screen persona that makes a star," Hansen writes, "Valentino's female admirers in effect became part of that legend. Never before was the discourse on fan behaviour so strongly marked by the terms of sexual difference, and never again was spectatorship so explicitly linked to the discourse on female desire" (259).

Depp and Reeves proffer appealing masculine hero types whose enlarged gender discourse at century's end invite less gender determined "cinematic identificatory fantasies," in Jackie Stacey's terminology ("Feminine" 149). For Stacey, cinematic identification concerns women fans' fluid movement from (her) self to (the star) other in the pleasurable loss of oneself in the film. Or, more simply put, "The spectator's identity merges with the star in the film, or the character she is portraying" ("Feminine" 152). Adapted to Reeves's and Depp's nineties films and characters, Stacey's formulation points the way for us to address these young male stars' contribution to forms of non-gender and non-sexually determined cinematic identificatory practices that apparently resonated well with third wave and postfeminist female and queer-identified filmgoers of the 1990s.

★★★★★ On Female Fandom and Reception

Writing in the March 1996 issue of *Mademoiselle*, journalist and self-professed fan Lauren David Peden highlights an important element of Reeves's allure and mesmerizing powers for female fans:

> *What Is It About Him, Anyway?* I'll tell you: It's the Vulnerable Puppy Syndrome. Everything we read about Reeves contributes to an urge to protect him: His fatherless upbringing (he never saw his half-Chinese, half-Hawaiian father after age 13); his rootless childhood (the family moved five times, about as many times as Reeves changed high schools); his homeless lifestyle (he lives in hotels, out of a suitcase). Then, of course, there's his exuberant physicality—his lumbering walk in *Parenthood*, his big gestures and heart-stopping grin in both *Bill & Ted* movies, his sleek strength in *Speed*. (Fans of his action-hero persona should look for his upcoming thriller *Dead Drop*.)
>
> ("In Search of Keanu," 110)

The girl-centric protection and rescue fantasies informing Reeves's irresistible "Vulnerable Puppy Syndrome" could just as easily apply to Depp, with perhaps one key difference. That difference appears bound up with Reeves's unique biography and clearly discernable mixed-race heritage and facial features that resonate with the era's expanding global media audiences and their increasing fascination with nonwhite stars and multiracial celebrity. And despite Hilary de Vries's disclosure about Depp's own multi-racial bloodline, Depp's racial identity registers as normative whiteness to a degree that Reeves's, arguably, does not ("The Normalization of Johnny Depp," *Los Angeles Times*, 12 December 1998, 3). Another salient element of Reeves's growing, if sometimes unfathomable, popularity in the early nineties is a resilient transgenerational sex appeal that captivates the actor's feverish female fan bases even as he matures and explores new acting roles and challenges into the decade's midway point.

Unveiling this unanticipated scope of Reeves's often-disparaged—yet enduring—stardom for women and girl spectators is Heidi Losleben's marginalia item that accompanies Peden's *Mademoiselle* article for the "Arts" section of the magazine. In "Reeves Fever," Losleben extracts juicy quotes from what she describes as "more fan mail about Keanu Reeves than about all other Hollywood actors put together." She asked *Mademoiselle* readers to say exactly what they saw in Reeves that put him over the top in their 1996 star-gazing polls. Unsurprisingly, Losleben found a way to distill Reeves's magnetism down to an "astonishing lyricism, insight, honesty and, well, lust," as she honestly put it. Losleben's characterizations are telling:

> "He's masculine and well-built. It's a commando-type thing"—Vicky, 26. "I thought he looked quite good naked in *My Own Private Idaho*. He has lovely skin"—Randi, 33. "That whole elusive-rebel thing and the fact that he's from several ethnic backgrounds makes him stand out from the rest of the crowd"—Leslie, 29. "He's the ideal bimbo. It's like that saying, he 'should be seen and not heard'—but I mean that in a nice way"—Carol, 26. "Deep in my heart, I know he's really smart underneath it all"—Selena, 25.
>
> ("Reeves Fever")

What is striking in these utterances from Reeves's older demographic fan base, besides a tenor expected more from teen girls, is how the sentiments betray a female gaze that objectifies the star in terms that could be said to turn Mulvey's visual pleasure thesis on its head (Mulvey). If, for argument's sake, you grant me this allusion to gender parity, then postmodern women filmgoers in the nineties make it clear that they have no compunction about acknowledging Reeves's undeniable sex appeal and asserting their own visual pleasure in consuming his enticing cinematic image, as these quotations confirm. Taken in isolation, it appears that women and girls of this era enjoyed scopic pleasures of male-star gazing (to invoke Jackie Stacey once again) that past generations could not or did not express so freely in public. But, as we know, earlier female fan communities devoted to Rudolph Valentino traversed this terrain of fandom first.

While it is the case that Reeves's exotic good looks translate into an intergenerational allure for female fans, his appeal is not restricted to their gaze. In fact, his homoeroticism has been duly noted both onscreen and off. In "Much Ado about Keanu," Karen S. Schneider points out that speculation about Reeves's sexuality has followed the star since his "small-town triumphs in Toronto to Hollywood." It was Reeves's 1984 professional debut in a local play entitled "Wolfboy," a work suffused with "homoerotic undertones" and pushed to cult status by Toronto's gay community, that linked the actor with homosociality from the start. Even in the wake of his phenomenal success in the blockbuster powerhouse film *Speed* (1994) more than a decade later, the "bisexual buzz" on Reeves had persisted to the point that out gay "entertainment mogul David Geffen commented to *Time* magazine on the innuendo publicly. 'I hear that I'm supposed to be married to Keanu Reeves. . . . I never met or even laid eyes on him.' Reeves seems little bothered by the bisexual buzz." Schneider quotes Reeves's sister Kim as saying the actor "doesn't care one bit about it." Schneider continues: "Indeed, the talk brings out his mischievous side. Asked by *Interview* magazine in 1990 if he was gay, Reeves said no. 'But,' he coyly added, 'ya never know'" (*People*, 5 June 1995). What we do know is that by the decade's end Reeves had reached the pinnacle of Hollywood stardom, earning more than $10 million per film after *Speed* and generating adoration from fans around the world, as evidenced by such elaborate fansites as "Keanu's Fever."[1]

From the moment that Johnny Depp reluctantly agreed to appear in "21 Jump Street," the twenty-three-year-old "caught the eyes and hearts of fans." In fact, by the series' second year, "much to Depp's surprise and dread," he was reportedly receiving approximately 10,000 letters weekly (Blitz and Krasniewicz 25), although he was dismayed that he was getting "mail from very young girls, 13 and 14," clamoring for autographs, handshakes, kisses, and shouting their love and devotion. In the article "Baby Face" for *Sky Magazine*, Tony Fletcher gives an indication of Depp's whitehot appeal for female fans in 1990 at the Baltimore premiere of *Cry-Baby*. Despite an obvious doting on his then-fiancée Winona Ryder, whom he was escorting to the screening, "legions of young female followers" did not mute their star-struck frenzy. Fletcher puts it thus:

> The star was mobbed by hordes of screaming girls. . . . Even the sight of Winona Ryder clinging happily to his arm failed to deter their undying love for this high school dropout and failed rock musician. Depp's co-stars . . . are no less subtle in their admiration of his physique. Amy Locane, an innocent 18-year-old from a Catholic girls' school in suburban New Jersey, who plays his leading lady Allison, confesses that she almost fainted when required to

do a love scene with Depp during the second day of rehearsals. . . . And Rikki Lake . . . simply describes Depp as, "One of the most beautiful men I've ever seen."   (June 1990, n.p.)

For female fans in the nineties, postmodern spectatorship practices are not determined or delimited by patriarchal enforcement of a "taboo on female scopophilia" that Jackie Stacey interrogates in terms of what she calls the "Valentinian gaze" (*Star* 264). This is because, as Stacey points out, spectatorship, visual pleasure, and its gendered identification problematic have been complicated by contemporary feminist theorists who refashion male gaze and cinema identification theories through "differences of class and race, with cultural and historical specificity" (*Star* 266). Not only can female moviegoers in the nineties be said to build upon the fan practices in the twenties surrounding Rudolph Valentino, but they transform them according to a progression of change agents impinging on the cinema: these include changes in social values, norms, and mores, changes in film and other media industries, changes in global media flows and transnational cultural exchanges, changes in media technologies, and changes in attitudes about stardom where race and ethnicity intersected.

☆☆★★★ Star Quality, Multiculturalism, and the New Ethnic Exoticism

What Keanu Reeves and Johnny Depp contributed to new masculine star images and types, and to new fan and reception practices (particularly the online fansites and web/home pages phenomena), was equally matched by their participation in decentering a purist Anglo-American whiteness as the privileged passport to A-list male stardom in Hollywood. Their career fortunes came at a time of intensifying globalization that exerted special leverage on Hollywood and independent films' box office receipts, and an increasing racial tolerance throughout all sectors of society. In fact, most of the reportage, in print and online, carries comments about the racial and ethnic backgrounds of Depp and Reeves. This point is not insignificant when coupled with the growing significance of the international box office grosses on the economic bottom line of America's film industry and the career fortunes of the period's most successful stars. Increasingly, part of that success was bound up with stars' abilities to appeal across diverse audience demographics nationally and internationally. And Depp's and Reeves's star texts were quite emblematic of America's changing subject positions, multicultural identity politics, and new attitudes about desirable star bodies. An extant Reeves fan website created in the nineties makes the case perfectly.

The fansite, "Keanu's Fever," was developed around 1998 by Charlize Reeves (no relation) with the assistance of her mom and a committed cadre of contributors. Most pertinent to our study is the "Keanu Around the World" section devoted to understanding the far-flung reach of the star's fan base. Charlize describes this portion of the site as "making a kind of research, to know how far does the name Keanu Reeves, makes people sigh and dream [sic]." From 1998 to 2007, Reeves's fans, hailing from locales including America, Singapore, Malaysia, India, Canada, England, Germany, Ireland, Italy, Puerto Rico, Australia, Poland, Turkey, the Bahamas, Brazil, South Africa, South Korea, Dubai, and Russia, among others, posted commentary mostly about how much they love him and his films. A few suggest that his appeal is tied to his exotic or racially ambiguous looks, as Cosmo from Finland gushes (the posts are reproduced verbatim here):

> I'm 27 years old female from Finland. I like Keanu cos *he's so unique as persona and unique by his looks, he looks so different* [my emphasis] everything seems to suit him: he looks so good with long and short hair and has this look in his eyes, but I don't like him only for his bea[u]ty or looks, he's more, far more . . . he's not a Hollywood type of person. He's really talented and hard working, and does really his best as a actor. . . . *Matrix, My Own Private Idaho, Speed, Point Break* (that surfing) are the films's I like best. Nice to see how many fans all over the world share the same passion to Keanu :).

In 1999, Apologia in Germany posted:

> I first saw Keanu in one of those extremely beautiful Gorman pictures (that was in . . . hmm, 1994—i think). I didn't know who he was or *what he was*. . . . he was just the most beautiful human being i've ever seen. I don't know if he's like the way i picutre him at all. And still i love the mere idea of him . . . don't know if that sounds crap.

Although not explicit, these posts strongly insinuate a racial or ethnic difference associated with Reeves's unique appearance. Most striking, however, is the fact that this presumptive racial ambiguity is not viewed as a problem or impediment. Far from it. Rather, as Mary Beltrán and Camilla Fojas note, "Multiracial action heroes in fact have become a trend in their own right. . . . Vin Diesel, Dwayne Johnson (the Rock), Keanu Reeves, and Jessica Alba are a few of the actors of mixed racial heritage whose recent careers have been boosted by their portrayal of such enigmatic and heroic figures" (11). Certainly Reeves's Neo in the *Matrix* trilogy, the eponymous Johnny Mnemonic, and John ("Johnny") Utah in *Point Break* fit the bill.

Depp's Edward Scissorhands and Don Juan DeMarco roles might be suited to such characterizations as well. For just as Johnny Depp's Cherokee racial heritage gets mentioned routinely in his ubiquitous media coverage, so too do columnists and reviewers make a point of foregrounding Reeves's "Hawaiian-Chinese descent" as Lyle Slack's "keanu's excellent adventure" article appearing in *Maclean's* demonstrates (23 January 1995, 52).

Following *Wired* magazine's discursive lead, Leilani Nishime proffers that Reeves may well be "the new face of globalization" (303). If Reeves and, by extension, Depp are representatives of a racially hybrid globalization, then their "heroic" characters construct for Western visual culture a cinematic constellation of mixed-race character archetypes that recode or jettison the stereotypical tragic mulatto, primitive, and savage dramatis personae and de rigueur villain to the white protagonist (cowboys versus Indians; Tarzan versus cannibalistic, superstitious natives; and the white colonial master versus the devious oriental/yellow peril, among other racial binary oppositions). Beltrán and Fojas make this cogent observation in the introduction to their excellent and timely anthology *Mixed Race Hollywood*. They also contextualize this important shift in historical and hegemonic representations of race on film in terms of some formidable demographic shifts occurring in American democratic society, including changed immigration patterns and increased interracial families and romantic relationships (Beltrán and Fojas 8–9).

At the same time, this argument does not claim that the progressive development of heroic mixed-race imagery is a panacea for enduring problems around race and representation. Rather, it is a clarion call to "rethink normative discourses about the representation of race and racial categories," especially in film, TV, and other visual media (Beltrán and Fojas 11). After all, in her astute analysis of Reeves and issues of mixed race identity in the *Matrix* films in the same volume, Nishime reminds us that for many critics and moviegoers Reeves's "Neo is destined to save, and lead the battle against the machines because of his whiteness" (293), or that "for many viewers Reeves's body does not 'speak' its race" (308). Further complicating this issue are the stars' own positions on their racial/ethnic status. In an August 1991 *Details* magazine interview with Chris Heath, Reeves self-identifies as white. In that article, entitled "The Pursuit of Excellence," he is quoted as saying, "I'm a middle-class white boy . . . a bourgeois middle-class white boy with an absent father, a strong-willed mother, and two beautiful younger sisters." This quotation has been picked up by countless numbers of online sources, including the websites of the Biography Channel and Turner Classic Movies, to name only two. By contrast, Depp claimed not to be white in a 1997 *Vanity Fair* interview with gay author Kevin Sessums, who posed a "woman question": "The ones that have been highly publicized are white, yeah. That just says more about the press than my tastes. I ain't fucking 'white,' that's for sure. Kate [Moss]'s definitely not. She's about the furthest thing from 'white' there is. She's got that high water booty," he brags. "A high-water booty is important . . . And feet. Feet are very important" (qtd. on JohnnyDeppfan.com). It is difficult to know whether or not Depp is serious here, or if he is performing rebelliousness that during this period defined his personal and star images. In some ways, Depp's utterance, facetious or otherwise, is authorized by the type of racial shifts and new multicultural realities obtaining in the 1990s that Hollywood's media industries at once reflect and promote during this era. Jane Parks makes an insightful observation that pertains to both Reeves and Depp's identity claims. "Racially ambiguous characters in science fiction action films," she notes, "complicate the white appropriation of racial difference . . . what I call '*virtual race*,' or the idea of racial and ethnic identity as an ornamental product that can be marketed and consumed, put on and taken off . . . with mixed race bodies blurring the boundaries between whiteness and nonwhiteness even as they receive certain privileges that historically have been conferred upon those with white bodies" (in Beltrán and Fojas 186). With Depp and Reeves, the notion of blurring racial boundaries seemed to register as much for their fans and the media publicists and reporters as for the stars themselves. Despite the movement of Hollywood's mixed-race characters from tragic to heroic, as Beltrán and Fojas note, notions of race according to familiar racial scripts of white privilege and dominance persist in American popular media culture (9–12). Nonetheless, Reeves's and Depp's distinctive careers and subsequent superstardom are testament to the evolution of mixed-race and ethnic portrayals in Hollywood films throughout the ensuing decades after Valentino and Sessue Hayakawa set the mold for exotic, sexually desirable "woman made" matinee idols from the twenties (Beltrán and Fojas 12; Miyao 192).

☆☆☆☆☆ Peck's Bad Boy Redux

So far, we have discussed Keanu Reeves's and Johnny Depp's constructions of new, sensitive masculine types, and their impact on emerging cinematic discourses of mixed race and ethnic identity politics in U.S. civil society and on practices of female spectatorship. We now turn to a particular feature of Depp's and Reeves's star personas and charismatic appeals for their diverse fan communities. Through their respective enactments of the classic American bad-boy personality onscreen and in real life, they effectively counterbalance their new age sensitive male performativities.

Reeves's and Depp's backgrounds are uncannily similar. Both are products of broken homes, high school dropouts, musicians in rock bands, and reluctant heartthrobs at the center of young Hollywood at the same time. Moreover, both received extensive coverage for what Chris Willman called "the anti-star mentality" ("From Baby Face to 'Cry-Baby' Profile," *Los Angeles Times*, 4 April 1990, 1). It is interesting that among their contemporaries—Brad Pitt, Tom Cruise, Leonardo DiCaprio, Ewan McGregor, among others—it is Depp and Reeves whom the celebrity media and film critics often compare or yoke together. Consider, for instance, Willman's remark: "Despite his handsome, all-American TV image, Depp in person is long-haired, loosely funky and unglamorous enough to seem more a Keanu Reeves type than a James Dean type." Also yoking Depp and Reeves together is *Los Angeles Times* writer Steve Hochman in his 1997 review of their respective alternative rock bands Dogstar and P. "Among rock bands, there's none easier to sell than P. . . . What better bait can you have than heartthrob actor Johnny Depp? Unless you're talking Keanu Reeves" ("Depp Leppard? Nah," *Los Angeles Times*, 30 July 1995, 57).

For all their similarities, they were individualists. In effect, Johnny Depp's and Keanu Reeves's separate careers during the decade generated a mutually reinforcing star constellation or celebrity parallel universe that seemed highly beneficial for both young stars on the rise. This suggests that their coterminous but partitioned roads to stardom evoked a sort of professional sibling rivalry. The fact that Reeves and Depp have not, at this writing, appeared or co-starred in a single film together—yet were considered for some of the same high-profile roles, such as in *Point Break*, *Speed*, *Bram Stoker's Dracula* (1992), *Legends of the Fall* (1994), and even *The Matrix* (1999)—supports this notion of sibling rivalry, by design or by chance. Reeves and Depp have recoded Hollywood teen idolatry each in his own star image and through his particular cinematic oeuvre as the decade progressed.

What Depp and Reeves share is a propensity to adopt or embody masculine types in films that revive America's quintessential naughty/bad boy figure created in the nineteenth century by newspaper journalist-owner and politician George W. Peck in a series of short stories in his newspaper *Peck's Sun*. "Peck's Bad Boy" was a sensational and popular persona that circulated through the era's newspapers and books, and later was adapted to the stage and magic lantern shows and then films from 1883 to 1934. The irreverent but popular fictional bad boy was named Hennery. His outlandish antics and pranks captivated readers, theatergoers, and subsequent film audiences alike, clearly an early iteration of a transmedia star. Over the years, Peck's Bad Boy character came to signify any incorrigible rule-breaker. In 1884, the *New York Tribune* castigated the bad boy character for his "distressing examples of the crimes against good taste and decency that are committed in the name of American humor." This historicizing of the bad boy figure is meant to explore his origins and enduring allure in popular culture, and especially to juxtapose the charm of the *bad boy* against the menace of the *bad man*.[2]

Gwendolyn Audrey Foster has made a fascinating study of cinematic bad man performativity in her book *Performing Whiteness: Postmodern Re/Constructions in the Cinema*. Moving beyond one key figure from the Orrin Klapp typology of social types, particularly the tough guy as contextualized by Richard Dyer, Foster gives us the bad man or bad guy whose social significance is inflected in terms of dominant or normative whiteness. "In much of cinema," as she puts it, "badness in men is routinely linked to female influence," typified by James Cagney's performance of obsessive attachment to his mother in *White Heat* (1949). She also singles out Dennis Hopper's mad bomber in *Speed* and Anthony Hopkins's cannibalistic madman in *The Silence of the Lambs* (1991) as illustrative of the bad man's pathology linked to "an unfit white mother as a root cause" (127). "Bad white men," she continues, "are routinely associated with blackness and darkness. They are often involved in the realm of the body. . . . The gaze of the bad white is routinely associated with mastery over others" (127–29).

Given this context, when we think of Depp's and Reeves's onscreen performances of the bad boy, and the media coverage of their real-life bad-boy behaviors, we can imagine how women fans' rescue fantasies might be invoked as they consume the endless reportage and imagine that, if only these celluloid bad boys could meet them or some other good women, they could be rescued from descent into the realm of the bad man. Women's putative rescue fantasies aside, Reeves and Depp's postmodern redux of Peck's Bad Boy retains the trope's historical allure, and above all is entertaining, exciting, humorous, enigmatic, and fun. In *Cry-Baby, Don Juan DeMarco, Ed Wood, Edward Scissorhands, Donnie Brasco* (1997), *Fear and Loathing in Las Vegas* (1998), and *Sleepy Hollow* (1999), Depp's virtuoso performances adeptly reinscribe this by now tried-and-true, naughty but lovable bad-boy persona for the tastes and expectations of nineties-era film audiences. Perhaps most striking about Depp's incorrigible rule-breaker characters Don Juan DeMarco, Edward Scissorhands, Ichabod Crane, and Donnie Brasco is how much they fuse with the much-publicized rebelliousness, unconventionality, and

Depp as lovable bad-boy Wade "Cry-Baby" Walker in his first starring film role. Depp's fifties-era juvenile delinquent captures the affections of good-girl Allison (Amy Locane) in *Cry-Baby* (John Waters, Universal, 1990). Digital frame enlargement.

volatility ascribed to Depp's own personal life throughout the decade. From reports of his repeated confrontations with police, trashing of a hotel room, chain smoking, drinking, and drug use, to his multiple engagements to such glamorous women as supermodel Kate Moss and Hollywood starlet Winona Ryder and others, we clearly see a perfect fit between Depp's nonconformist star image and his repertoire of outsider characters discussed above. In fact, Depp's careful selection of characters and films is legendary (Elizabeth McCracken, "Depp Charge," *Elle*, 6 January 1998, 106–08). His practice of selecting roles based on an intellectual appeal rather than box office potential has resulted in Depp being regarded as "the best actor of his generation" (106). Underscoring that "perfect fit" between actor and character, Depp's remarks are telling in this lengthy quote from his 1997 interview with Sessums:

> "*Donnie Brasco* was a motherfucker of a movie," Depp deadpans. "I spent a lot of time with the real Donnie Brasco, Joe Pistone. Brasco was his undercover name. He's got an interesting rhythm to his speech. I did my best to get that. I put great pressure on myself to make it fucking right for the guy. He lived it. I was just pretending." . . ."I've never consciously played into any image," insists Depp. "I never wanted to emulate anybody else. Every young actor

who comes out of the blocks, they say, 'James Dean,' because it's easy." . . . "I'm not 'Blockbuster Boy.' I never wanted to be. I wasn't looking for that," Depp says, having turned down the role of Lestat in *Interview with the Vampire* before Tom Cruise accepted it, passed on the Brad Pitt romantic lead in *Legends of the Fall*, and declined the offer of the action hero in *Speed*, a part which made Keanu Reeves a star. "I mean, it would be nice to get a whole shitpile of money so you can throw it at your family and friends. . . . I just don't know if movies can ever be considered art, because there's so much money involved," he continues, perhaps protesting a tad too much, since he himself recently crossed the $4-million-per-picture threshold. "It's all about commerce. I don't think art can come from that place. But I aspire to be an artist someday. Maybe I'll be 70. I don't know if it will come from being in a movie, though. Maybe I'll just whittle something."

(Sessums, "Johnny Be Good," JohnnyDeppFan.com)

As for Keanu Reeves, his real-life bad-boy behavior prior to his acting career comported more with Peck's bad boy trope of the Victorian era. Lyle Slack reports that Reeves's childhood years in public school were "mostly well-behaved," with the star reflecting on "building go-carts . . . [and slinging] chestnuts at teachers' heads . . . and in Grade 8 hash started to come around, and LSD kinda." Slack reports that early on in his acting career, Reeves was not the most disciplined. "As his career grew, so did complaints about his self-absorption. Reeves would show up late on the set or not take direction"; most important, Slack reveals, Reeves's agents told him "either shape up or ship out," at which point Reeves took the work seriously and began taking classes in earnest in Canada, his home during childhood and early adulthood (Lyle Slack, "Keanu's Excellent Adventure," *Macleans*, 23 January 1995). And whereas Johnny Depp's acting talents have been celebrated, Reeves's rarely have, with Reeves's performances being characterized as "largely one-dimensional compared with the complex work of such contemporaries as Johnny Depp, Eric Stoltz or Jason Patric. Yet," Slack admits, "Reeves has thrived, principally because, as Robert M. Eaves noted in London's *The Observer*, 'he has the indefinable essence that is called star quality. When he's on the screen, you watch, however bad his acting may sometimes be'" (Slack).

Reeves's contribution to the bad-boy type inheres mainly in his memorable character portrayals in the *Bill & Ted* comedies, *Tune in Tomorrow, My Own Private Idaho, Much Ado About Nothing* (1993), *Bram Stoker's Dracula*, and *The Devil's Advocate* (1997). As Ted Logan and as Martin Loader, Reeves demonstrates his comedic skills along two registers of the genre, the buffoonish, clueless teen rebel college slacker dude and inept villainous doppelgänger in *Bill & Ted*; and the lovesick straight man to Peter Falk's hilariously impish comedic lead in *Tune in Tomorrow*. Like Peck's bad boy, these characters are essentially harmless pranksters who simultaneously lampoon the laidback California lifestyle, the science fiction genre's time-travel convention, and the stereotypes of southern society in *Bill & Ted* and *Tune in Tomorrow*, respectively. As Scott Favor, Don John, and Kevin Lomax, Reeves's bad boys border on the darker side of the trope with a tinge of the bad-man persona as outlined by Foster above.

As the decade progressed and ultimately came to a close, both Depp and Reeves reaped the benefits of their smart career choices that, by and large, saw each star remaining as true to his sense of personal integrity as possible in the Hollywood firmament. With their combination of memorable independent films and extremely successful blockbusters they became the industry's most sought after and best-known iconoclasts, navigating the Hollywood thickets on their own relatively outsider terms.

NOTES

1. See Charlize Reeves's unofficial Keanu Reeves website, Keanu's Fever, including "Keanu Around the World" at keanusfever.tripod.com/karound.html. Accessed 15 July 2010.

2. Histories and wikis of Peck's Bad Boy are easily found on the web. See, for example, "Peck's Bad Boy" at www.infoplease.com/biography/var/pecksbadboy.html.

In the Wings

ANNA EVERETT

The select top women stars "in the wings" during the 1990s were Meg Ryan, Sandra Bullock, Angelina Jolie, Cameron Diaz, Whitney Houston, Salma Hayek, and Jennifer Lopez; the select top men stars were Will Smith, Brad Pitt, Jim Carrey, and Mike Meyers. Clearly these charismatic individuals represent the tip of stardom's proverbial iceberg, suggesting what David Lusted in a different context calls "the glut of the personality" (251). Although Lusted is referencing an economic imperative of the television industry, his insights are instructive. "Personalities," Lusted notes, "are central to the institution of television. A stock of recognized names acts as an assurance that audiences will return again (and again) to their role as viewers, perpetuating . . . the flow of cash to maintain the institution" (251). The film industry's glut of stars, if you will, performs an analogous function. We are a star-struck nation, and the growing import of global cinema and media culture makes it clear that we are not alone.

Unlike expatriate international stars between World War I and World War II who emigrated to the United States, postwar international stars in the 1990s were free to retain citizenship in their native countries and make public and even trade on their dual citizenships. It seems that popular stars not hailing from the United States helped Americans to accept the concept of globalization and the notion of the "global village" more favorably. After all, if we like foreign stars, particularly as representatives of their distant homelands, then perhaps their cultures, commodities, and countries are not so bad after all, right? Consider some of the blockbuster "international" film stars who became familiar to and beloved by American audiences in the nineties: Chow Yun Fat and Jackie Chan (China); Nicole Kidman, Hugh Jackman, Charlize Theron, Cate Blanchett, and Russell Crowe (Australia); Hugh Grant, Elizabeth Hurley, Kenneth Branagh, Emma Thompson, Jude Law, Thandie Newton, Colin Firth, Kate Winslet, Helena Bonham Carter, Ewan McGregor (Great Britain); Liam Neeson (Ireland); and Juliette Binoche and Gérard Depardieu (France). This group is not comprehensive, but it indicates how the business of globalization was very much represented in the culture industries as well as in manufacturing industries. American film audiences embraced these actors whether appearing in American films or in films produced elsewhere. We might note that as this grouping of international stars indicates, Americans, perhaps understandably, seem to be ardent Anglophiles.

Meg Ryan co-starred with Billy Crystal in the surprise hit *When Harry Met Sally* (1989), after some initial success on television in such shows as "Rich and Famous" (1981) and the soap opera "As the World Turns" (1982–1984) and the films *Top Gun* (1986) and *The Presidio* (1988); but *Harry/Sally* catapulted her career. Her star billing opposite Tom Hanks in the wildly popular romantic comedies *Sleepless in Seattle* (1993) and *You've Got Mail* (1998), among other films of that ilk, established Ryan as the darling of the chick flick. Ryan's disarmingly charming and bubbly star image endeared her to national and international audiences alike throughout the decade.

Sandra Bullock, though she toiled in a few failed television series, including "Working Girl" and "Lucky Chances" (both in 1990), and in such films as *Love Potion No. 9* (1992), *The Vanishing* (1993), and *Demolition Man* (1993), became America's celluloid sweetheart with her stunning performance in the blockbuster action thriller *Speed* (1994), opposite Keanu Reeves. Bullock's sweet, unassuming, perky, and unthreatening pretty-girl-next-door persona sustained her throughout the decade in such films as *While You Were Sleeping* (1995), *Two If by Sea* (1996), *Speed 2: Cruise Control* (1999), and *Hope Floats* (1998). In the 2000s, Bullock's lead roles in *Miss Congeniality* (2000), *Miss Congeniality 2: Armed and Fabulous* (2005), *The Proposal*, and *The Blind Side* (both in 2009), and her production of the TV show "George Lopez" (2002–2004), established unequivocally her role as a major player atop the Hollywood star heap.

Angelina Jolie's breakthrough film was *Hackers* (1995), where her tough, edgy, tomboy computer-hacker character Kate Libby/Acid Burn embodied much of the decade's postfeminist "girl power" zeitgeist. Bound up with the technophilia of computer-savvy young girl gamers and sexually awakening teen boy computer geeks, Jolie's Acid Burn hacker babe persona became her calling card for securing the starring role in the highly anticipated and successful film adaptation of the Lara Croft videogame. Prior to her lead role in the film *Lara Croft* (2001), Jolie won the Best Supporting Actress Oscar in 2000 for her critically acclaimed performance in the Winona Ryder star vehicle *Girl, Interrupted* (1999). Despite a few missteps, Jolie, with her so-called "exotic good looks," went on to be widely regarded as one of the most beautiful women in Hollywood, and an ideal spokesperson for a number of global charities focusing on needy children.

Cameron Diaz's star image in the nineties was as a consummate sexy ingénue in such top-grossing films as *The Mask* (1994), *My Best Friend's Wedding* (1997), and *There's Something About Mary* (1998). A consistent star presence in many films of the era, Diaz had her most successful vehicles come in the 2000s as she gives voice to Princess Fiona of the lucrative animated *Shrek* (2001) film franchise, including *Shrek 2* (2004), *Shrek the Third* (2007), and *Shrek Forever After* (2010).

Whitney Houston, one of the most successful and talented popular music divas of the decade, had star turns in *The Bodyguard* (1992), *Waiting to Exhale* (1995), and *The Preacher's Wife* (1996) that recall similar but not equal film sensations Diana Ross in the 1970s and Madonna in the 1980s. *The Bodyguard* was the seventh highest grossing film of 1992, with a total box-office gross of nearly $122 million in the United States and $410 million worldwide. Not bad for a film debut. The other two fared well at the box office also, positioning the singer as a bona fide A-list movie star during the decade, helping to raise Hollywood executives' perception of black women actors as viable crossover romantic leads in big-budget mainstream films.

Will Smith, whose full name is Willard Christopher Smith Jr., became one of Hollywood's most bankable film stars in the 1990s. He achieved remarkable successes in popular music as rapper "The Fresh Prince" (winning the first Grammy Award for Rap music in 1989 as the partner of Jeffrey "DJ Jazzy Jeff" Townes for the single "Parents Just Don't Understand"); and then on network television with the popular sitcom based on Smith's own life "The Fresh Prince of Bel-Air" (1990–1996). Smith's apparent Midas touch extended to his early film work as well, including his critically acclaimed performance in *Six Degrees of Separation* (1993) and the financially successful *Bad Boys* (1995). In 1996, Smith's action/adventure/science fiction film, *Independence Day*, captured the number-one slot at the box office for the year. *Men in Black* (1997), *Enemy of the State* (1998), and *Wild Wild West* (1999) were other notable vehicles for Smith, with *Men in Black* set for a lucrative sequel franchise.

At the decade's end, Will Smith had in fact become a megastar, and Hollywood's $14 million man—his salary for opening *Enemy of the State*. Smith turned down the role of Neo in the Matrix film franchise but expressed no regrets. By 2008, *Newsweek*, Britain's *Daily Mail*, and others regarded Smith as the most powerful man in Hollywood, with *Newsweek* labeling him "the $4 billion dollar man." As Donna Porter reported in April

2007: "Will Smith is the only thing in this business—the only thing—that represents a guaranteed opening weekend." He may be even bigger than that. "Let's put it this way," said one studio head, "there's Will Smith, and then there are the mortals" ("Will Smith, Hollywood's Most Powerful Actor," associatedcontent.com).

When William Bradley Pitt (aka "Brad") appeared in *Thelma & Louise* (1991), his matinee-idol looks caused a stir, and a string of substantial roles in big-budget Hollywood films followed. Pitt starred in such films as *A River Runs Through It* (1992), *Interview with the Vampire* (1994), *Legends of the Fall* (1994), *Se7en* (1995), *Twelve Monkeys* (1995), *Meet Joe Black* (1998), and *Fight Club* (1999), among others. More than simply a pretty face, Pitt had acting talent that garnered him numerous award nominations over the years and a Golden Globe for his supporting role in *Twelve Monkeys*.

Jim Carrey and Mike Myers, Canadians who began in Canadian television, both contributed substantially to the American comedy film. Carrey was quite a dominant comedic force in Hollywood with such blockbusters as *Dumb and Dumber* (1994), *The Mask* (1994), *Ace Ventura: Pet Detective* (1994), *Batman Forever* (1995), *Ace Ventura: When Nature Calls* (1995), *Liar Liar* (1997), and the unexpected dramatic tour de force *The Truman Show* (1998). Myers's films included *Wayne's World* (1992), *So I Married an Axe Murderer* (1993), *Wayne's World 2* (1993), *Austin Powers: International Man of Mystery* (1997), *54* (1998), and *Austin Powers: The Spy Who Shagged Me* (1999). They effectively translated their standup and television comedy backgrounds into family-friendly films.

For Jennifer Lopez and Salma Hayek, 1997 was an important year. Each reached a career milestone not only personally but for Latina actresses in mainstream American films. With her breakout role in the biopic *Selena* (based on the true story of murdered tejano singer Selena Quintanilla-Perez), Lopez's career reached a level of stardom in Hollywood that eluded other Latina actresses. Her other high-profile films *Anaconda* (1997), *U Turn* (1997), and *Out of Sight* (1998) established her as a lead female star not necessarily racially marked as Latina. Hayek starred opposite Matthew Perry in *Fools Rush In* (1997), a romantic comedy in which she played the Mexican love interest of an Anglo. Unlike Lopez, Hayek's celebrity seems absolutely bound up with her Latina-ness in films such as *Breaking Up* (1997) with Russell Crowe, *Dogma* (1999), an ensemble film with Ben Affleck and Matt Damon, and *The Wild, Wild West* (1999) with Will Smith and Kevin Kline. In *Desperado* (1995), with Antonio Banderas, Hayek instantiates a strong-willed, sexy character type, which she reprises in most of her American films. Lopez and Hayek's significance are as particular post-feminist constructs whose sexuality and ethnic otherness simultaneously reify and challenge the hot Latina stereotype in mainstream and independent films at the moment when borderland culture and anti-affirmative action discourses escalate throughout U.S. society.[1]

NOTE

1. For this discussion of Salma Hayek and Jennifer Lopez, I am indebted to Cynthia Fuchs.

WORKS CITED

☆☆☆☆☆☆☆☆☆☆☆

Adler, M. "Stardom and Talent." *American Economic Review* 75:1 (1985): 208–12.

Albert, Steven. "Movie Stars and the Distribution of Financially Successful Films in the Motion Picture Industry." *Journal of Cultural Economics* 22:4 (1998): 249–70.

Aparicio, Frances. "Jennifer as Selena: Rethinking Latinidad in Media and Popular Culture." *Latino Studies* 1 (2003): 90–105.

Bakarkjieva, Maria. *Internet Society: The Internet in Everyday Life.* London: Sage Publications, 2005.

Baldwin, James. *The Devil Finds Work.* New York: Dial, 1976.

Balio, Tino. "'A Major Presence in All of the World's Important Markets': The Globalization of Hollywood in the 1990s." *Contemporary Hollywood Cinema.* Ed. Steve Neale and Murray Smith. London: Routledge, 1998. 58–73.

Barnhart, Robert, ed. *Chambers Dictionary of Etymology.* Edinburgh: Chambers, 2008.

Bates, Karen Grigsby. "Angela Bassett Is *Not* a Diva!" *Essence* December 1995: 78, 117–18.

Bauman, Zygmunt. "Consuming Life." *Journal of Consumer Culture* 1:1 (2001): 9–29.

Beckerman, Gal. "Product Placement: It's Everywhere, It's Everywhere." *Columbia Journalism Review Daily* www.cjr.org. 29 September 2005.

Beltrán, Mary C. "The Hollywood Latina Body as a Site of Social Struggle: Media Constructions of Stardom and Jennifer Lopez's 'Cross-over Butt.'" *Quarterly Review of Film & Video* 19:1 (2002): 71–86.

———. *Latina/o Stars in U.S. Eyes: The Making and Meaning of Film and TV Stardom.* Urbana: U of Illinois P, 2009.

Beltrán, Mary, and Camilla Fojas, eds. *Mixed Race Hollywood.* New York: New York UP, 2008.

Bennett, James. "The Television Personality System: Television Stardom Revisited after Film Theory." *Screen* 49:1 (2008): 32–50.

Bennett, Tony, and Janet Woollacott. *Bond and Beyond: The Political Career of a Popular Hero.* Basingstoke, U.K.: Macmillan, 1987.

Berg, Charles Ramírez. *Latino Images in Film: Stereotypes, Subversion, & Resistance.* Austin: U of Texas P, 2002.

Berrettini, Mark. "Can 'We All' Get Along?: Social Difference, the Future, and *Strange Days.*" *Camera Obscura* 50, 17:2 (2002): 154–89.

Berry, Sarah. *Screen Style: Fashion and Femininity in 1930s Hollywood.* Minneapolis: U of Minnesota P, 2000.

Bingham, Dennis. "Kidman, Cruise, and Kubrick: A Brechtian Pastiche." *More than a Method: Trends and Traditions in Contemporary Film Performance.* Ed. Cynthia Baron, Diane Carson, and Frank Tomasulo. Detroit: Wayne State UP, 2004. 247–74.

Blitz, Michael, and Louise Krasniewicz. *Johnny Depp: A Biography.* Westport, Conn.: Greenwood, 2008.

Bogle, Donald. *Toms, Coons, Mulattoes, Mammies, and Bucks.* New York: Continuum, 2001.

Boykoff, Maxwell T., and Michael K. Goodman. "Conspicuous Redemption? Reflections on the Promises and Perils of the 'Celebritization' of Climate Change." *Geoforum*40 (2009): 395–406.

Braudy, Leo. *The Frenzy of Renown: Fame and Its History*. Oxford: Oxford UP, 1986.

Briggs, Asa, and Peter Burke. *A Social History of the Media: From Gutenberg to the Internet*. Cambridge, Mass.: Polity, 2003.

Brockington, Dan. "Powerful Environmentalisms: Conservation, Celebrity and Capitalism." *Media, Culture & Society* 30:4 (2008): 551–68.

Brode, Douglas. *Denzel Washington: His Films and Career*. Secaucus, N.J.: Carol Publishing, 1997.

Bronner, Simon J. "Menfolk." *Manly Traditions: The Folk Roots of American Masculinities*. Ed. Simon J. Bronner. Bloomington: Indiana UP, 2005. 1–58.

Brown, Terry. "The Butch Femme Fatale." *Lesbian Post Modern*. Ed. Laura Dean. New York: Columbia UP, 1994. 229–43.

Butler, Judith. *Gender Trouble: Feminism and the Subversion of Identity*. New York: Routledge, 1990.

Cameron, Julia. "The Burden of the Gift." *American Film* 16:10 (November/December 1991): 44–8.

Carr, Brian. "*Strange Days* and the Subject of Mobility." *Camera Obscura* 50, 17:2 (2002): 190–217.

Chartier, Roger. "Texts, Printings, Readings." *The New Cultural History*. Ed. Lynn Hunt. Berkeley: U of California P, 1989. 154–75.

Chung, Kee H., and Raymond A. K. Cox. "A Stochastic Model of Superstardom: An Application of the Yule Distribution." *Review of Economics and Statistics* 76:4 (1994): 771–75.

Clover, Carol. *Men, Women, and Chainsaws: Gender in the Modern Horror Film*. Princeton, N.J.: Princeton UP, 1992.

———. "White Noise." *Sight and Sound* (May 1993): 6–9.

Cohan, Steven. *Masked Men: Masculinity and the Movies in the Fifties*. Bloomington: Indiana UP, 1997.

Corbett, Charles J., and Richard P. Turco. *Sustainability in the Motion Picture Industry*. Report prepared for the Integrated Waste Management Board of the State of California by the University of California, Los Angeles, Institute of the Environment, 2006. personal. anderson.ucla.edu/charles.corbett/papers/mpis_report.pdf.

Cornea, Christine. "Arnold Schwarzenegger." *Contemporary American Cinema*. Ed. Linda Ruth Williams and Michael Hammond. London: Open UP and McGraw-Hill, 2006. 284–86.

———. *Science Fiction Cinema between Fantasy and Reality*. Edinburgh: Edinburgh UP, 2007.

Cose, Ellis. *The Envy of the World: On Being a Black Man in America*. New York: Washington Square, 2002.

Cox, Cathy R., Jamie L. Goldenberg, Jamie Arndt, and Tom Pyszczynski. "Mother's Milk: An Existential Perspective on Negative Reactions to Breast-Feeding." *Personality and Social Psychology Bulletin* 33:1 (2007): 110–22.

Crimp, Douglas. "Right On, Girlfriend!" *Social Text* 33 (1992): 2–18.

Cunningham, Michael. "Just Your Ordinary (Gay) Guy." *New York Times* 7 May 1994: 17.

Davies, Jude. "Gender, Ethnicity and Cultural Crisis in *Falling Down* and *Groundhog Day*." *Screen* 36:3 (1995): 214–32.

———. "'I'm the Bad Guy?' *Falling Down* and White Masculinity in 1990s Hollywood." *Journal of Gender Studies* 4:2 (1995): 145–52.

Davies, Jude, and Carol R. Smith. *Gender, Ethnicity and Sexuality in Contemporary American Film*. Edinburgh: Keele UP, 1997.

Dávila, Arlene. *Latinos, Inc.: The Marketing and Making of a People*. Berkeley: U of California P, 2001.

De Angelis, Therese. *Jodie Foster*. Philadelphia: Chelsea House, 2001.

De Vany, Arthur S., and W. David Walls. "The Market for Motion Pictures: Rank, Revenue, and Survival." *Economic Inquiry* 35:4 (1997): 783–97.

———. "Uncertainty and the Movie Industry: Does Star Power Reduce the Terror of the Box Office?" *Journal of Cultural Economics* 23:4 (1999): 285–318.

Del Río, Esteban. "All of Us Americanos: Cultural Exhibition and the Rise of Latino/as within a National Imaginary." Ph.D. diss., University of Massachusetts, 2006.

Deleyto, Celestino. "The Margins of Pleasure: Female Monstrosity and Male Paranoia in *Basic Instinct*." *Film Criticism* 21:3 (Spring 1997): 20–42.

Diawara, Manthia. "Black Spectatorship: Problems of Identification and Resistance." *Screen* 29:4 (1988): 66–79.

Distefan, Janet M., Elizabeth A. Gilpin, James D. Sargent, and John P. Pierce. "Do Movie Stars Encourage Adolescents to Start Smoking? Evidence from California." *Preventive Medicine* 28:1 (1999): 1–11.

Donalson, Melvin. *Masculinity in the Interracial Buddy Film*. Jefferson, N.C.: McFarland, 2006.

Drake, Philip. "Jim Carrey: The Cultural Politics of Dumbing Down." *Hollywood Stars and Beyond*. Ed. Andy Willis. Manchester: Manchester UP, 2004.

Dyer, Richard. "Don't Look Now: The Male Pin-up." *The Sexual Subject: A* Screen *Reader in Sexuality*. London: Routledge, 1992. 265–76.

———. *Heavenly Bodies: Film Stars and Society*. 2nd ed. New York: Routledge, 2004.

———. *Stars: New Edition*. London: BFI/Palgrave Macmillan, 1998.

———. "Stereotyping." *Gays and Film*. Ed. Richard Dyer. London: BFI, 1977. 27–39.

Edwards, Tim. *Men in the Mirror: Men's Fashion, Masculinity and Consumer Society*. London: Cassell, 1997.

Ehrenstein, David. *Open Secret: Gay Hollywood 1928–1998*. New York: William Morrow, 1998.

Elias, Norbert. *The Civilizing Process: The History of Manners and State Formation and Civilization*. Trans. Edmund Jephcott. Oxford: Blackwell, 1994.

Ellerby, Janet Mason. "Deposing the Man of the House: Terry McMillan Rewrites the Family." *Mellus* 22:2 (Summer 1997): 105–17.

Ellis, John. *Visible Fictions*. London: Routledge, 1992.

Elsaesser, Thomas. "Specularity and Engulfment: Francis Ford Coppola and *Bram Stoker's Dracula*." *Contemporary Hollywood Cinema*. Ed. Steve Neale and Murray Smith. London: Routledge, 1998. 191–208.

Epstein, Rebecca L. "Sharon Stone in a Gap Turtleneck." *Hollywood Goes Shopping*. Ed. David Desser and Garth S. Jowett. Minneapolis: U of Minnesota P, 2000. 179–204.

Essence: 40 of the Most Inspiring African-Americans. New York: Essence Books/Time Inc., 2002.

Fernandes, Sujatha. *Cuba Represent!: Cuban Arts, State Power, and the Making of New Revolutionary Cultures*. Durham, N.C.: Duke UP, 2006.

Fiedler, Leslie A. *Love and Death in the American Novel*. New York: Criterion, 1960.

Foster, Buddy, and Leon Wagener. *Foster Child: An Intimate Biography of Jodie Foster by Her Brother*. New York: Penguin, 1997.

Foster, Gwendolyn Audrey. *Performing Whiteness: Postmodern Re/constructions in the Cinema*. Albany: State U of New York P, 2003.

Foster, Jodie. "Introduction." *Maverick,* by Burl Barer. Boston: Charles E. Tuttle, 1994. xv–xvi.

Fregoso, Rosa Linda. *The Bronze Screen: Chicana and Chicano Film Culture*. Minneapolis: U of Minnesota P, 1993.

French, Sean. *The Terminator*. London: BFI, 1996.

Fuqua, Joy Van. "'Can You Feel It, Joe?': Male Melodrama and the Feeling Man." *Velvet Light Trap* 38 (Fall 1996): 28–38.

Gabilondo, Joseba. "Our Man in Hollywood: Antonio Banderas's Seduction." *Hopscotch: A Cultural Review* 1:1 (1999): 70–77.

Gabriel, John. "What Do You Do When Minority Means You? *Falling Down* and the Construction of 'Whiteness.'" *Screen* 37 (1996): 129–52.

Galician, Mary-Lou, and Peter G. Bourdeau. "The Evolution of Product Placements in Hollywood Cinema: Embedding High-Involvement 'Heroic' Brand Images." *Journal of Promotion Management* 10:1–2 (2004): 15–36.

Gallagher, Mark. *Action Figures Men, Action Films, and Contemporary Adventure Narratives*. New York: Palgrave Macmillan, 2006.

Gamson, Joshua. *Claims to Fame: Celebrity in Contemporary America*. Berkeley: U of California P, 1994.

García, María Cristina. "Exiles, Immigrants, and Transnationals: The Cuban Communities of the United States." *The Columbia History of Latinos in the United States since 1960*. Ed. David G. Gutiérrez. New York: Columbia UP, 2004. 146–86.

Gledhill, Christine. "Signs of Melodrama." *Stardom: Industry of Desire*. Ed. Christine Gledhill. New York: Routledge, 1991. 207–29.

Goffman, Erving. *Forms of Talk*. Philadelphia: U of Pennsylvania P, 1981.

Gormley, Paul. *The New-Brutality Film: Race and Affect in Contemporary Hollywood Cinema*. Bristol: Intellect, 2005.

Green, Philip. *Cracks in the Pedestal: Ideology and Gender in Hollywood*. Amherst: U of Massachusetts P, 1998.

Greenberg, Harvey R. "Review: My Own Private Idaho." *Film Quarterly* 46:1 (Autumn 1992): 23–25.

Griswold, A. B. "King Mongkut in Perspective." *Journal of the Siam Society* 45:1 (1957): 1–41.

Gross, Larry. "Big and Loud." *Sight and Sound* 5:8 (August 1995): 6–10.

Guerrero, Edward. "Black Men in the Movies: How Does It Feel to Be a Problem (and an Answer)?" *Traps: African American Men on Gender and Sexuality*. Ed. Rudolph P. Byrd and Beverly Guy-Sheftall. Bloomington: Indiana UP, 2001. 270–77.

Guglielmo, Thomos. *White on Arrival: Italians, Race, Color, and Power in Chicago*. London: Oxford UP, 2004.

Hairston, Andrea. "Driving Mr. Lenny: Notes on Race and Gender as a Transport to Another Reality, Another Dimension." *Foundation* 33:92 (2004): 5–16.

Hansen, Miriam. *Babel and Babylon: Spectatorship in American Silent Film*. Cambridge, Mass.: Harvard UP, 1991.

Harris, Thomas. "The Building of Popular Images: Grace Kelly and Marilyn Monroe." *Stardom: Industry of Desire*. Ed. Christine Gledhill. New York: Routledge, 1991. 40–44.

Harris, Tina. "Interrogating the Representation of African American Female Identity in the Films *Waiting to Exhale* and *Set It Off*." *Popular Culture Review* 10:2 (August 1999): 43–53.

Haug, W. F. *Critique of Commodity Aesthetics: Appearance, Sexuality and Advertising in Capitalist Society*. Trans. Robert Bock. Cambridge, Mass.: Polity, 1986.

Herzog, Charlotte Cornelia, and Jane Marie Gaines. "'Puffed Sleeves before Tea-time': Joan Crawford, Adrian, and Women Audiences." *Stardom: Industry of Desire*. Ed. Christine Gledhill. New York: Routledge, 1991. 74–91.

Higson, Andrew. "Film Acting and Independent Cinema." *Screen* 27:3–4 (May–August 1986): 110–32.

Holland, Sharon. "On Waiting to Exhale: Or What to Do When You're Feeling Black and Blue, a Review of Recent Black Feminist Criticism." *Feminist Studies* 26:1 (Spring 2000): 101–12.

Hollinger, Karen. "Angela the Icon: Angela Bassett." *The Actress: Hollywood Acting and the Female Star*. New York: Routledge, 2006.

Holmes, Su. "'All You've Got to Worry about Is the Task, Having a Cup of Tea, and Doing a Bit of Sunbathing: Approaching Celebrity in *Big Brother*." *Understanding Reality TV*. Ed. Su Holmes and Deborah Jermyn. London: Routledge, 2004. 111–35.

Horton, Robert. "Life Upside Down." *Film Comment* (January/February 1991): 38–39.

Hunter, Ian. "Providence and Profit: Speculations in the Genre Market." *Southern Review* 22:3 (1988): 211–23.

Ignatiev, Noel. *How the Irish Became White*. New York: Routledge, 1995.

Indiana, Gary. *Schwarzenegger Syndrome Politics and Celebrity in the Age of Contempt*. New York: New Press, 2005.

Iverem, Esther. *We Gotta Have It: Twenty Years of Seeing Blacks at the Movies, 1986–2006*. New York: Thunder's Mouth, 2007.

Jeffords, Susan. "The Big Switch: Hollywood Masculinity in the Nineties." *Film Theory Goes to the Movies*. Ed. Jim Collins, Hilary Radner, and Ava Preacher Collins. New York: Routledge, 1993. 196–208.

———. "Can Masculinity Be Terminated?" *Screening the Male: Exploring Masculinities in Hollywood Cinema*. Ed. Steven Cohan and Ina Rae Hark. London: Routledge, 1993. 245–62.

———. *Hard Bodies: Hollywood Masculinity in the Reagan Era*. New Brunswick, N.J.: Rutgers UP, 1994.

Jenkins, Henry. *Fans, Bloggers, and Gamers: Exploring Participatory Culture*. New York: New York UP, 2006.

Johnstone, Emma, and Christopher A. Dodd. "Placements as Mediators of Brand Salience within a UK Cinema Audience." *Journal of Marketing Communications* 6:3 (2000): 141–58.

Jones, Sandra C., and John D. Rossiter. "Young Adults' Perceptions of Smoking Actors." *Health Education* 108:6 (2008): 450–62.

Jory, Patrick. "The King and Us: Representations of Monarchy in Thailand and the Case of *Anna and the King*." *International Journal of Cultural Studies* 4:2 (June 2001): 201–18.

"Julia Roberts." *International Dictionary of Films and Filmmakers*. 4th ed. Ed. Tom Pendergast and Sara Pendergast. Detroit: St. James, 2000.

Kaplan, Caren. "'Getting to Know You': Travel, Gender, and the Politics of Representation in *Anna and the King of Siam* and *The King and I*." *Late Imperial Culture*. Ed. Roman de la Campa, E. Ann Kaplan, and Michael Sprinkler. London: Verso, 1995. 22–52.

Kendall, Lori. "Colin Mochrie vs. Jesus H. Christ: Messages about Masculinities and Fame in Online Video Conversations." *Proceedings of the 40th Hawaii International Conference on System Sciences* (2007).

Kennedy, Randall. *Nigger: The Strange Career of a Troublesome Word*. New York: Vintage, 2003.

Kepner, Susan. "Anna (and Margaret) and the King of Siam." *Crossroads* 10:2 (1997): 1–32.

Kimmel, Michael. *Manhood in America: A Cultural History*. New York: Free Press, 1996.

King, Barry. "Embodying an Elastic Self." *Contemporary Hollywood Stardom*. Ed. Thomas Austin and Martin Barker. Oxford: Hodder and Arnold, 2003. 45–61.

Lambert, A., J. D. Sargent, S. A. Glantz, and P. M. Ling. "How Philip Morris Unlocked the Japanese Cigarette Market: Lessons for Global Tobacco Control." *Tobacco Control* 13:4 (2004): 379–87.

Landy, Marcia. *Stardom Italian Style: Screen Performance and Personality in Italian Cinema.* Bloomington: Indiana UP, 2008.

Lane, Christina. "The Liminal Iconography of Jodie Foster." *Journal of Popular Film and Television* 22:4 (Winter 1995): 149–53.

Latour, Bruno. *We Have Never Been Modern.* Trans. Catherine Porter. Cambridge, Mass.: Harvard UP, 1993.

Leamer, Laurence. *Fantastic: The Life of Arnold Schwarzenegger.* London: Pan Macmillan, 2006.

"Lestat Lives!" *Scarlet Street: The Magazine of Mystery and Horror* 16 (Fall 1994): 28–33.

Looseleaf, Victoria. *Leonardo: Up Close and Personal.* New York: Ballantine, 1998.

Lusted, David. "The Glut of the Personality." *Stardom: Industry of Desire.* Ed. Christine Gledhill. New York: Routledge, 1991. 251–58.

Macherey, Pierre. "Culture and Politics: Interview with Pierre Macherey." Trans. and ed. Colin Mercer and Jean Radford. *Red Letters* 5 (1977): 3–9.

Mandel, Ernest. *Delightful Murder: A Social History of the Crime Story.* London: Pluto, 1984.

Mapp, Edward. *African Americans and the Oscar: Seven Decades of Struggle and Achievement.* Lanham, Md.: Scarecrow, 2003.

Marshall, P. David. *Celebrity and Power: Fame in Contemporary Culture.* Minneapolis: U of Minnesota P, 1997.

Mask, Mia. "Halle Berry in *Monster's Ball*: Black Womanhood, Miscegenation, and the Prison Industrial Complex." *Abafazi* 12:1 (Spring 2003): 7–13.

Mauss, Marcel. "Fragment d'un plan de sociologie générale descriptive." *Annales sociologiques* (1934).

———. "Les techniques du corps." *Journal de Psychologie* 23:3–4 (1936).

McConachie, Bruce A. "The 'Oriental' Musicals of Rodgers and Hammerstein and the U.S. War in Southeast Asia." *Theatre Journal* 46:3 (October 1994): 385–98.

McDonagh, Maitland. "*Philadelphia.*" *The Motion Picture Guide: 1994 Annual.* Ed. James Pallot. New York: Cinebooks, 1994. 210–11.

McDonald, Paul. *The Star System: Hollywood's Production of Popular Identities.* London: Wallflower, 2000.

Mera, Miguel. "Invention/Re-invention." *MSMI* 3:1 (2009): 1–20.

Miller, Toby. *The Avengers.* London: BFI, 1997.

———. *Makeover Nation: The United States of Reinvention.* Columbus: Ohio State UP, 2008.

———. *Spyscreen: Espionage on Film and TV from the 1930s to the 1960s.* Oxford: Oxford UP, 2003.

Mirandé, Alfredo. "*Quegacho* es ser macho: It's a Drag to Be a Macho Man." *Aztlán* 17:2 (Fall 1986): 63–89.

Mitchell, Stacey. *Big-Box Swindle: The True Cost of Mega-Retailers and the Fight for America's Independent Business.* Boston: Beacon, 2007.

Miyao, Daisuke. *Sessue Hayakawa: Silent Cinema and Transnational Stardom.* Durham, N.C.: Duke UP, 2007.

Mizejewski, Linda. *Hardboiled and High Heeled: The Woman Detective in Popular Culture.* New York: Routledge, 2004.

Moffat, Sandra. "Learning to Re-Imagine: Uncovering Affective Investments in Female Film Characters." *Gender and Education* 10:1 (March 1998): 93–99.

Morag, Raya. "Defeated Masculinity: Post-Traumatic Cinema in the Aftermath of the Vietnam War." *Communication Review* 9 (2006): 189–219.

Morin, Edgar. *The Stars*. 1972. Trans. Richard Howard. Foreword by Lorraine Mortimer. Minneapolis: U of Minnesota P, 2005.

Morton, Andrew. *Tom Cruise: An Unauthorized Biography*. New York: St. Martin's, 2008.

Moynihan, Daniel Patrick. "The Negro Family: The Case for National Action." Office of Policy Planning and Research, U.S. Department of Labor. March 1965. www.dol.gov/oasam/programs/history/webid-moynihan.htm.

Mulvey, Laura. "Visual Pleasure and Narrative Cinema" [1975]. *Visual and Other Pleasures*. Bloomington: Indiana UP, 1989.

Naremore, James. *Acting in the Cinema*. Berkeley: U of California P, 1988.

Nash, Melanie, and Martti Lahti. "'Almost Ashamed to Say I Am One of Those Girls': *Titanic*, Leonardo DiCaprio, and the Paradoxes of Girls' Fandom." *Titanic: Anatomy of a Blockbuster*. Ed. Kevin S. Sandler and Gaylyn Studlar. New Brunswick, N.J.: Rutgers UP, 1999. 64–88.

Neale, Steve. *Genre and Hollywood*. London: Routledge, 2000.

Newman, Kathleen. "Latino Sacrifice in the Discourse of Citizenship: Acting Against the 'Mainstream' 1985–1988." *Chicanos and Film: Essays on Chicano Representation and Resistance*. Ed. Chon A. Noriega. New York: Garland Publishing, 1992. 67–82.

Newsmakers. Edition 1991. Detroit: Gale, 1991.

Nishime, Leilani. "The Matrix Trilogy, Keanu Reeves, and Multiraciality at the End of Time." *Mixed Race Hollywood*. Ed. Mary Beltrán and Camilla Fojas. New York: New York UP, 2008. 290–312.

Noriega, Chon A. *Shot in America: Television, the State, and the Rise of Chicano Cinema*. Minneapolis: U of Minnesota P, 1997.

Norment, Lynn. "Waiting to Exhale." *Ebony* 51:2 (December 1995): 24–28.

Pachon, Harry, Louis DeSipio, Rodolfo de la Garza, and Chon A. Noriega. *Missing in Action: Latinos In and Out of Hollywood*. Claremont, Calif.: Tomás Rivera Policy Institute, 1999.

Parish, James Robert. *Today's Black Hollywood*. New York: Pinnacle Books, 1995.

Perriam, Chris. "Antonio Banderas." *Stars and Masculinities in Spanish Cinema from Banderas to Bardem*. Oxford: Oxford UP, 2003. 45–69.

Pfeil, Fred. *White Guys: Studies in Postmodern Domination and Difference*. London: Verso, 1995.

Phillips, Kendall R. "Unmasking Buffalo Bill: Interpretive Controversy and *The Silence of the Lambs*." *RSQ: Rhetoric Society Quarterly* 28:3 (Summer 1998): 33–47.

Pomerance, Murray. "Hitchcock and the Dramaturgy of Screen Violence." *New Hollywood Violence*. Ed. Steven Jay Schneider. Manchester: Manchester UP, 2004. 34–56.

———. *Johnny Depp Starts Here*. New Brunswick, N.J.: Rutgers UP, 2005.

———. "A Royal Audience: Voyages of Involvement in David Fincher's *The Game*." *Quarterly Review of Film and Video* 21:3 (July-September 2004): 187–98.

Prince, Stephen. *A New Pot of Gold: Hollywood under the Electronic Rainbow, 1980–1989*. Berkeley: U of California P, 2000.

Rall, Veronika. "'This Isn't Filmmaking, It's War': A Gendered Gaze on the Tom Cruise Phenomenon." *Visual Anthropology Review* 9:1 (Spring 1993): 93–104.

Rand, Ayn. *The Romantic Manifesto: A Philosophy of Literature*. New York: Signet, 1971.

Rich, B. Ruby. "Nobody's Handmaid." *Sight and Sound* (December 1991): 7–10. Originally published as "Jodie Foster: Growing Up On-Screen." *Jodie Foster: Growing Up On-Screen: A Retrospective by The Walker Art Center*. Minneapolis: Walker Art Center, 1991. 3–21.

Rodríguez, Ana P. "As the Latino/a Word Turns: The Literary and Cultural Production of Translatinidades." *Latina/osin the United States: Changing the Face of America*. Ed. Havidán Rodríguez, Rogelio Sáenz, and Cecilia Menjívar. New York: Springer, 2008. 210–24.

Rodríguez, Clara E. *Heroes, Lovers and Others: The Story of Latinos in Hollywood*. Washington, D.C.: Smithsonian Books, 2004.

Roper, Michael. *Masculinity and the British Organisation Man Since 1945*. Oxford: Oxford UP, 1995.

Rosen, David. "Crossover: Hispanic Specialty Films in the U.S. Movie Markets." *Chicanos and Film: Essays on Chicano Representation and Resistance*. Ed. Chon A. Noriega. Minneapolis: U of Minnesota P, 1992. 241–60.

Rosen, S. "The Economics of Superstars." *American Economic Review* 71:5 (1981): 845–57.

Roth, Kurt W., and Kurtis McKenny. *Energy Consumption by Consumer Electronics in U.S. Residences*. Final Report to the Consumer Electronics Association, www.ce.org. 2007.

Salzman, Marian, Ann O'Reilly, and Ira Matathia. *Future of Men: The Rise of the Übersexual and What He Means for Marketing Today*. New York: St. Martin's, 2006.

Sanello, Frank. *Halle Berry: A Stormy Life, The Unauthorized Biography*. London: Virgin Books, 2003.

———. *Julia Roberts*. Edinburgh: Mainstream Publishing, 2000.

Savran, David. "The Sadomasochist in the Closet: White Masculinity and the Culture of Victimization." *Differences* 8:2 (1996): 127–52.

Schwarzenegger, Arnold, and Douglas Kent Hall. *Arnold: The Education of a Bodybuilder*. 1977. New York: Simon and Schuster, 2005.

Serna, Laura Isabel. "As a Mexican I Feel It's My Duty': Citizenship, Censorship and the Campaign against Derogatory Films in Mexico, 1922–1930." *The Americas: A Quarterly Review of Inter-American Cultural History* 63:2 (October 2006): 225–44.

Sharrett, Christopher. "End of Story: The Collapse of Myth in Postmodern Narrative Film." *The End of Cinema as We Know It: American Film in the Nineties*. Ed. Jon Lewis. New York: New York UP, 2001. 319–31.

Shoos, Diane. "Representing Domestic Violence: Ambivalence and Difference in *What's Love Got to Do with It*." *NWSA Journal* 15:2 (Summer 2003): 57–75.

Silvera, David H., and Benedikte Austad. "Factors Predicting the Effectiveness of Celebrity Endorsement of Advertisements." *European Journal of Marketing* 38:11–12 (2004): 1509–26.

Silvestrini, Blanca. "The World We Enter When Claiming Rights: Claiming Latinos and Their Quest for Culture." *Latino Cultural Citizenship: Claiming Identity, Space, and Rights*. Ed. William V. Flores and Rina Benmayor. Boston: Beacon, 1997. 39–53.

Simonet, T. *Regression Analysis of Prior Experience of Key Production Personnel as Predictors of Revenue from High Grossing Motion Pictures in American Release*. New York: Arno, 1980.

Smithsonian Task Force on Latino Issues. *Willful Neglect: The Smithsonian Institution and U.S. Latinos*. Washington, D.C.: Smithsonian Institution, 1994.

Sørum, Kim André, Kjetil Marius Grape, and David Silvera. "Do Dispositional Attributions Regarding Peer Endorsers Influence Product Evaluations?" *Scandinavian Journal of Psychology* 44:1 (2003): 39–46.

Spada, James. *Julia: Her Life*. New York: St. Martin's, 2004.

Stacey, Jackie. "Feminine Fascinations: Forms of Identification in Star-Audience Relations." *Stardom: Industry of Desire*. Ed. Christine Gledhill. New York: Routledge, 1991. 141–63.

———. *Star Gazing: Hollywood Cinema and Female Spectatorship*. London: Routledge, 1994.

Staiger, Janet. "Taboos and Totems: Cultural Meanings of *The Silence of the Lambs*." *Film Theory Goes to the Movies*. Ed. Jim Collins, Hilary Radner, and Ava Preacher Collins. New York: Routledge, 1993. 142–54.

Steffans, Karrine. *Confessions of a Video Vixen*. New York: HarperCollins, 2009.

Stock, Paul. "Dial 'M' for Metonym: Universal Exports, M's Office Space and Empire." *National Identities* 2:1 (2000): 35–47.

Strick, Philip. "Strange Days." *Sight and Sound* 6:1 (1996): 53–55.

Studlar, Gaylyn. "Cruise-ing into the Millennium: Performative Masculinity, Stardom, and the All-American Boy's Body." *Ladies and Gentlemen, Boys and Girls: Gender in Film at the End of the Twentieth Century*. Ed. Murray Pomerance. Albany: State U of New York P, 2001. 171–83.

Tasker, Yvonne, ed. *Action and Adventure Cinema*. London: Routledge, 2004.

———. *Spectacular Bodies: Gender, Genre and the Action Cinema*. London: Routledge, 1993.

———. *Working Girls: Gender and Sexuality in Popular Cinema*. London: Routledge, 1998.

Tetzlaff, David. "Too Much Red Meat!" *New Hollywood Violence*. Ed. Steven Jay Schneider. Manchester: Manchester UP, 2004. 269–85.

Thompson, John O. "Screen Acting and the Commutation Test." *Stardom: Industry of Desire*. Ed. Christine Gledhill. London: Routledge, 1991. 183–97.

Thrall, A. Trevor, Jaime Lollio-Fakhreddine, Jon Berent, Lana Donnelly, Wes Herrin, Zachary Paquette, Rebecca Wenglinski, and Amy Wyatt. "Star Power: Celebrity Advocacy and the Evolution of the Public Sphere." *International Journal of Press/Politics* 13:4 (2008): 362–85.

Till, Brian D., Sarah M. Stanley, and Randi Priluck. "Classical Conditioning and Celebrity Endorsers: An Examination of Belongingness and Resistance to Extinction." *Psychology & Marketing* 25:2 (2008): 179–96.

Turner, Graeme. *Understanding Celebrity*. Thousand Oaks, Calif.: Sage Publications, 2004.

Van Scheers, Rob. *Paul Verhoeven*. London: Faber, 1997.

Vasey, Ruth. *The World According to Hollywood, 1918–1939*. Madison: U of Wisconsin P, 1997.

Vilanch, Bruce. "That's Myth Tom to You." *Advocate* 8:41 (3 July 2001): 40.

Wallace, Michele. "*Boyz N the Hood* and *Jungle Fever*." *Black Popular Culture*. Ed. Gina Dent. Seattle: Bay Press, 1992. 123–31.

Wallace, W. Timothy, Alan Seigerman, and Morris B. Holbrook. "The Role of Actors and Actresses in the Success of Films: How Much Is a Movie Star Worth?" *Journal of Cultural Economics* 17:1 (1993): 1–27.

Watkins, S. Craig. *Representing: Hip Hop and the Production of Black Cinema*. Chicago: U of Chicago P, 1998.

Wells, Peter, and Liz Heming. "Green Celebrity: Oxymoron, Fashion or Pioneering Sustainability?" *International Journal of Innovation and Sustainable Development* 4:1 (2009): 61–73.

Wheeler, Duncan. "The Representation of Domestic Violence in Popular English-Language Cinema." *New Cinemas Journal: Contemporary Film* 7:2 (2009): 155–75.

Wilkerson, Isabel. "Angela at the Crossroads." *Essence* (January 2003): 86–90.

Williams, Linda Ruth. *The Erotic Thriller in Contemporary Cinema*. Edinburgh: Edinburgh UP, 2005.

———. "Mother Courage." *Sight and Sound* 12:5 (May 2002): 12–14.

Willis, Sharon. *High Contrast: Race and Gender in Contemporary Hollywood Film*. Durham, N.C.: Duke UP, 1997.

Woledge, Elizabeth. "Intimatopia: Genre Intersections between Slash and the Mainstream." *Fan Fiction and Fan Communities in the Age of the Internet*. Ed. Karen Hellekson and Kristine Busse. Jefferson, N.C.: McFarland, 2006. 97–114.

Wolfe, George C. "Angela Bassett: The Showstopper." *Esquire* (August 1996): 91.

World Health Organization. *Smoke-Free Movies: From Evidence to Action*. Geneva: World Health Organization, 2009.

Wyatt, Justin. *High Concept: Movies and Marketing in Hollywood*. Austin: U of Texas P, 1994.

Young, Elizabeth. "*The Silence of the Lambs* and the Flaying of Feminist Theory." *Camera Obscura* 27 (1991): 5–35.

Zucker, Carole. "Passionate Engagement: Performance in the Films of Neil Jordan." *More than a Method: Trends and Traditions in Contemporary Film Performance*. Ed. Cynthia Baron, Diane Carson, and Frank Tomasulo. Detroit: Wayne State UP, 2004. 192–216.

CONTRIBUTORS
★★★★★★★★★★★★

MELVIN DONALSON is a professor at California State University–Los Angeles in both the Department of English and the Department of Pan African Studies. His critical books include *Black Directors in Hollywood* (2003), *Masculinity in the Interracial Buddy Film* (2006), and *Hip Hop in American Cinema* (2007). In addition, he is a screenwriter and filmmaker. He wrote, produced, and directed the short films *A Room without Doors* (1999) and *Performance* (2008), both of which were screened at numerous film festivals.

ANNA EVERETT is a professor of film, television, and new media as well as director of graduate studies in the Department of Film and Media Studies at the University of California, Santa Barbara. She has published numerous books and articles, including *Returning the Gaze, A Genealogy of Black Film Criticism, New Media: Theories and Practices of Digitextuality* (with John Caldwell), *Digital Diaspora: A Race for Cyberspace*, "Lester Walton's Ecriture Noir: Transcoding Cinematic Excess," and "Serious Play: Playing with Race in Computer Games." She founded *Screening Noir: A Journal of Film, TV, and Digital Culture*.

MARY BETH HARALOVICH is a professor in the School of Media Arts at the University of Arizona in Tucson. She teaches courses in television and film history and is director of internships and head of the university's Producing Division. Her essays on television include studies of the popular appeal of "Magnum, P.I." and the geopolitics of civil rights in "I Spy." She co-edited *Television, History, and American Culture: Feminist Critical Essays* and is a founder and board member of the International Conference on Television, Video, New Media, Audio and Feminism: Console-ing Passions. She also specializes in 1930s and 1940s posters; color in Sirk melodrama; the 1940s Sherlock Holmes film series; star and family in *Mildred Pierce*; and 1930s "proletarian" woman's films. Her book in progress is entitled *Marked Women: Local Promotion of "Scandalous Female" Films of the 1930s*.

KAREN HOLLINGER is a professor of film and literature at Armstrong Atlantic State University in Savannah, Georgia. She is the author of *The Actress: Hollywood Acting and the Female Star* and *In the Company of Women: Contemporary Female Friendship Films*, and co-editor of *Letter from an Unknown Woman*. She has also published numerous articles on women in film. She is currently working on a book on feminist film theory and criticism.

TRACEY HOOVER received her M.A. and Ph.D. in sociology at the University of California, Riverside. She did her undergraduate work at Cal Poly Pomona, where she received a degree in psychology. Dr. Hoover specializes in gender, family, and the media. Her dissertation explored the occupational roles of women in Hollywood films of the 1940s and 1950s, especially in regard to representations of motherhood and the formation of identity. Her scholarly interests are in the ways institutions influence identity formation. Dr. Hoover has been teaching since receiving her master's degree in 2005, and is currently in the Department of Sociology at Central Washington University, Ellensburg.

MIA MASK is an associate professor of film at Vassar College. She teaches African American cinema, documentary film history, horror film, feminist film theory, African national cinemas, and genre theory. She is the author of *Divas on Screen: Black Women in American Film*. Formerly an assistant editor and regular contributor at *Cineaste*, she has written film reviews and covered festival for *IndieWire.com*, *Village Voice*, *Abafazi: Simmons College Journal*, *Film Quarterly*, *Time Out New York*, *Brooklyn Woman*, and the *Poughkeepsie Journal*. In 1999, her criticism was anthologized in *Best American Movie Writing*.

TOBY MILLER is a professor of English, sociology, and women's studies and director of the Program in Film & Visual Culture, University of California, Riverside. He has published numerous books and articles, including *Spyscreen: Espionage on Film and TV from the 1930s to the 1960s*, *Sportsex*, and *The Avengers*. He also is co-editor of the Cultural Politics series for the University of Minnesota Press.

R. BARTON PALMER is Calhoun Lemon Professor of Literature and director of Film Studies at Clemson University, where he also serves as the interim chair of the English department. He is the author, editor, or general editor of nearly fifty volumes on various literary and cinematic subjects. Among his most recent edited books are *A Little Solitaire: John Frankenheimer and American Film* and, in the Star Decades series, *Larger than Life: Movie Stars of the 1950s*.

DONNA PEBERDY is a Senior Lecturer in Film and Television Studies at Southampton Solent University, UK. Her research and publications focus on performance and acting and masculinity and sexuality in American cinema. Recent publications include "Male Sounds and Speech Affectations: Voicing Masculinity," "Acting and Performance from Autism to Zissou," "Acting and Performance in Film Noir," and "Bipolar Masculinity and the Paradoxical

Performances of Tom Cruise." She is the author of *Masculinity and Film Performance: Male Angst in Contemporary American Cinema* (2011) and co-editor of *Tainted Love: Screening Sexual Perversities* (forthcoming, 2013).

MURRAY POMERANCE is a professor in the Department of Sociology at Ryerson University and the author of *Michelangelo Red Antonioni Blue: Eight Reflections on Cinema, Edith Valmaine, The Horse Who Drank the Sky: Film Experience Beyond Narrative and Theory, Johnny Depp Starts Here*, and *An Eye for Hitchcock*. He has edited or co-edited numerous volumes on cinema, including *Shining in Shadows: Movie Stars of the 2000s, A Little Solitaire: John Frankenheimer and American Film, A Family Affair: Cinema Calls Home, City That Never Sleeps: New York and the Filmic Imagination*, and *Cinema and Modernity*. He edits the Techniques of the Moving Image series at Rutgers and the Horizons of Cinema series at SUNY Press, and co-edits the Screen Decades and Star Decades series at Rutgers. His fiction has been awarded an O. Henry Prize.

LAURA ISABEL SERNA is an assistant professor of history at the University of Southern California. She is currently finishing *Making Cinelandia: American Films/Mexican Film Culture before the Golden Age, 1896–1936*. Her research interests include silent cinema in Latin America, historical reception studies, and Latina/o Media and Culture.

LINDA RUTH WILLIAMS is a professor of film in the English Department at the University of Southampton in the United Kingdom. She is the author of *The Erotic Thriller in Contemporary Cinema* and numerous articles on feminism, sexuality, censorship, and contemporary culture, as well as the co-editor of *Contemporary American Cinema*.

INDEX

☆☆☆☆☆☆☆☆☆★★